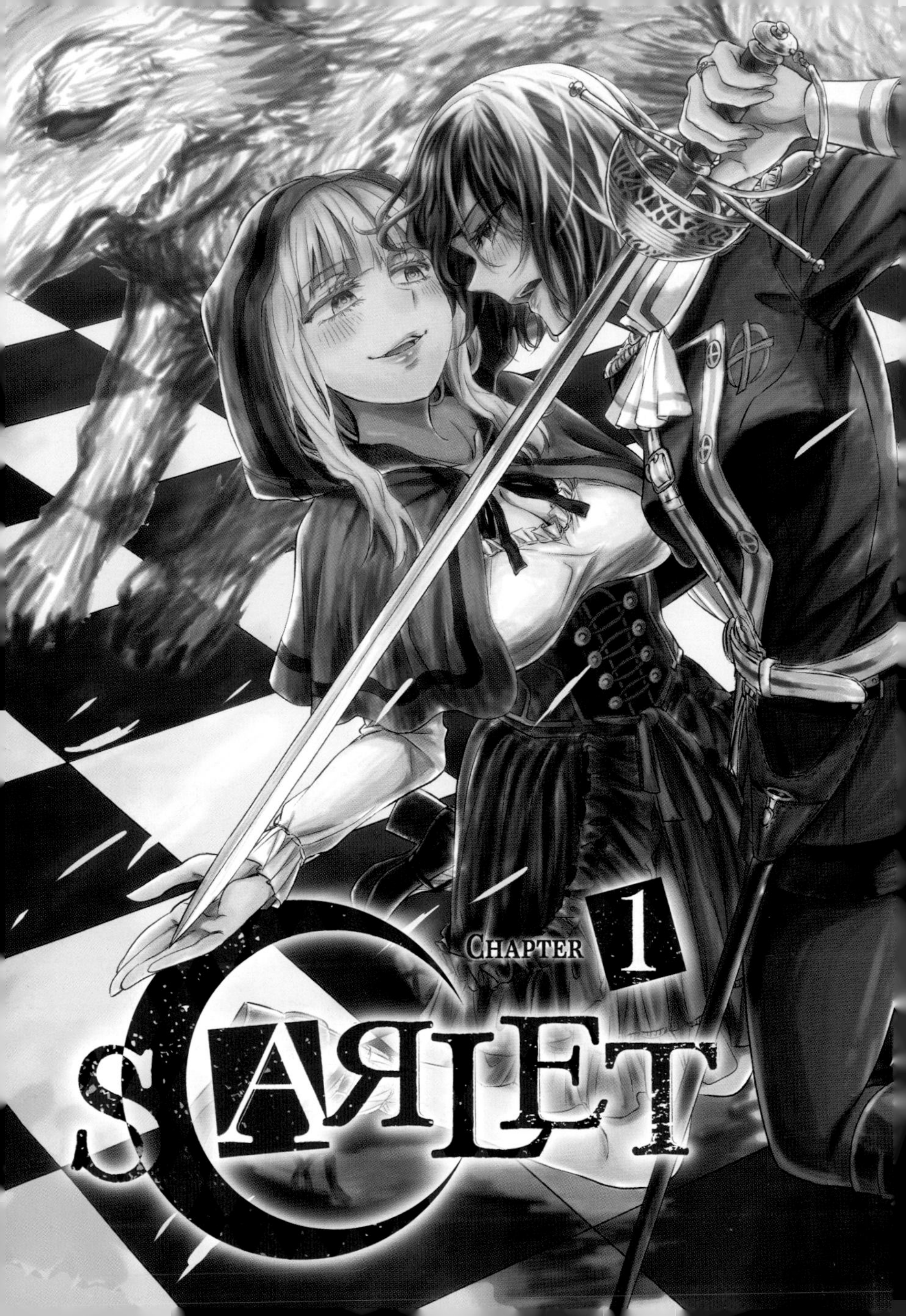
CHAPTER 1
SCARLET

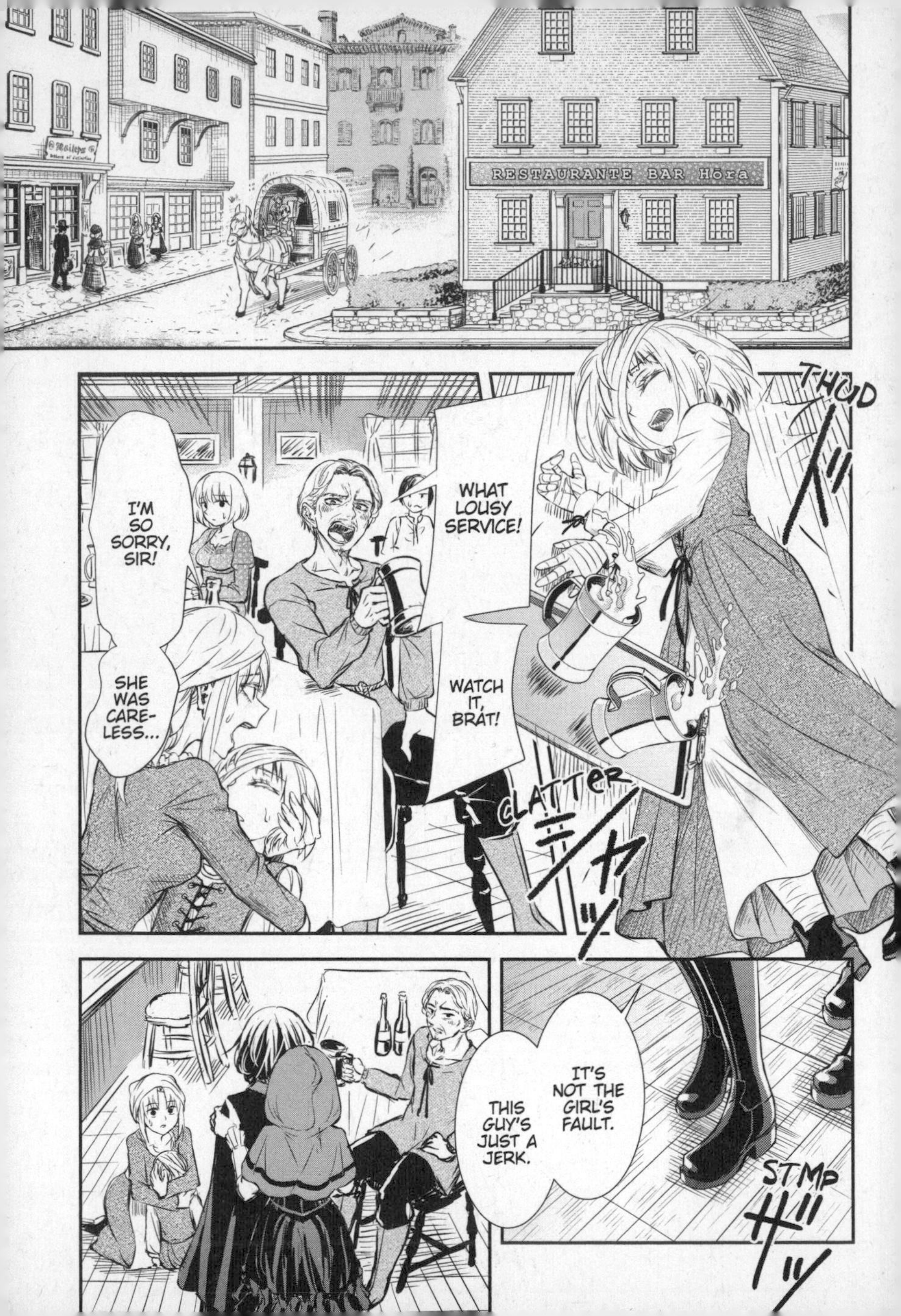
RESTAURANTE BAR Höra
THUD
WHAT LOUSY SERVICE!
WATCH IT, BRAT!
I'M SO SORRY, SIR!
SHE WAS CARELESS...
CLATTER
STMP
IT'S NOT THE GIRL'S FAULT.
THIS GUY'S JUST A JERK.

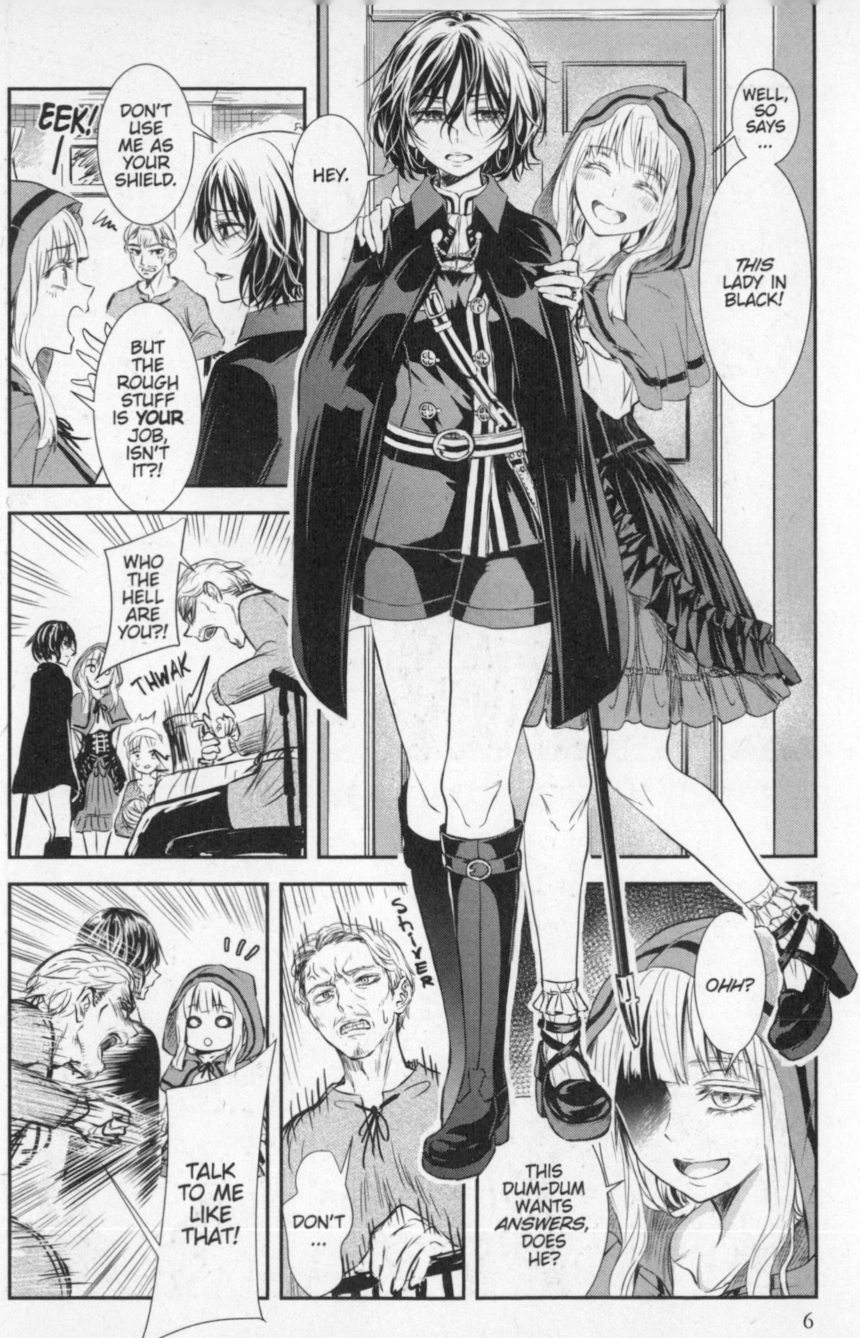
WELL, SO SAYS ...
THIS LADY IN BLACK!
HEY.
DON'T USE ME AS YOUR SHIELD.
EEK!
BUT THE ROUGH STUFF IS YOUR JOB, ISN'T IT?!
WHO THE HELL ARE YOU?!
THWAK
OHH?
THIS DUM-DUM WANTS ANSWERS, DOES HE?
SHIVER
DON'T ...
TALK TO ME LIKE THAT!

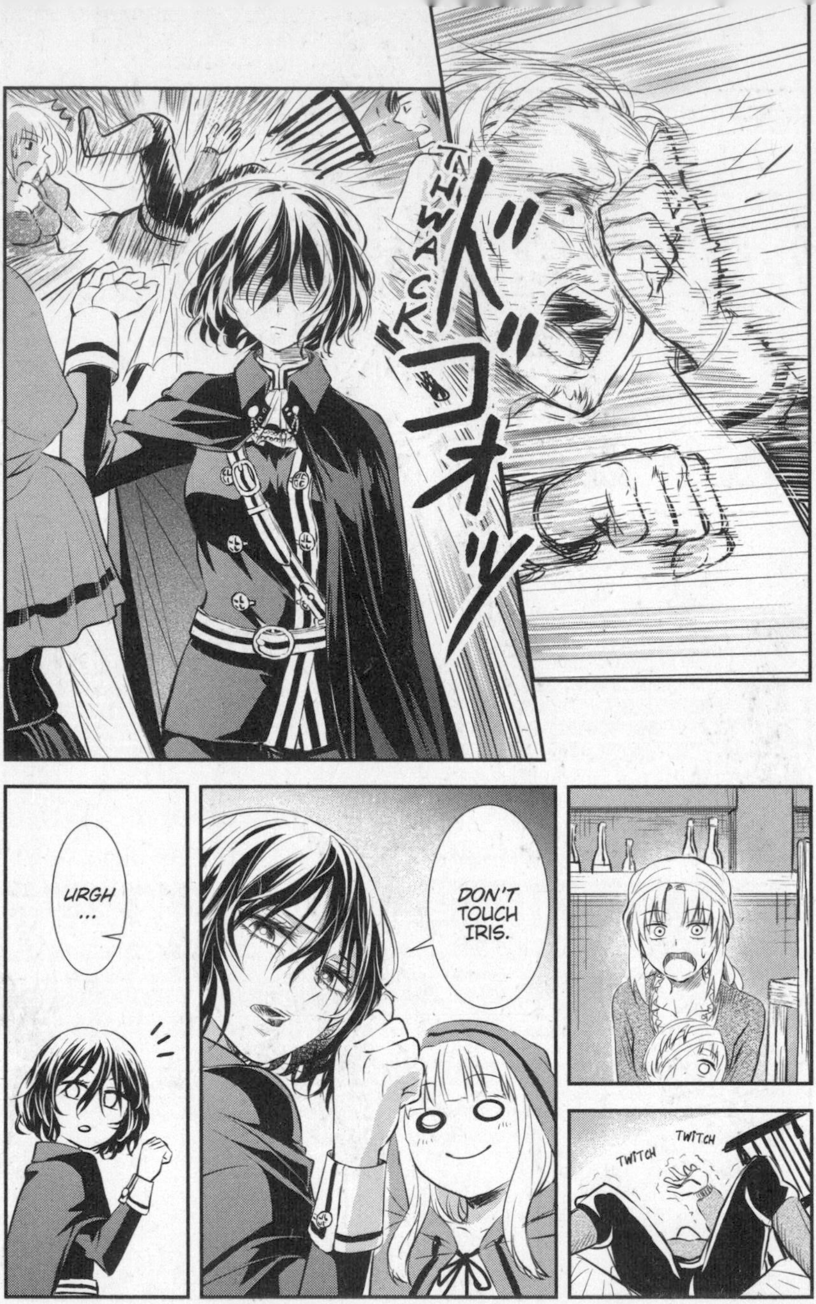
THWACK
ドゴオッ
TWITCH
TWITCH
DON'T TOUCH IRIS.
URGH ...

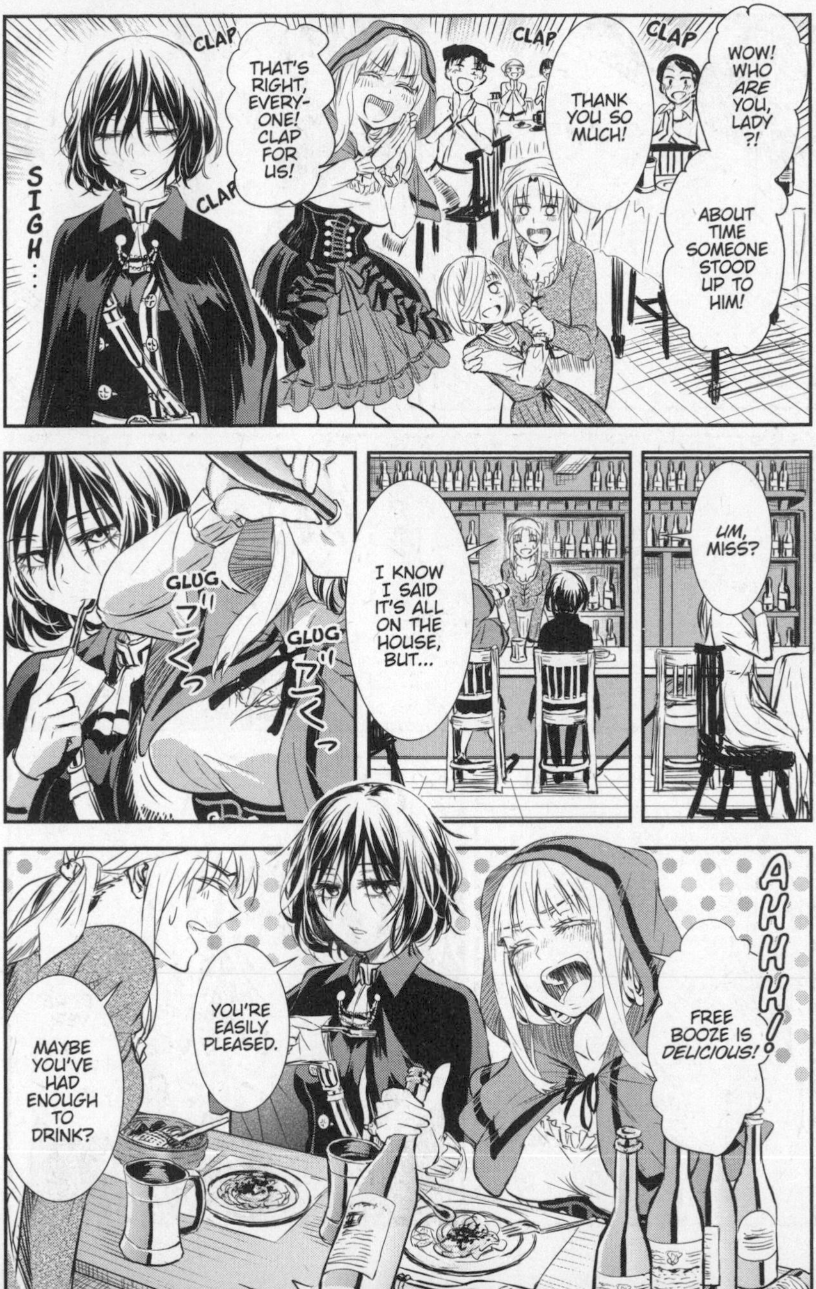
CLAP
WOW! WHO ARE YOU, LADY?!
CLAP
THANK YOU SO MUCH!
ABOUT TIME SOMEONE STOOD UP TO HIM!
CLAP
THAT'S RIGHT, EVERYONE! CLAP FOR US!
CLAP
SIGH...
UM, MISS?
I KNOW I SAID IT'S ALL ON THE HOUSE, BUT...
GLUG
GLUG
AHHHH!
FREE BOOZE IS DELICIOUS!
YOU'RE EASILY PLEASED.
MAYBE YOU'VE HAD ENOUGH TO DRINK?

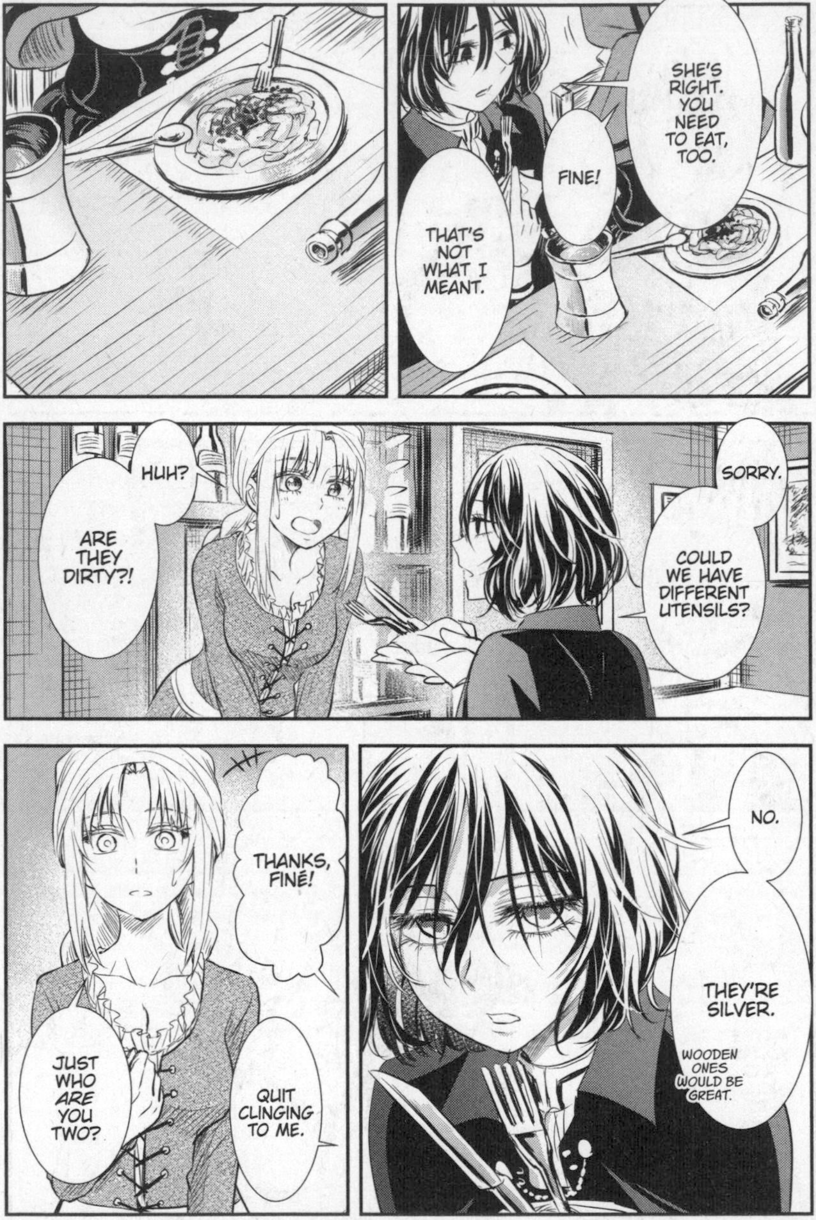
SHE'S RIGHT. YOU NEED TO EAT, TOO.
FINE!
THAT'S NOT WHAT I MEANT.
SORRY.
COULD WE HAVE DIFFERENT UTENSILS?
HUH?
ARE THEY DIRTY?!
NO.
THEY'RE SILVER.
WOODEN ONES WOULD BE GREAT.
THANKS, FINÉ!
QUIT CLINGING TO ME.
JUST WHO ARE YOU TWO?

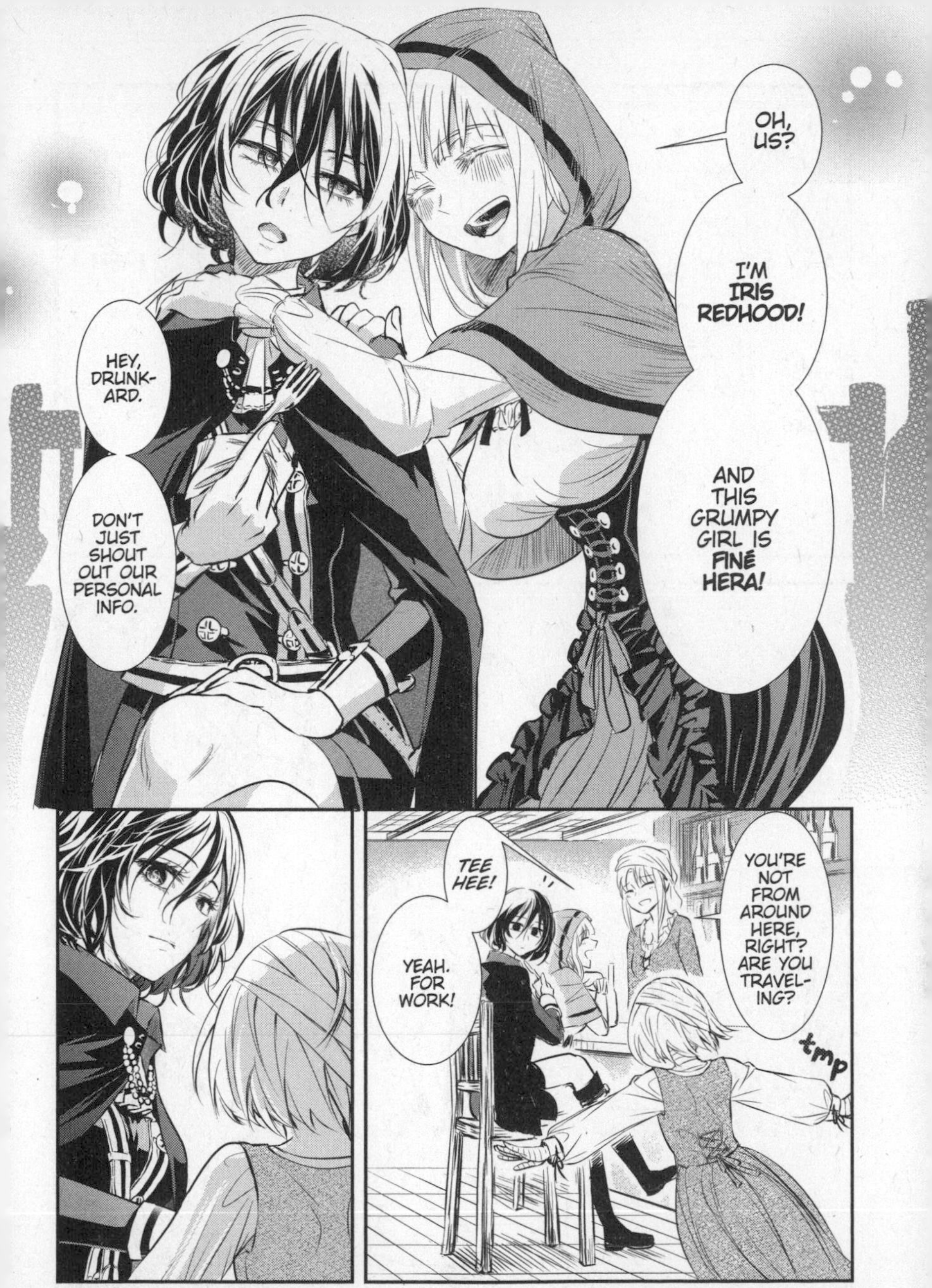
OH, US?
I'M IRIS REDHOOD!
AND THIS GRUMPY GIRL IS FINÉ HERA!
HEY, DRUNKARD.
DON'T JUST SHOUT OUT OUR PERSONAL INFO.
YOU'RE NOT FROM AROUND HERE, RIGHT? ARE YOU TRAVELING?
TEE HEE!
YEAH. FOR WORK!
tmp

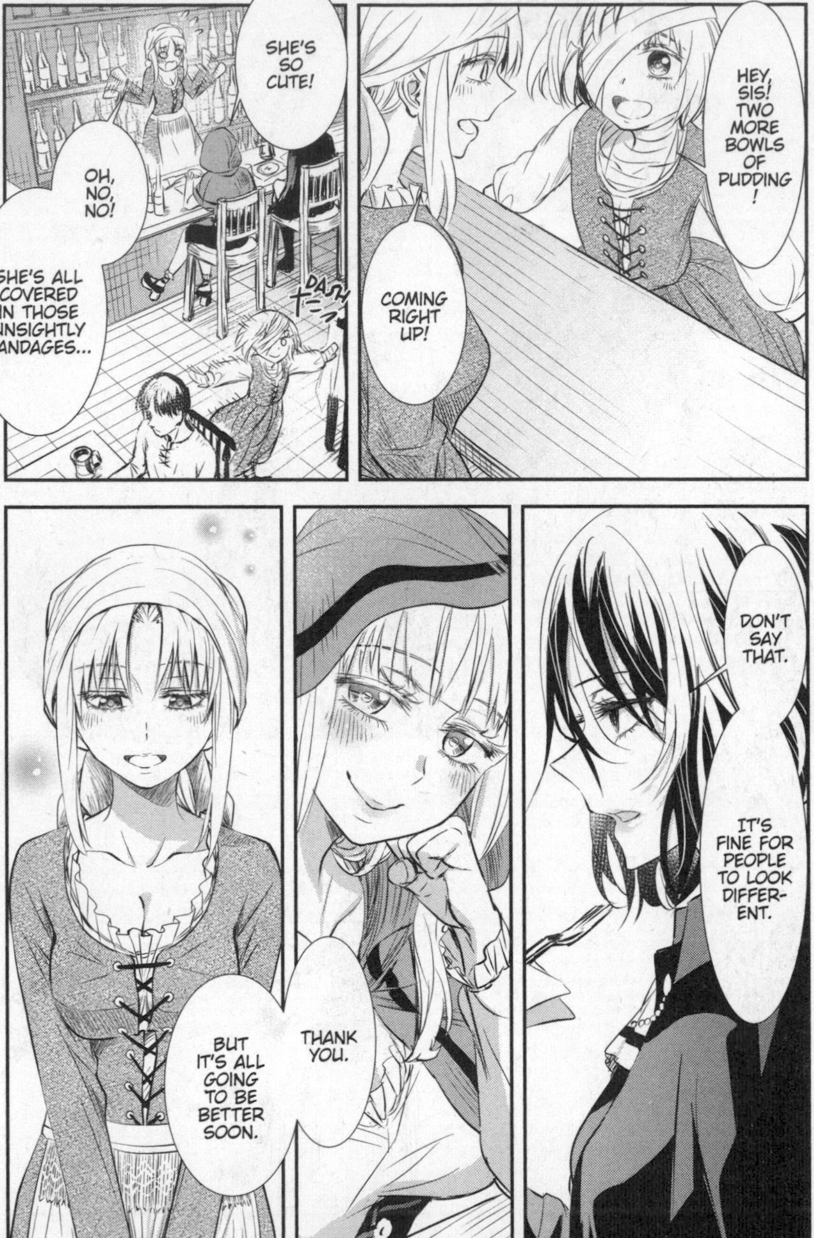
HEY, SIS! TWO MORE BOWLS OF PUDDING!
COMING RIGHT UP!
SHE'S SO CUTE!
OH, NO, NO!
SHE'S ALL COVERED IN THOSE UNSIGHTLY BANDAGES...
DASH
DON'T SAY THAT.
IT'S FINE FOR PEOPLE TO LOOK DIFFER-ENT.
THANK YOU.
BUT IT'S ALL GOING TO BE BETTER SOON.

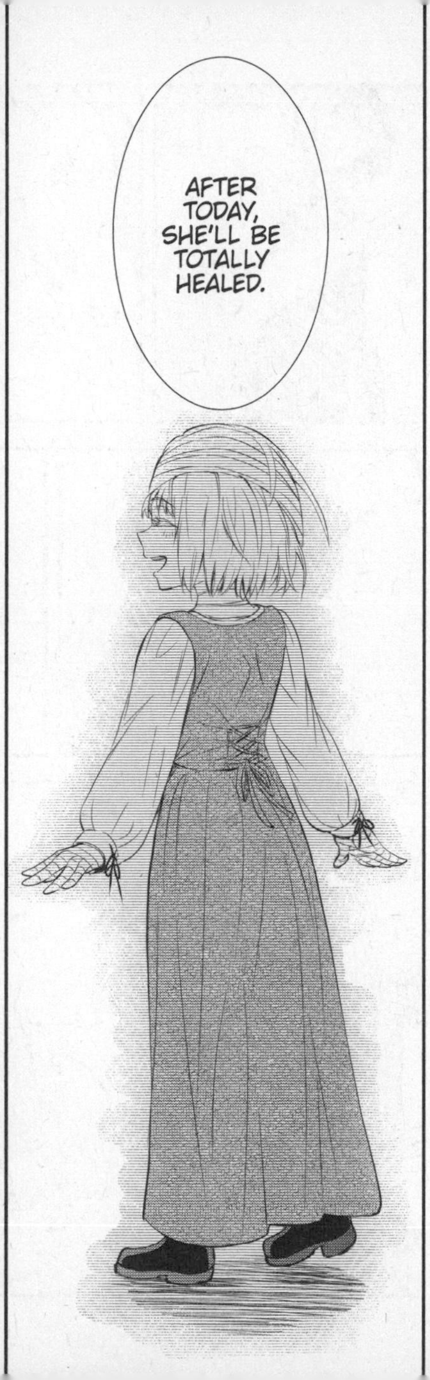
AFTER TODAY, SHE'LL BE TOTALLY HEALED.

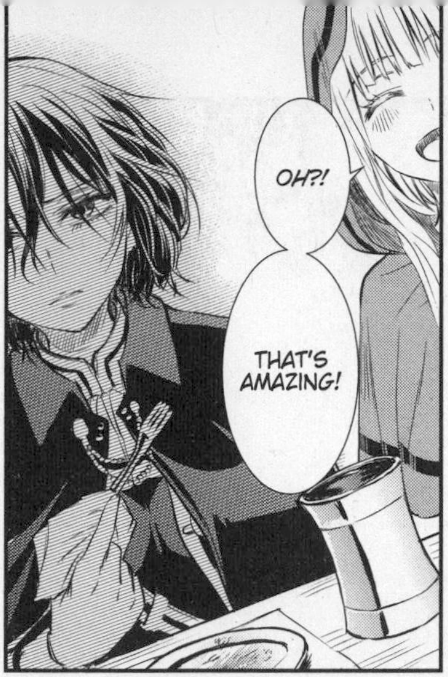
OH?!
THAT'S AMAZING!

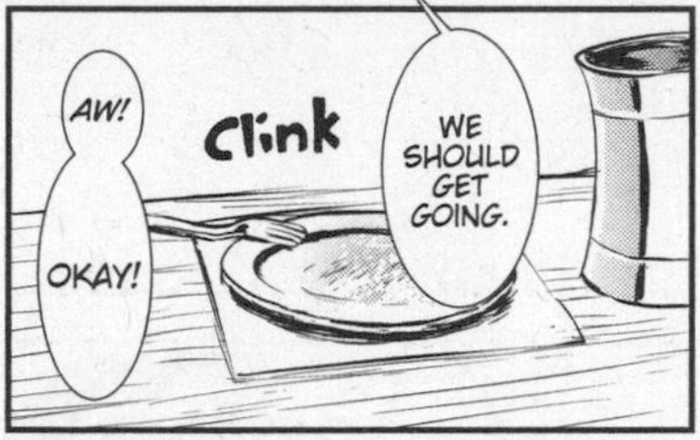
WE SHOULD GET GOING.
Clink
AW!
OKAY!

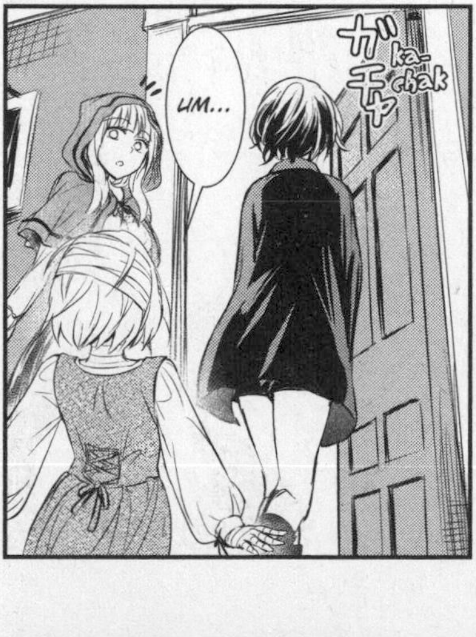
ガチャ
ka-chak
UM...

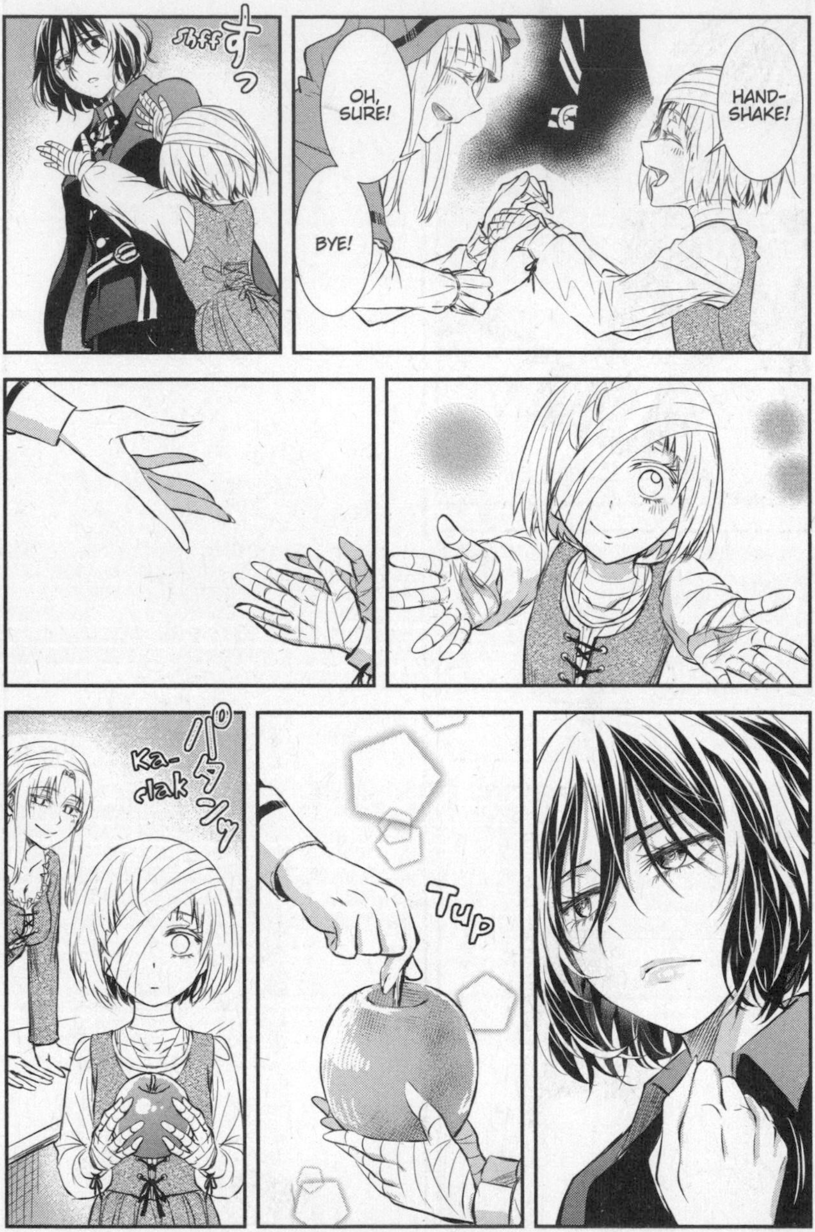
HAND-SHAKE!
OH, SURE!
BYE!
shff
すっ
Tup
Ka-clak
パタンッ

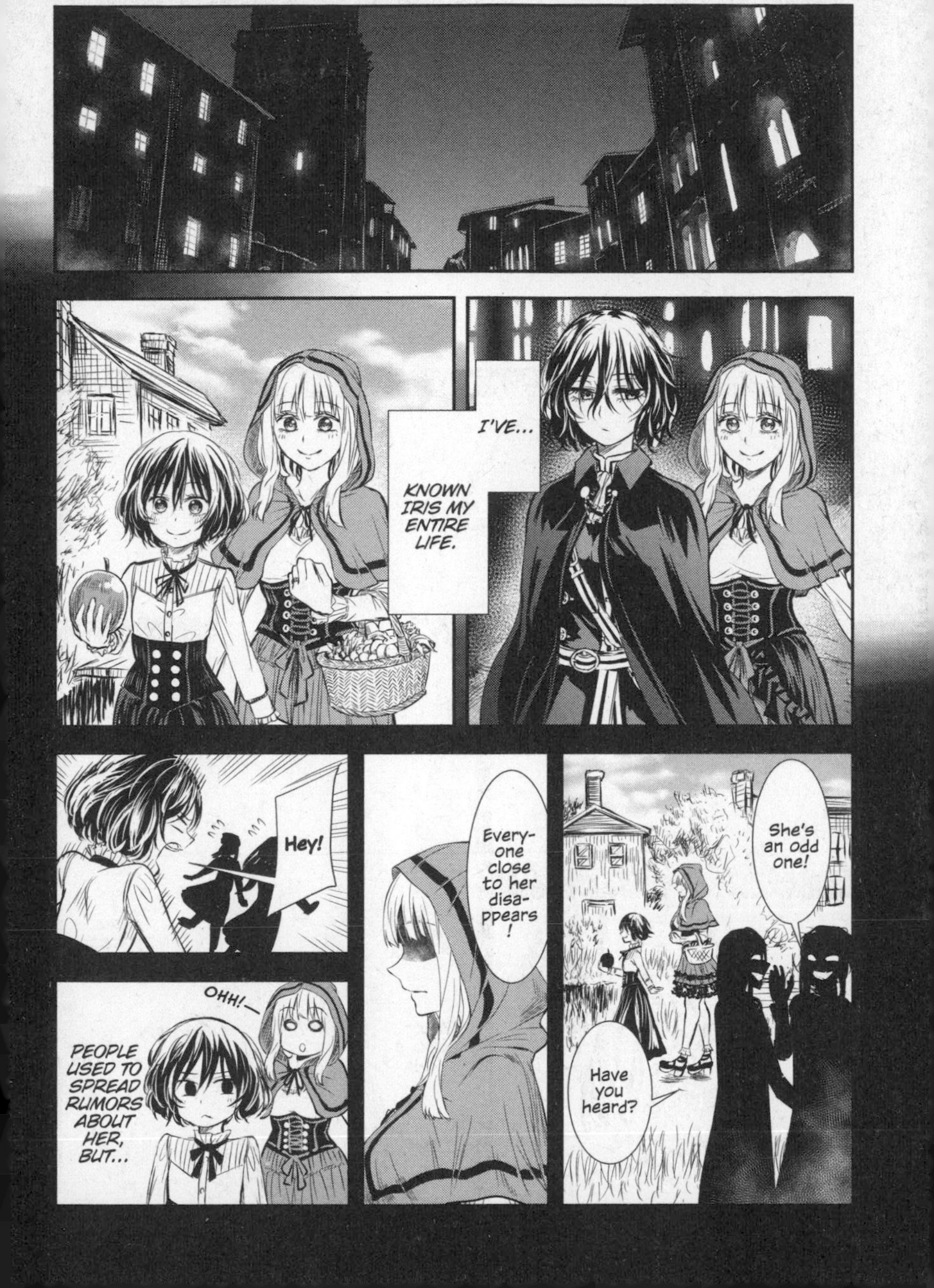
I'VE...
KNOWN IRIS MY ENTIRE LIFE.
She's an odd one!
Have you heard?
Every-one close to her disa-ppears!
Hey!
OHH!
PEOPLE USED TO SPREAD RUMORS ABOUT HER, BUT...

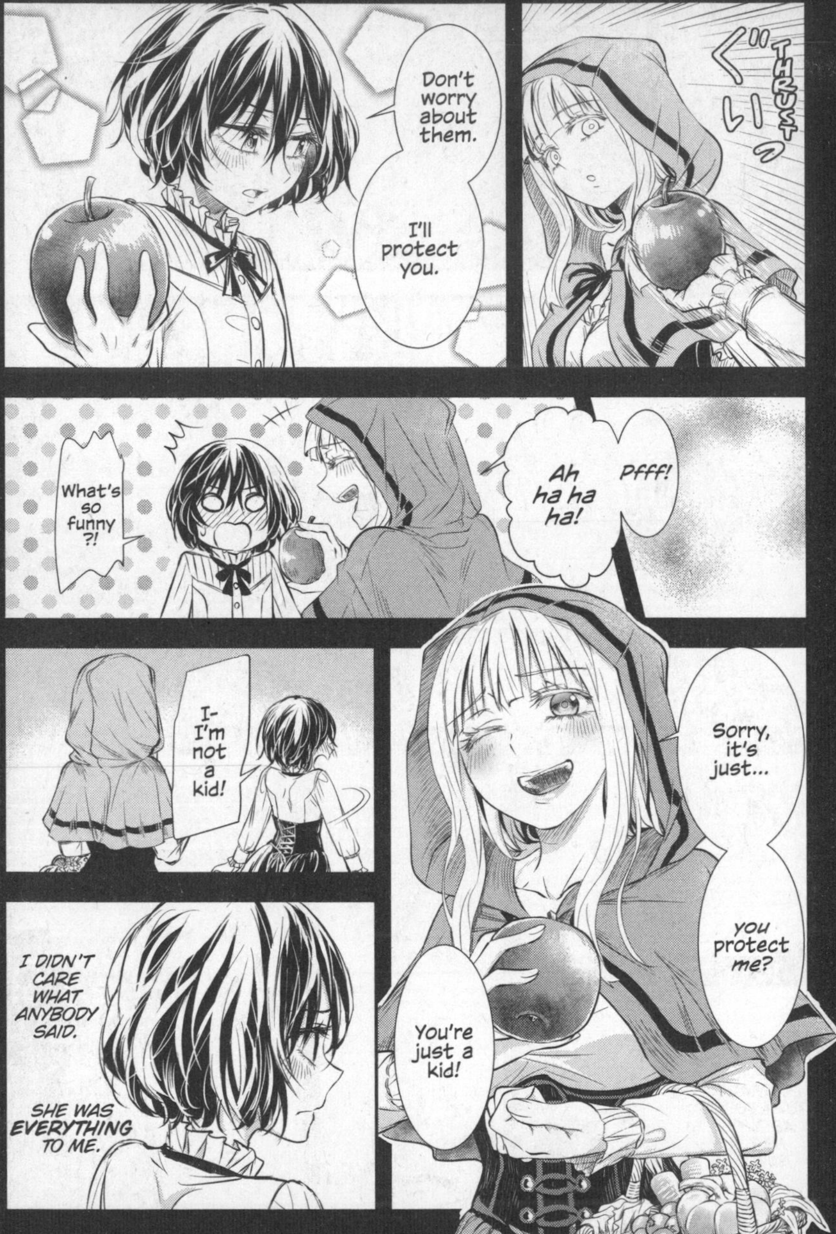
THRUST
Don't worry about them.
I'll protect you.
Pfff!
Ah ha ha ha!
What's so funny?!
Sorry, it's just...
you protect me?
You're just a kid!
I- I'm not a kid!
I DIDN'T CARE WHAT ANYBODY SAID.
SHE WAS EVERYTHING TO ME.

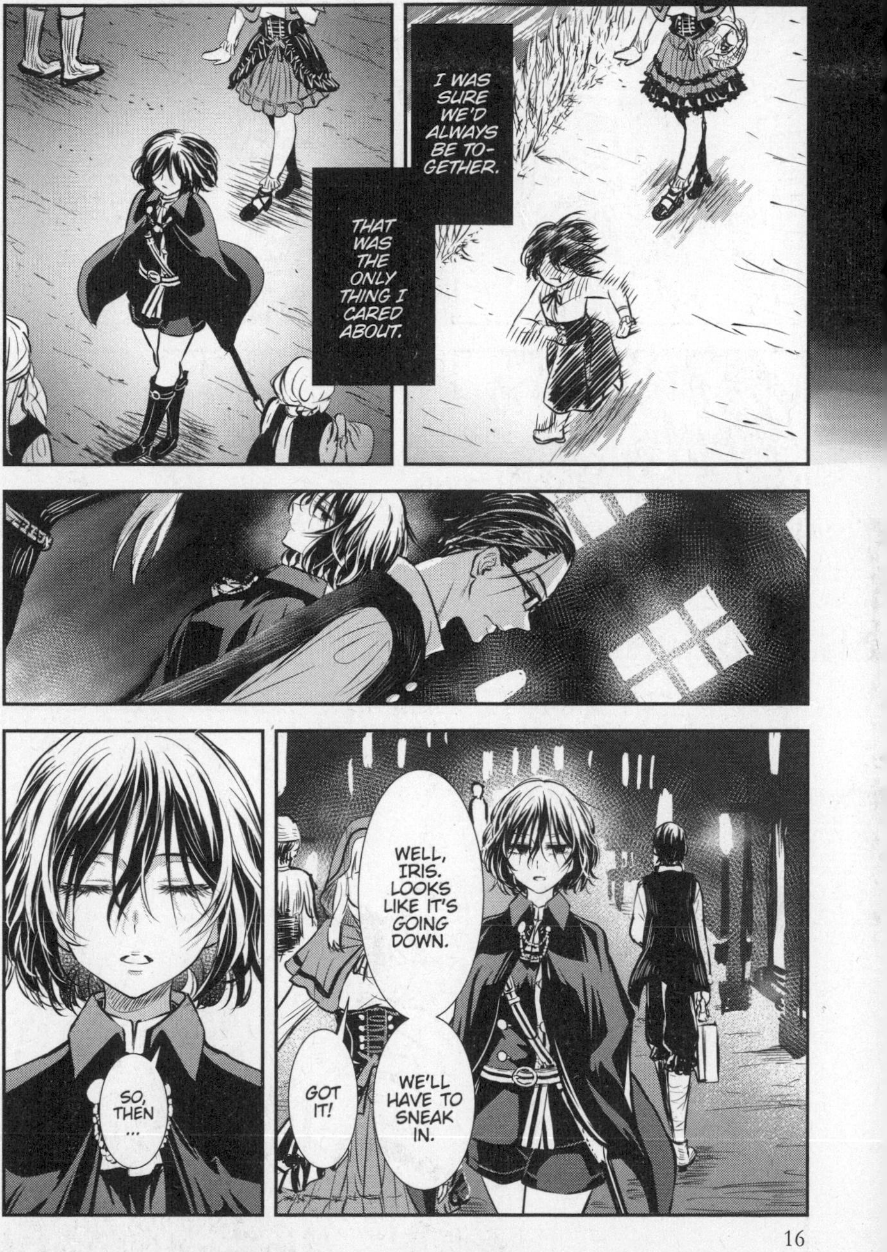
I WAS SURE WE'D ALWAYS BE TO-GETHER.
THAT WAS THE ONLY THING I CARED ABOUT.
WELL, IRIS. LOOKS LIKE IT'S GOING DOWN.
WE'LL HAVE TO SNEAK IN.
GOT IT!
SO, THEN ...

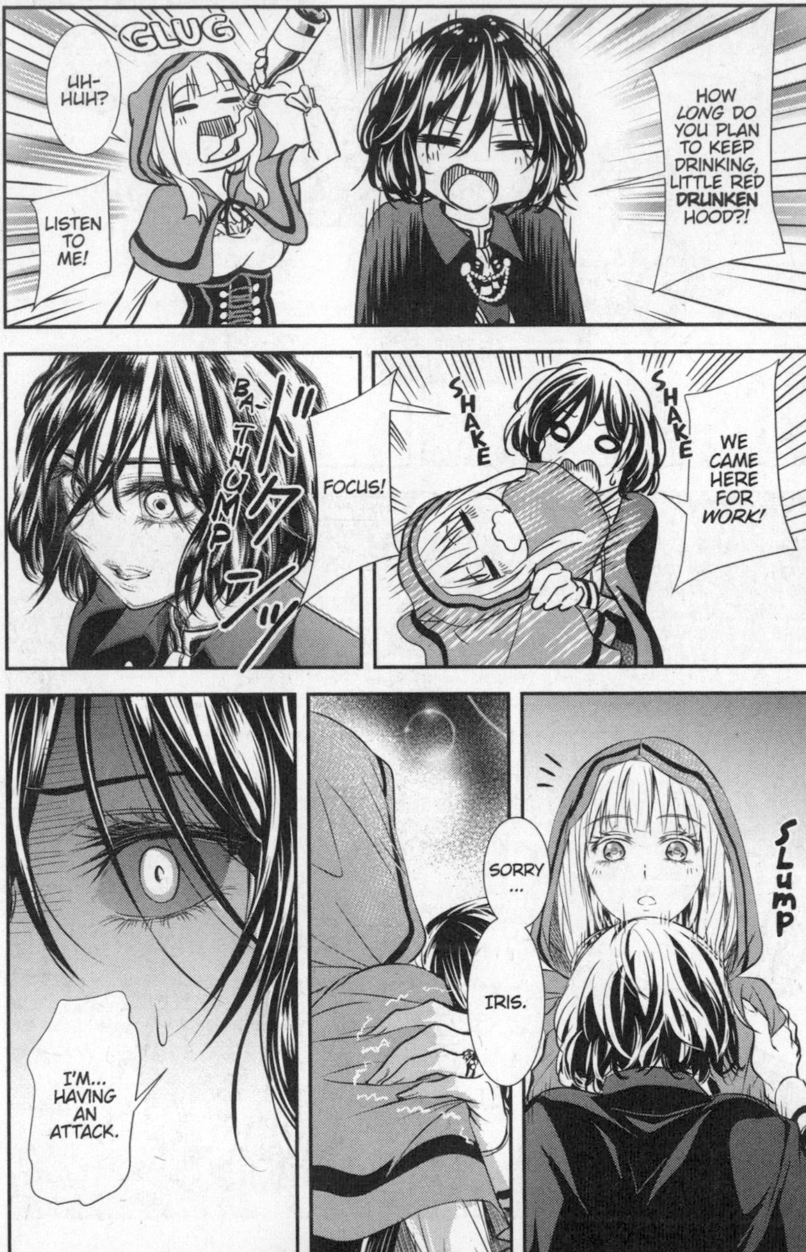
HOW LONG DO YOU PLAN TO KEEP DRINKING, LITTLE RED DRUNKEN HOOD?!
GLUG
UH-HUH?
LISTEN TO ME!
SHAKE
WE CAME HERE FOR WORK!
SHAKE
FOCUS!
BA-THUMP
SLUMP
SORRY...
IRIS.
I'M... HAVING AN ATTACK.

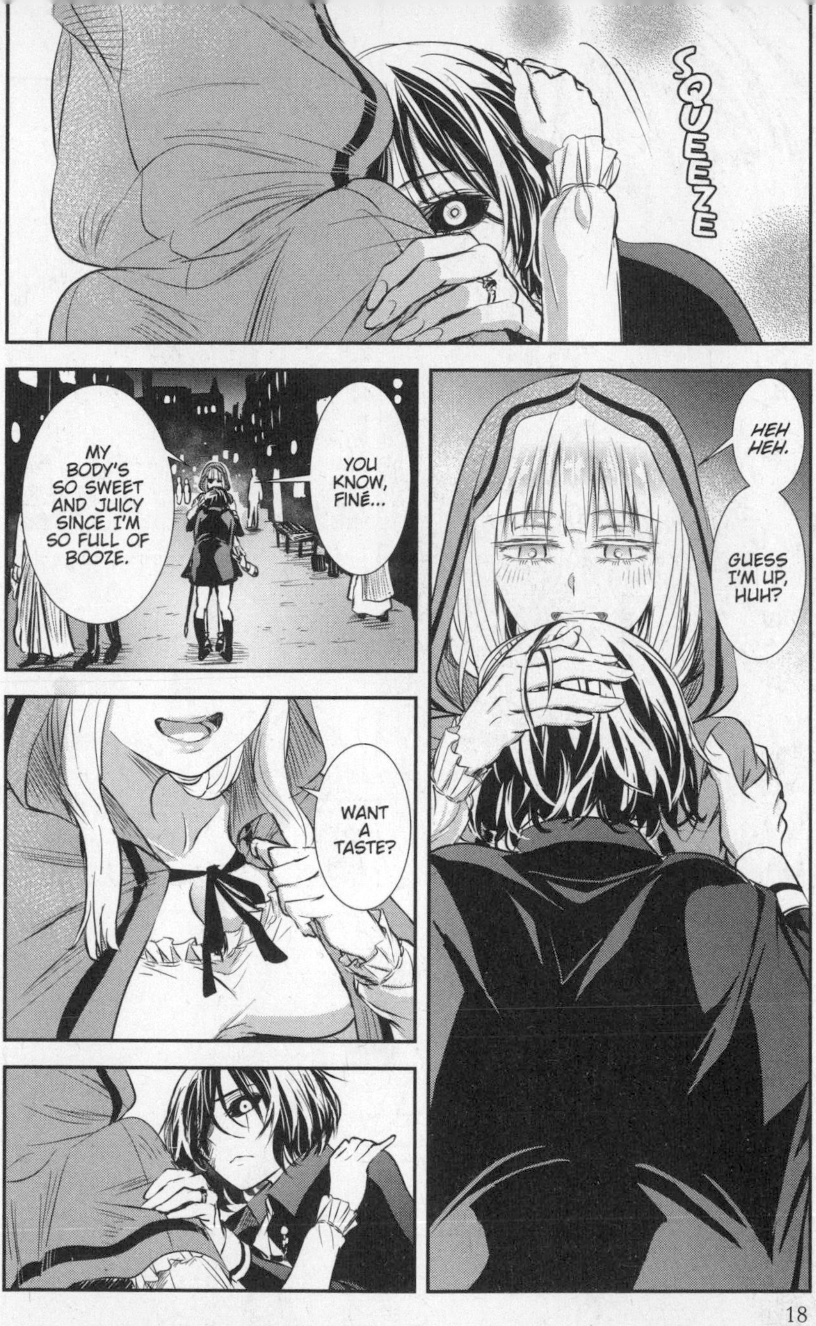
SQUEEZE
HEH HEH.
GUESS I'M UP, HUH?
YOU KNOW, FINÉ...
MY BODY'S SO SWEET AND JUICY SINCE I'M SO FULL OF BOOZE.
WANT A TASTE?

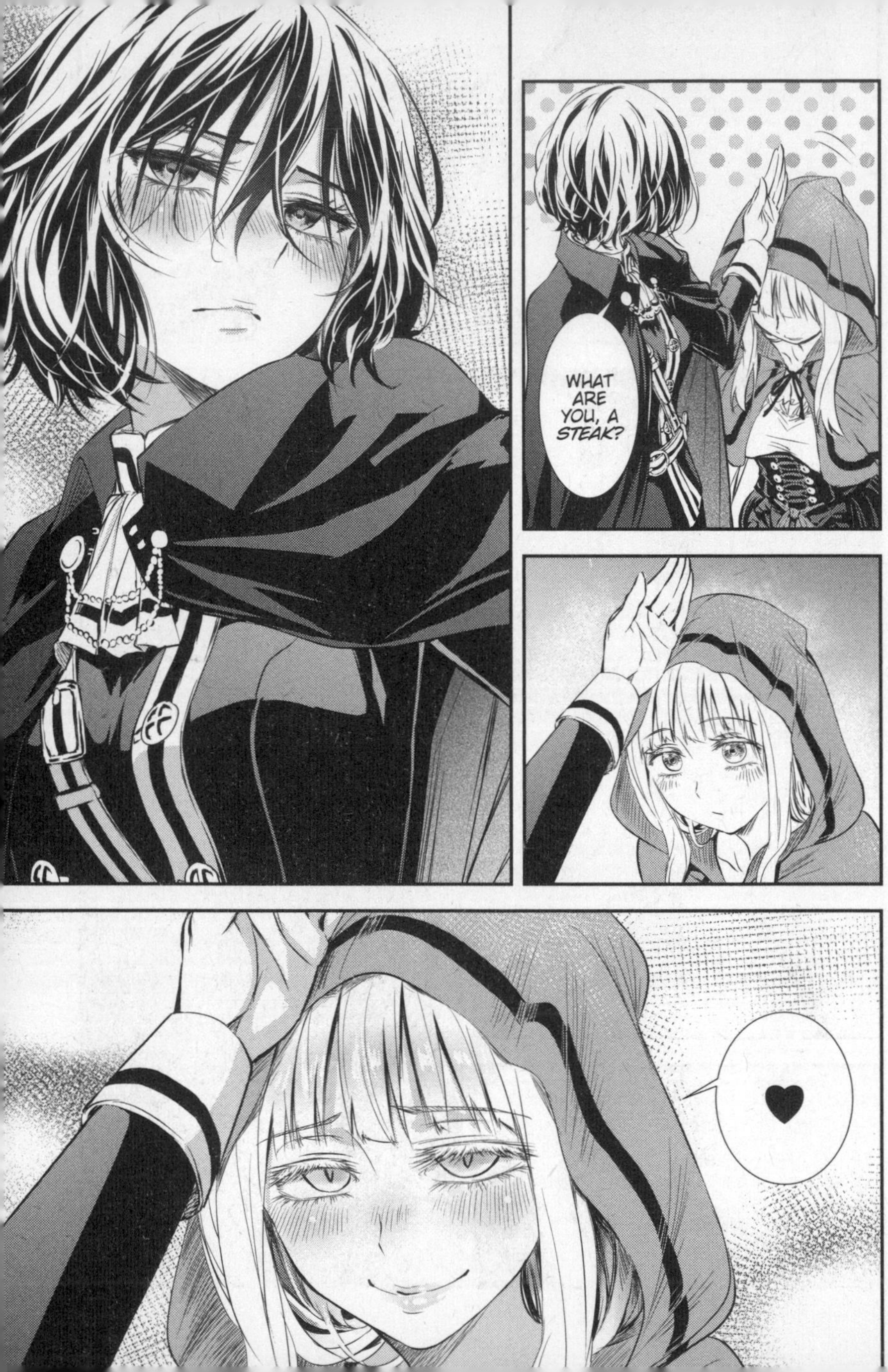
WHAT ARE YOU, A STEAK?
♥

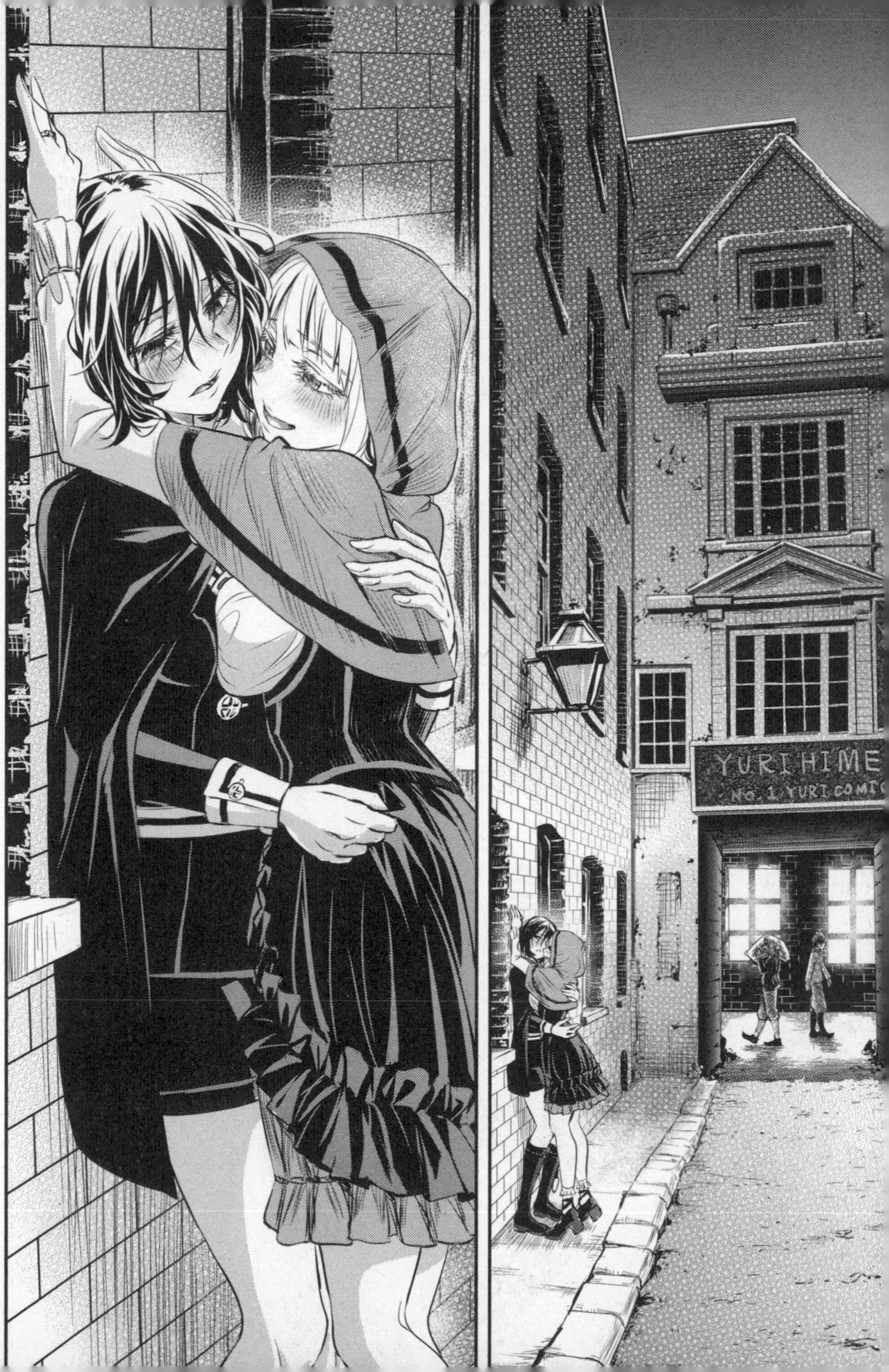
YURI HIME
No. 1 YURI COMI

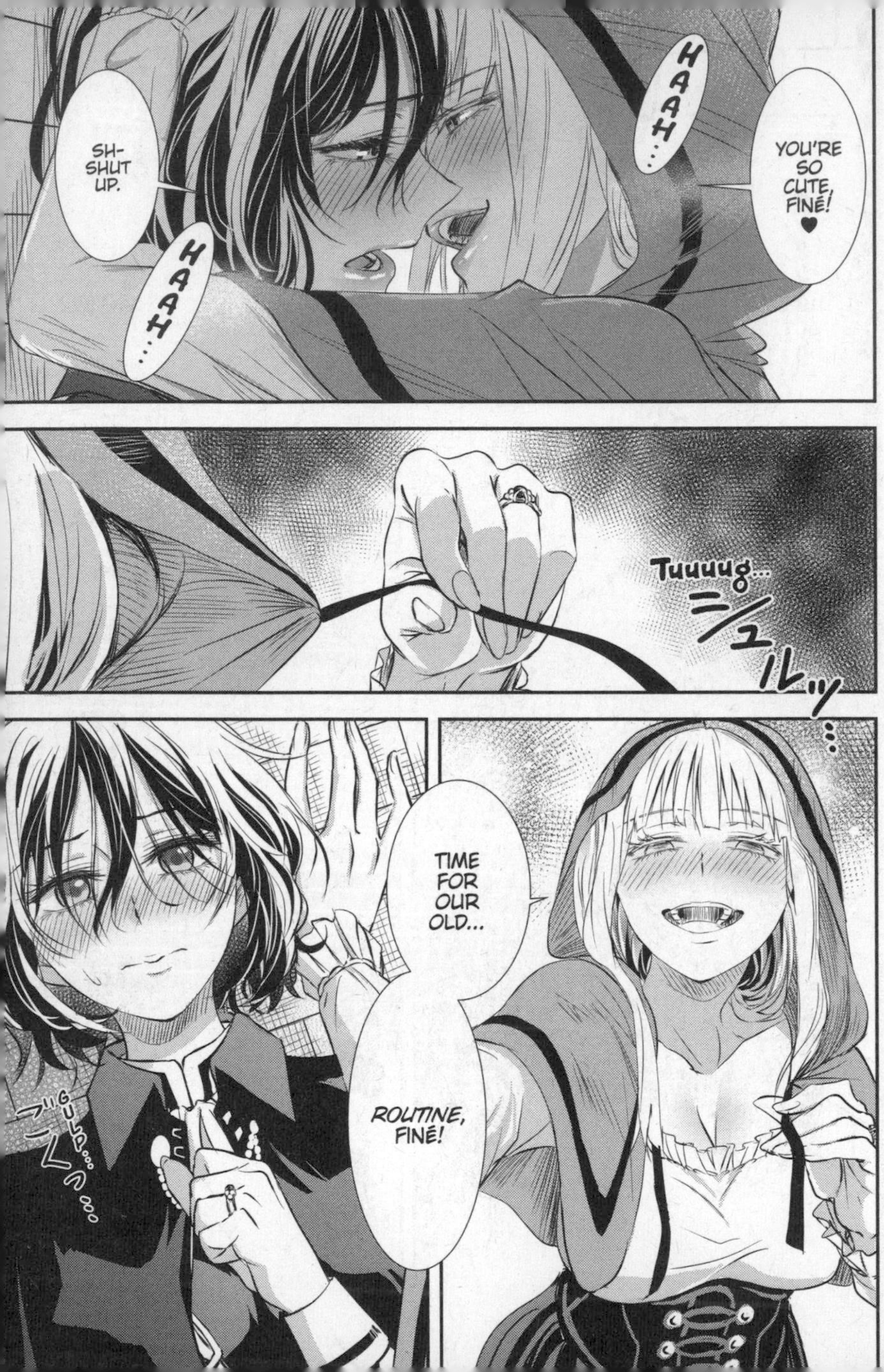
YOU'RE SO CUTE, FINÉ! ♥
HAAAH...
SH-SHUT UP.
HAAAH...
Tuuuug...
シュルッ...
TIME FOR OUR OLD...
ROUTINE, FINÉ!
GULP...

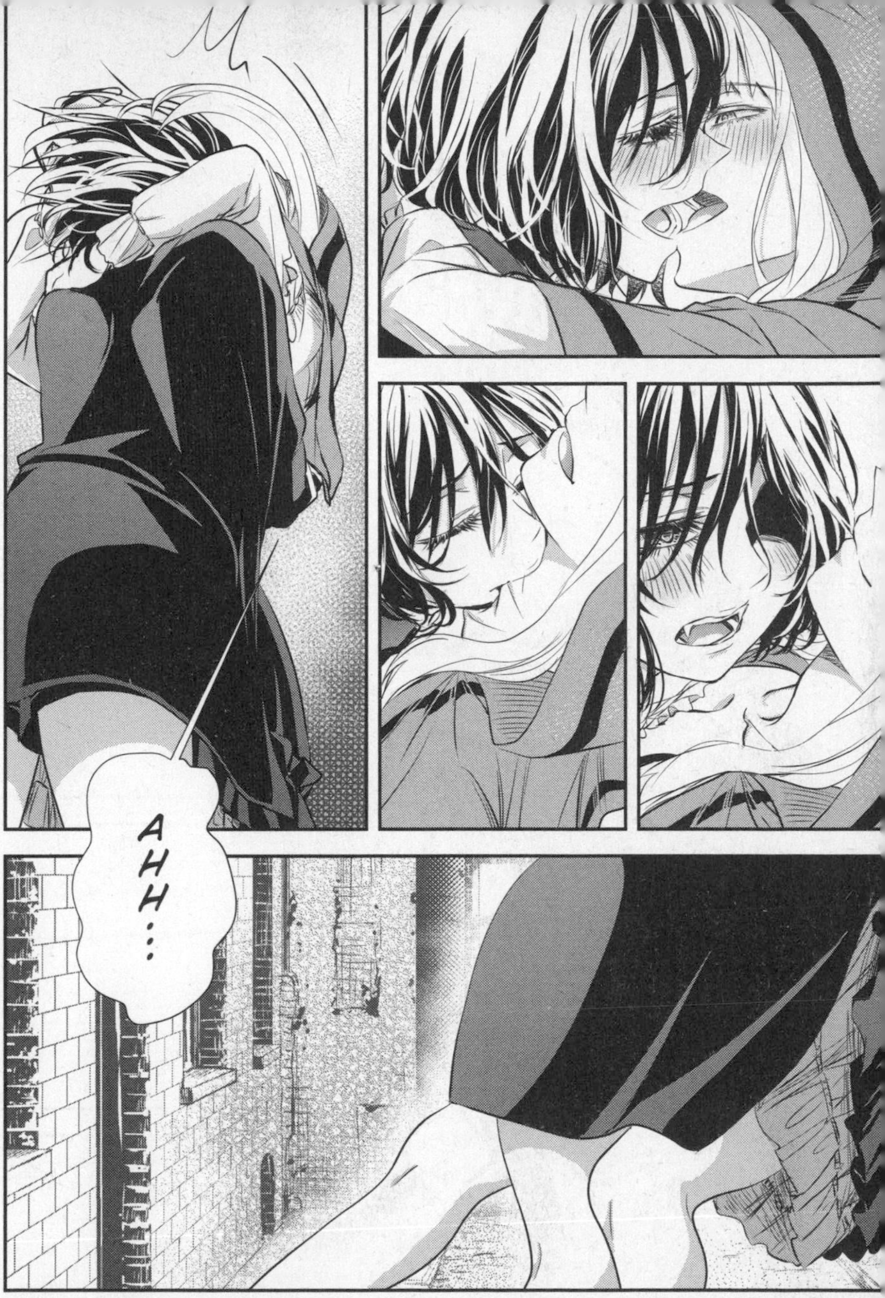
M
AHH...

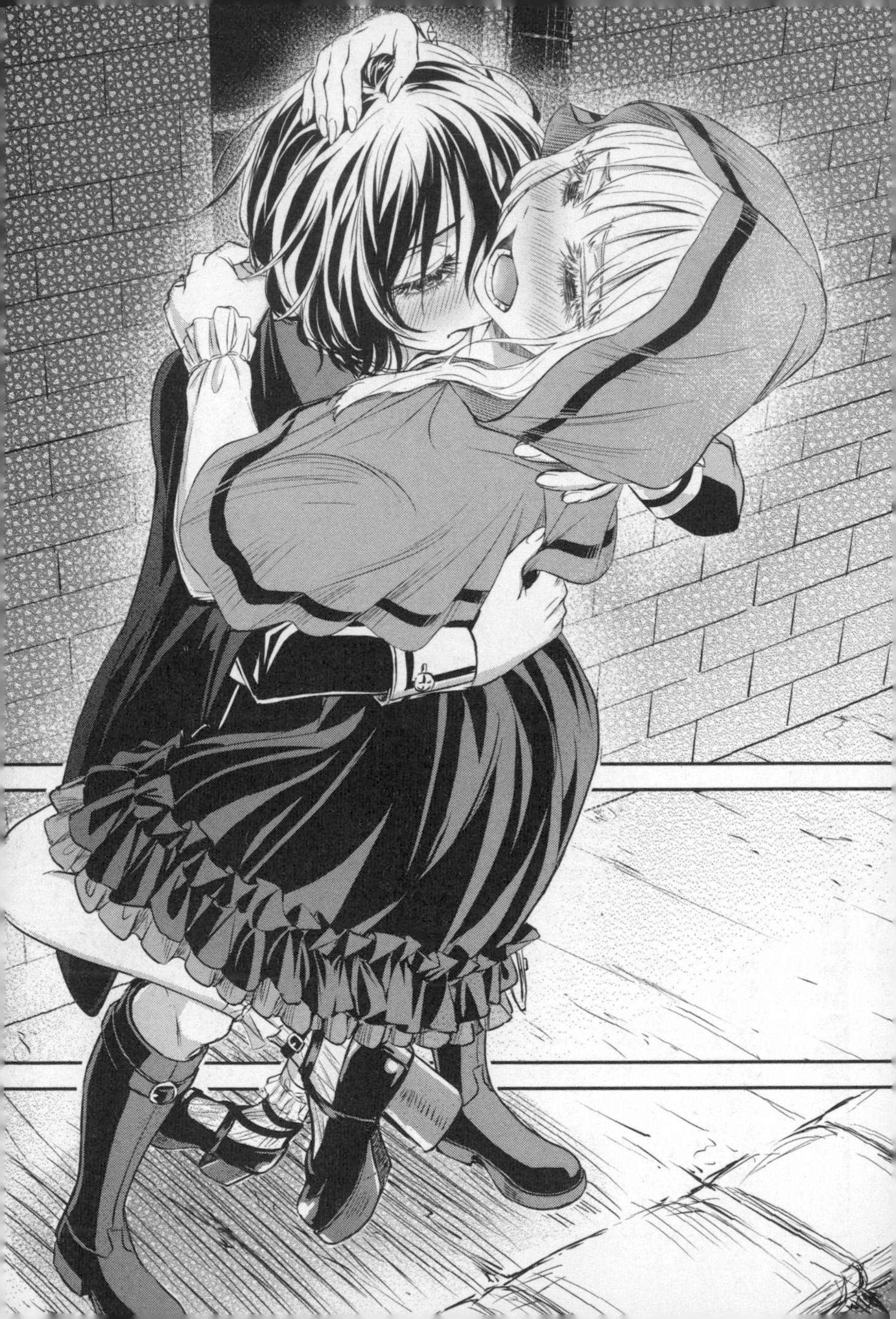

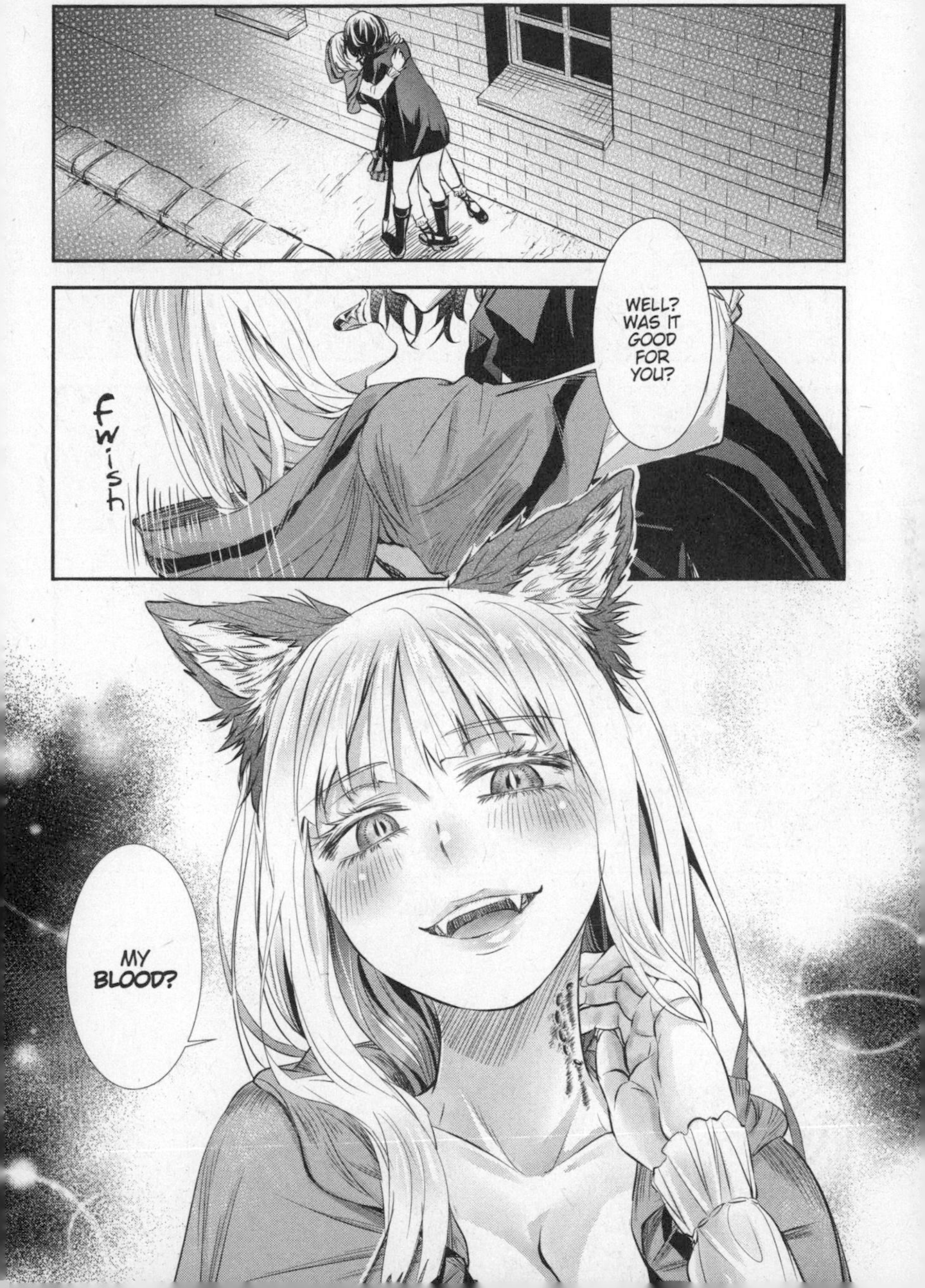
WELL? WAS IT GOOD FOR YOU?
fwish
MY BLOOD?

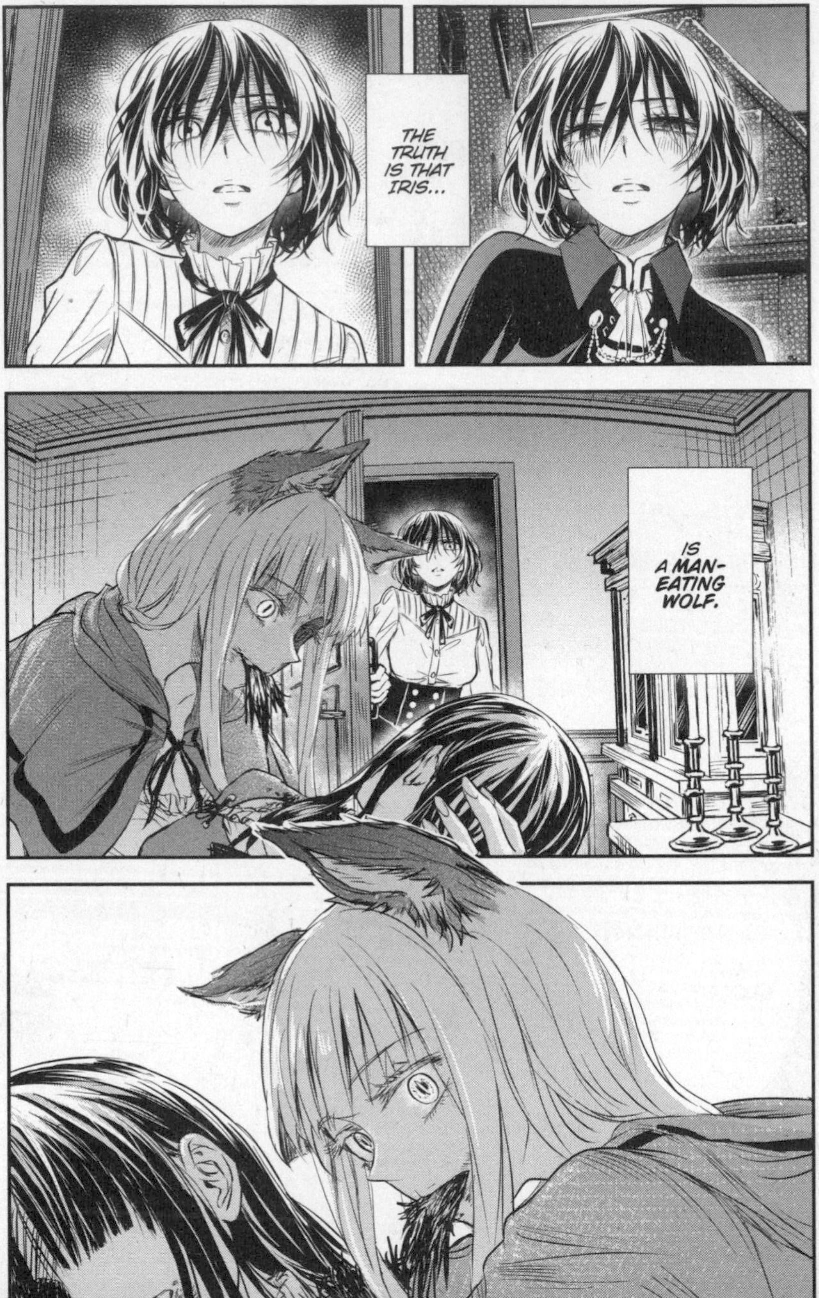
THE TRUTH IS THAT IRIS...
IS A MAN-EATING WOLF.

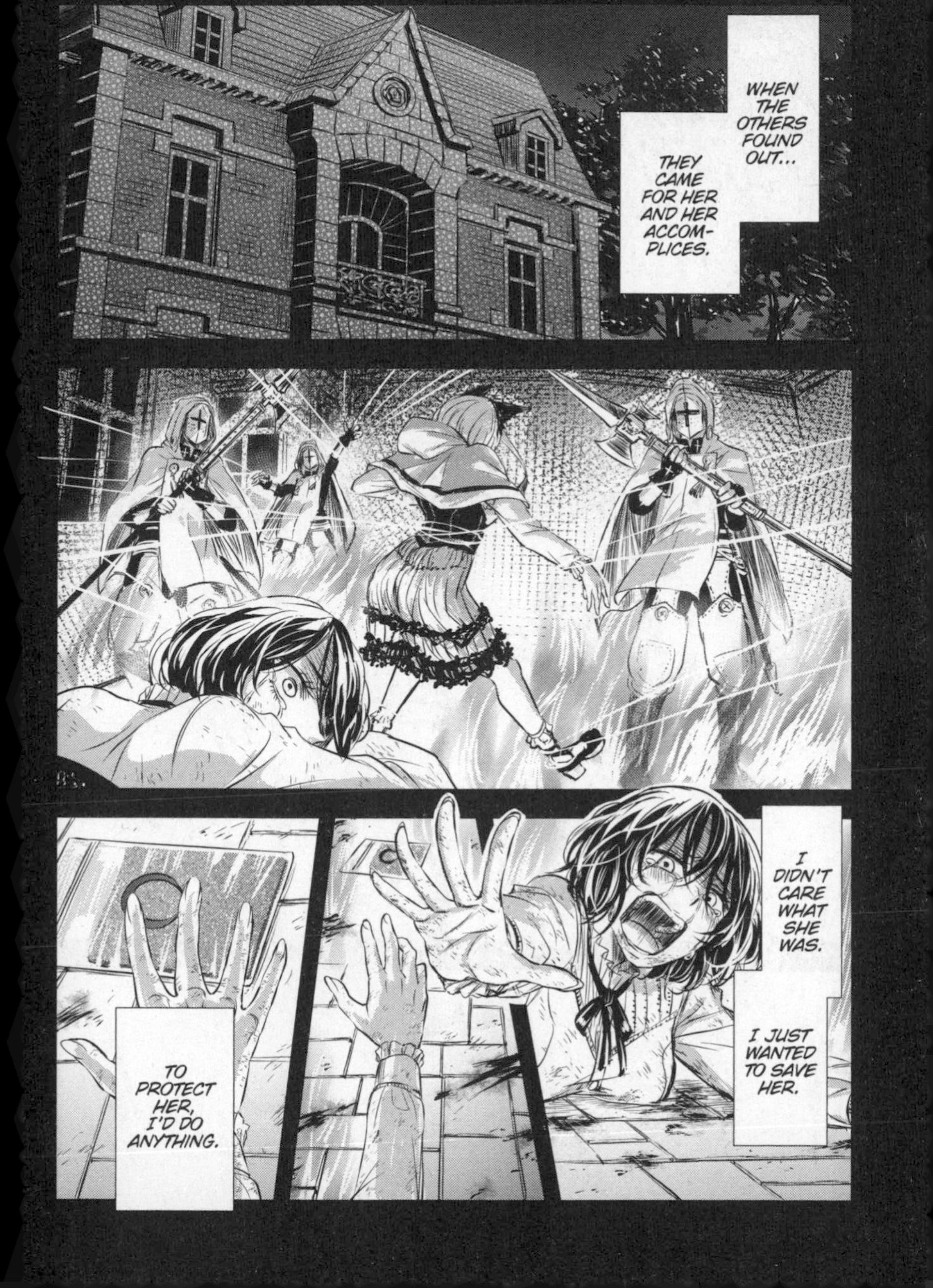
WHEN THE OTHERS FOUND OUT...
THEY CAME FOR HER AND HER ACCOMPLICES.
I DIDN'T CARE WHAT SHE WAS.
I JUST WANTED TO SAVE HER.
TO PROTECT HER, I'D DO ANYTHING.

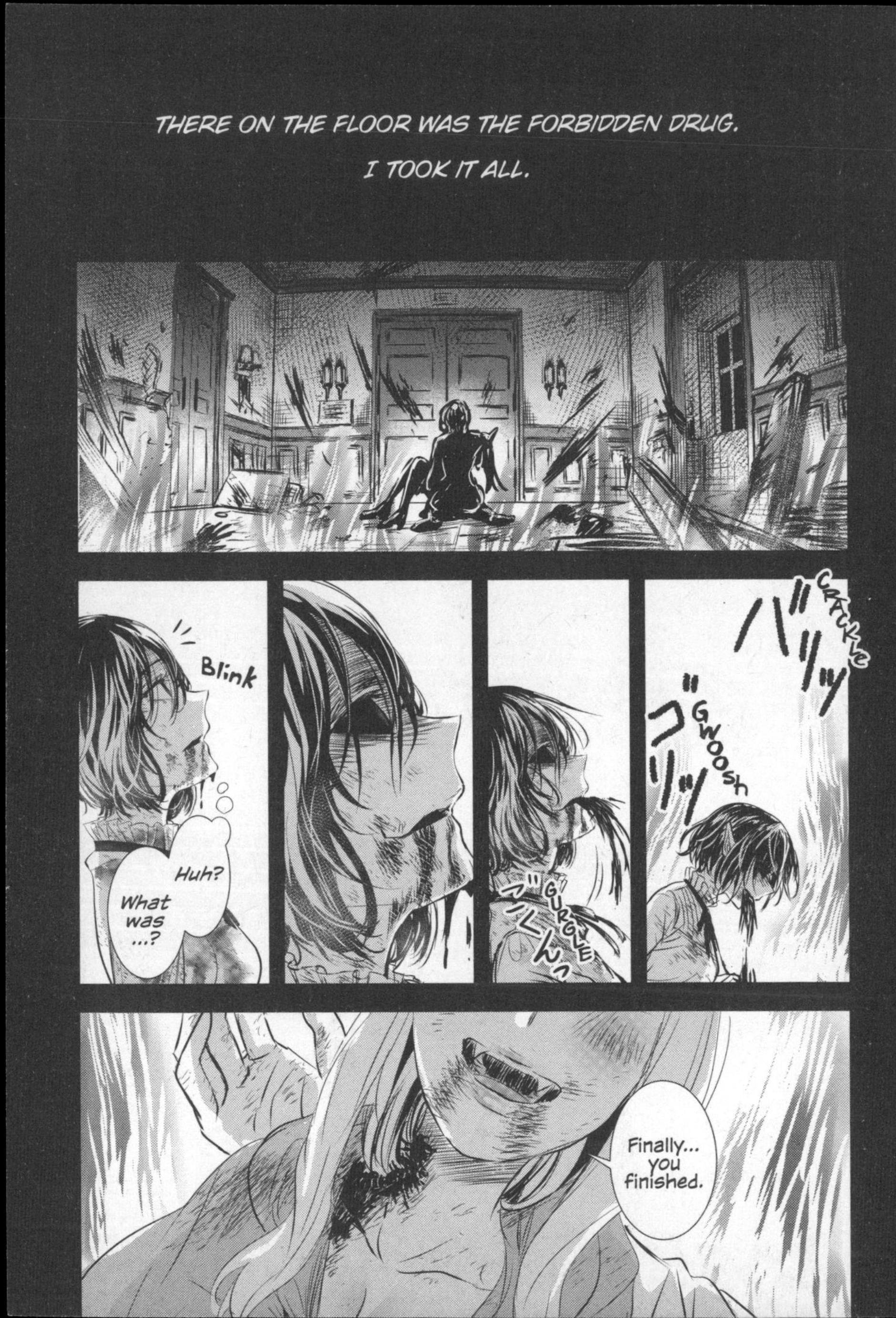
THERE ON THE FLOOR WAS THE FORBIDDEN DRUG.
I TOOK IT ALL.
バリッ
CRACKLE
ゴリッ
GWOOSH
ごくんっ
GURGLE
Blink
Huh? What was ...?
Finally... you finished.

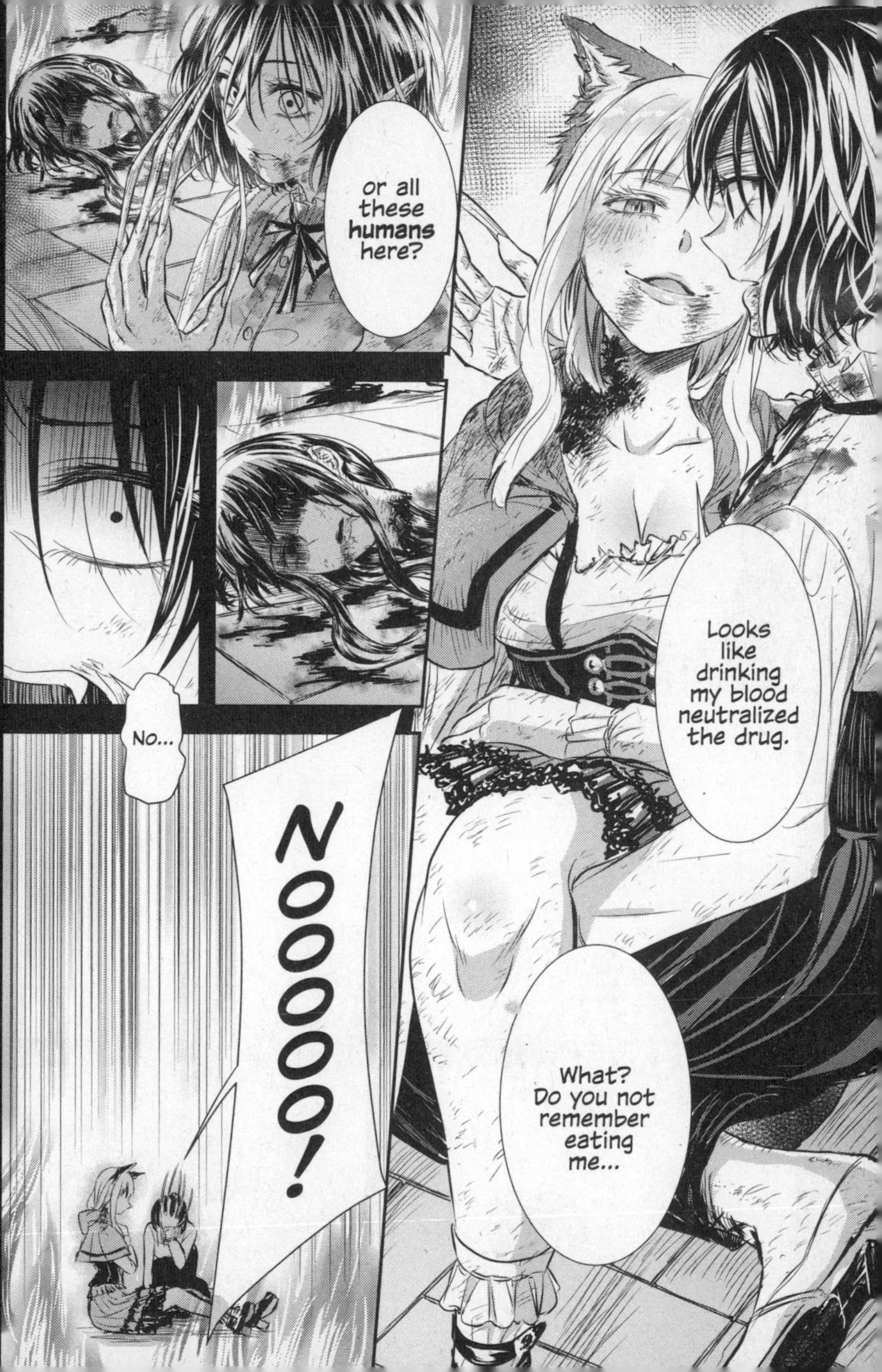
or all these humans here?
Looks like drinking my blood neutralized the drug.
What? Do you not remember eating me...
No...
NOOOOOO!

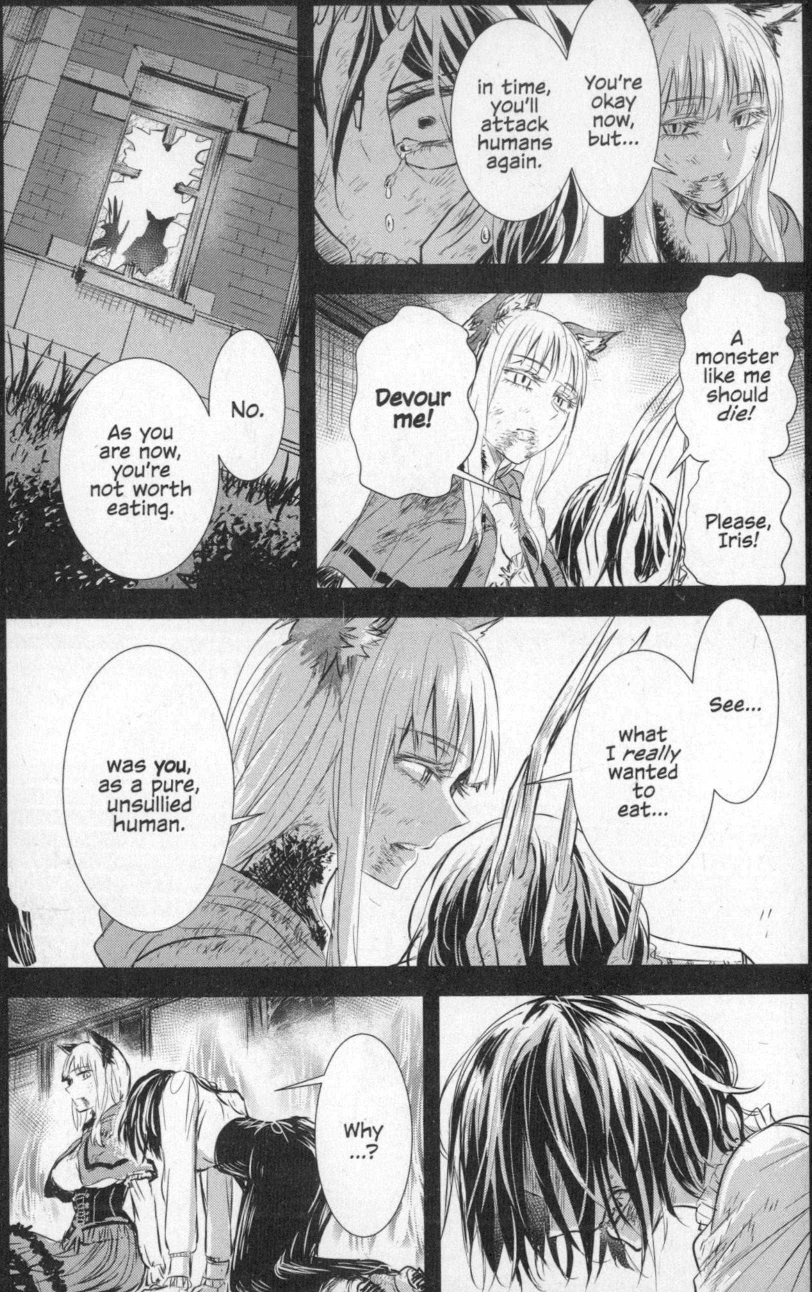
You're okay now, but...
in time, you'll attack humans again.
A monster like me should *die!*
Please, Iris!
Devour me!
No.
As you are now, you're not worth eating.
See...
what I *really* wanted to eat...
was you, as a pure, unsullied human.
!!
Why ...?

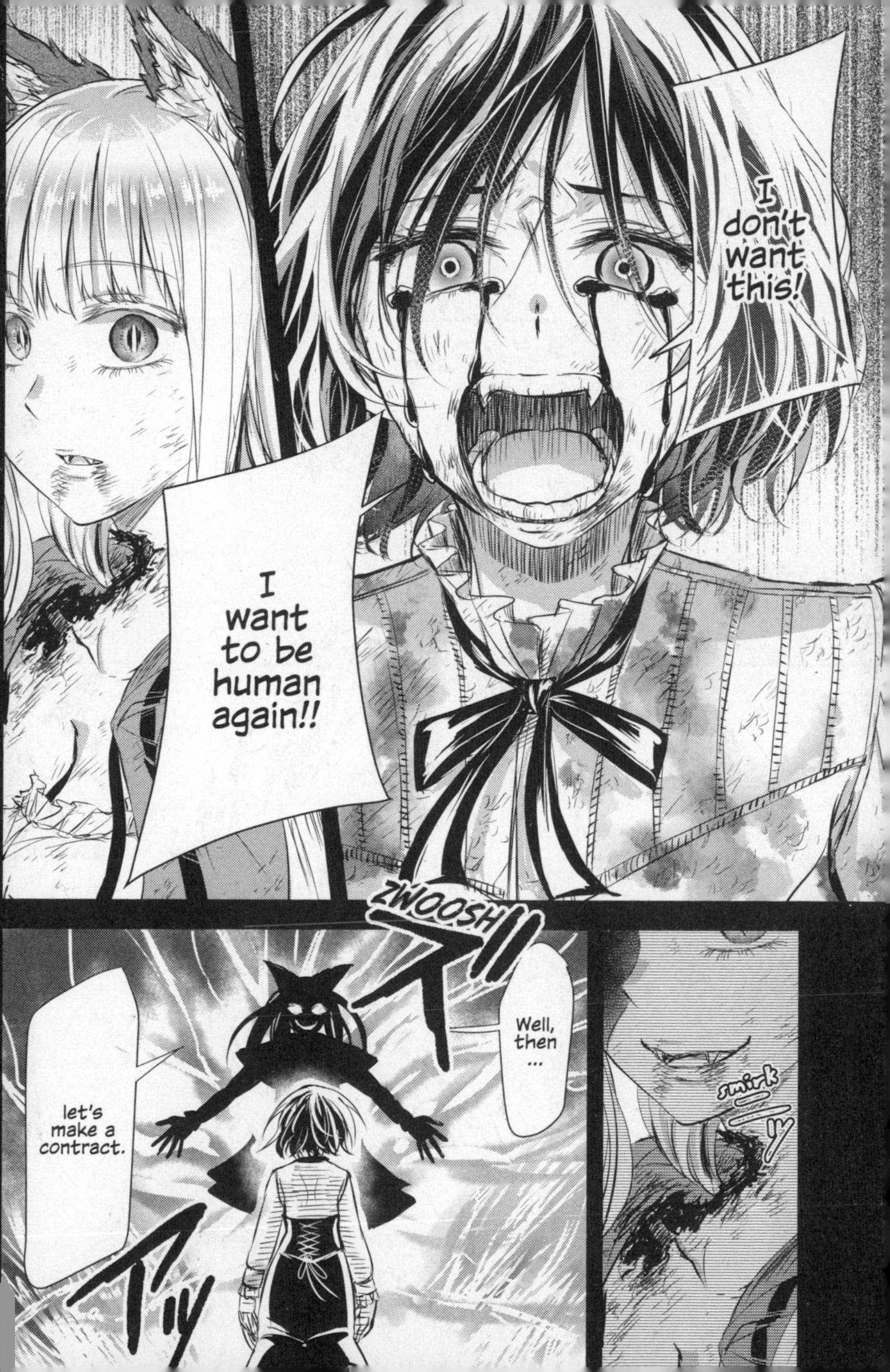
I don't want this!
I want to be human again!!
smirk
ZWOOSH
Well, then ...
let's make a contract.

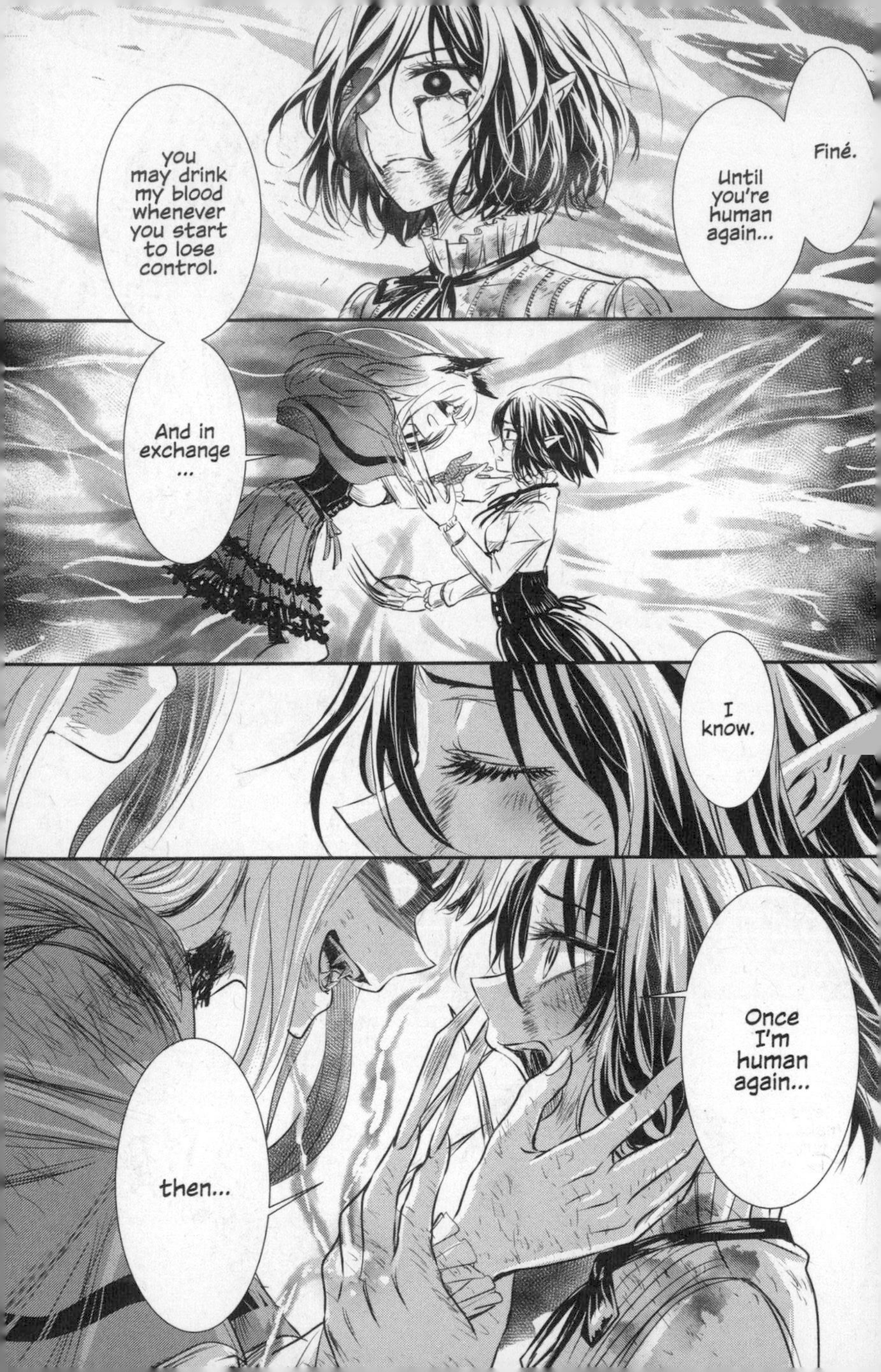
Finé.
Until you're human again...
you may drink my blood whenever you start to lose control.
And in exchange ...
I know.
Once I'm human again...
then...

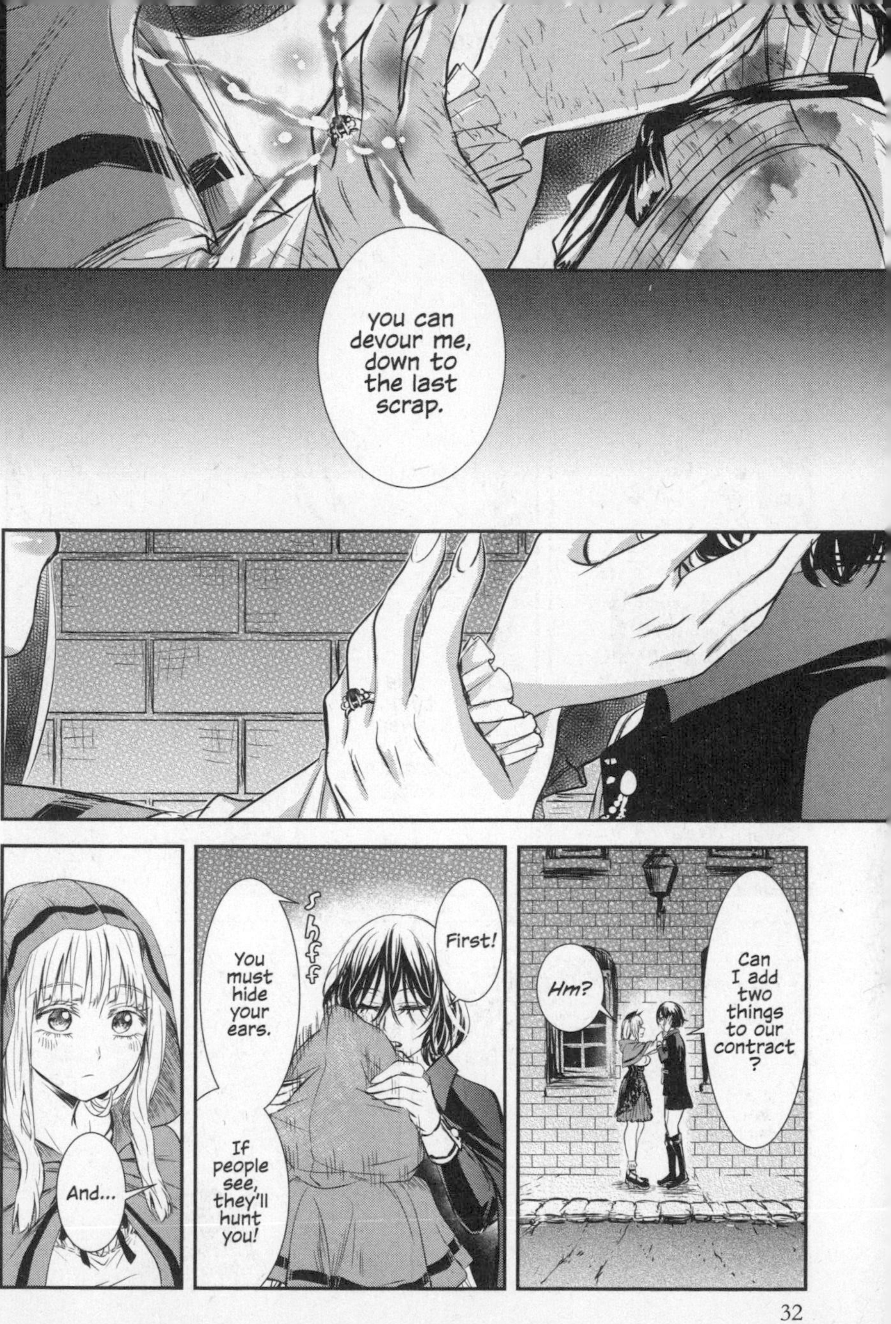
you can devour me, down to the last scrap.
Can I add two things to our contract?
Hm?
First!
You must hide your ears.
If people see, they'll hunt you!
And...

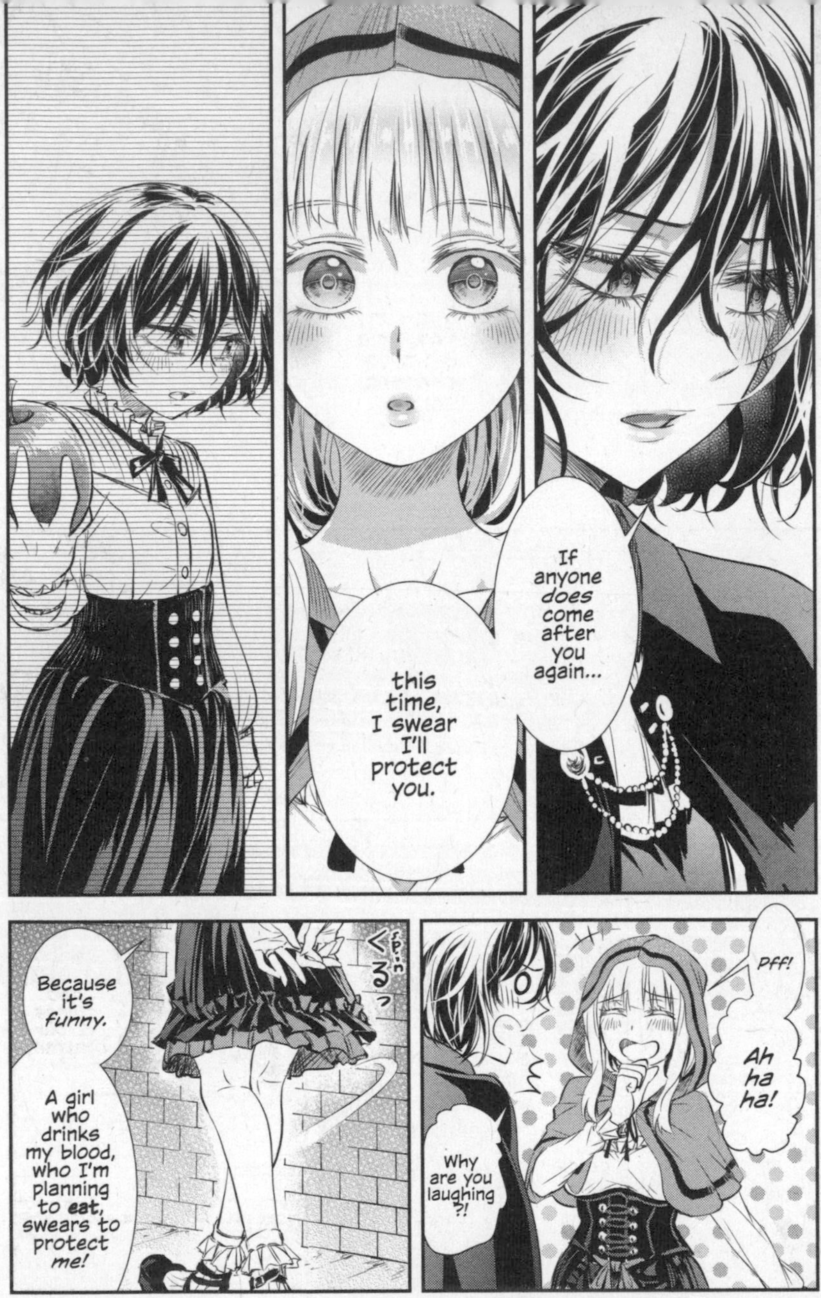
If anyone does come after you again...
this time, I swear I'll protect you.
Pff!
Ah ha ha!
Why are you laughing?!
くるっ spin
Because it's funny.
A girl who drinks my blood, who I'm planning to eat, swears to protect me!

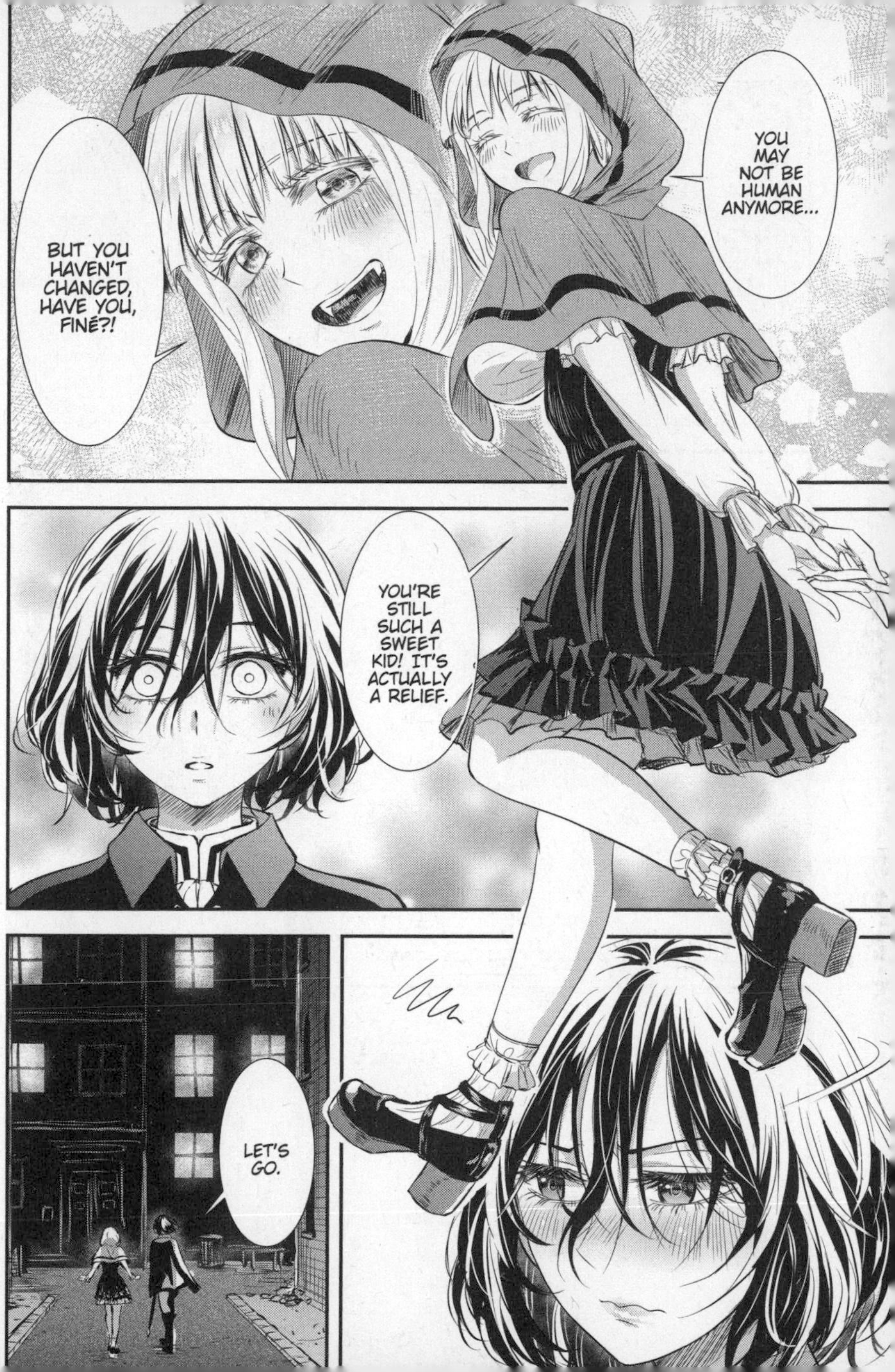
YOU MAY NOT BE HUMAN ANYMORE...
BUT YOU HAVEN'T CHANGED, HAVE YOU, FINÉ?!
YOU'RE STILL SUCH A SWEET KID! IT'S ACTUALLY A RELIEF.
LET'S GO.

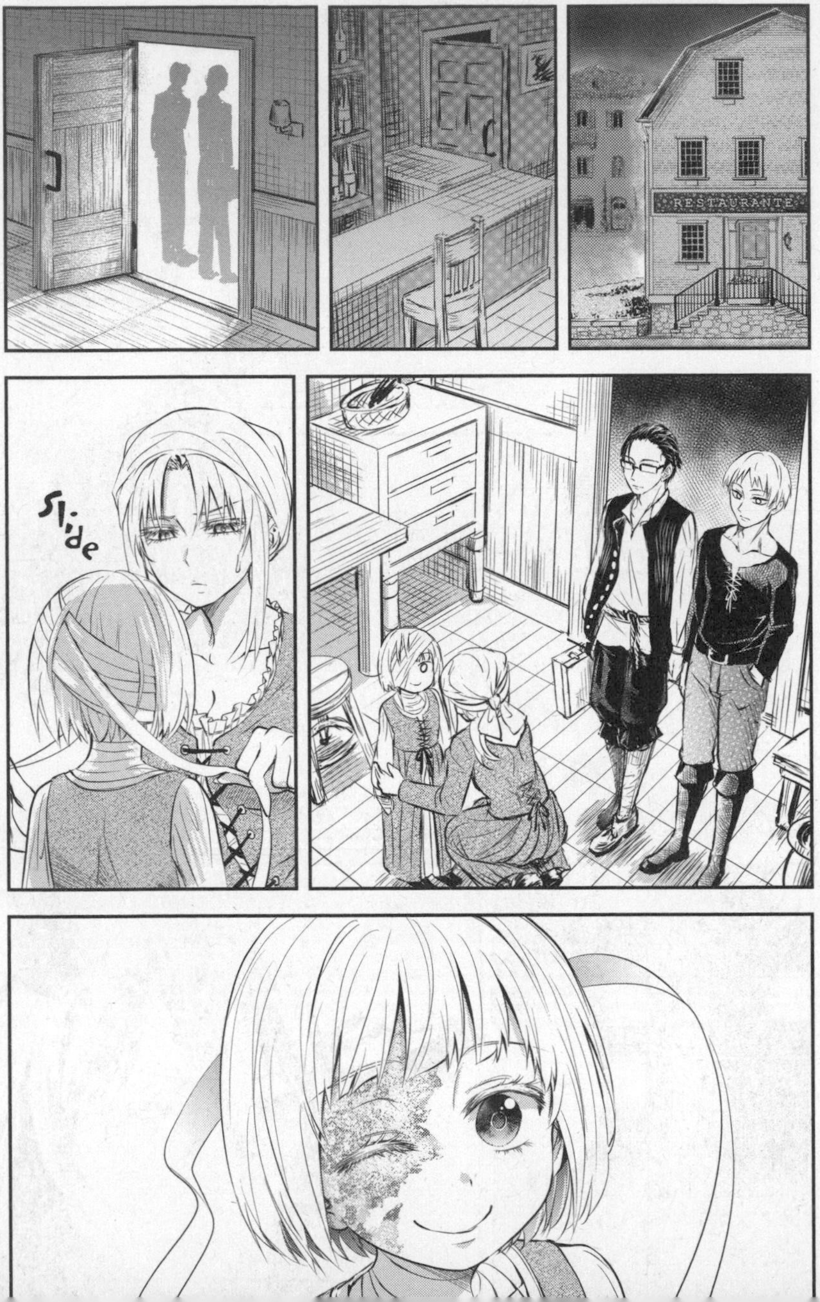
RESTAURANTE
Slide

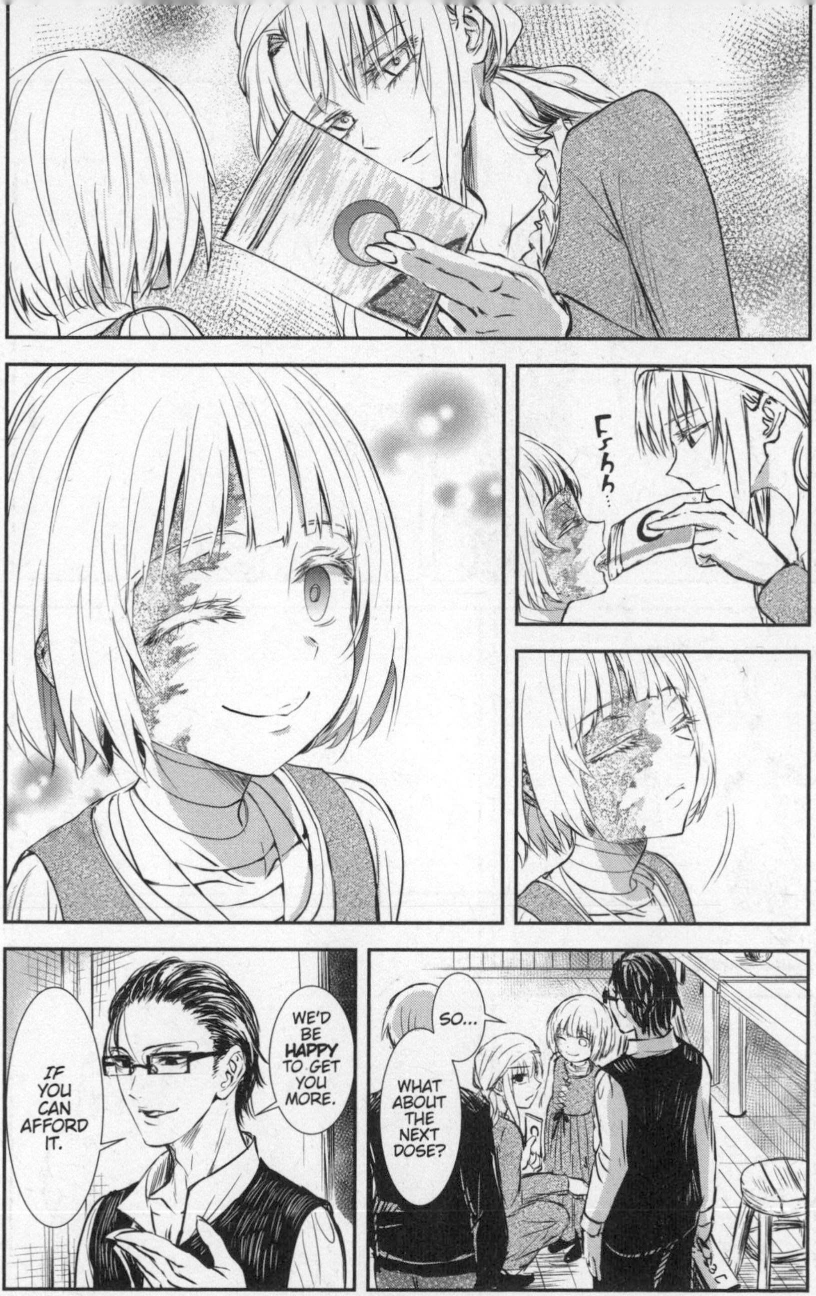
Fshh...
SO...
WHAT ABOUT THE NEXT DOSE?
WE'D BE **HAPPY** TO GET YOU MORE.
IF YOU CAN AFFORD IT.

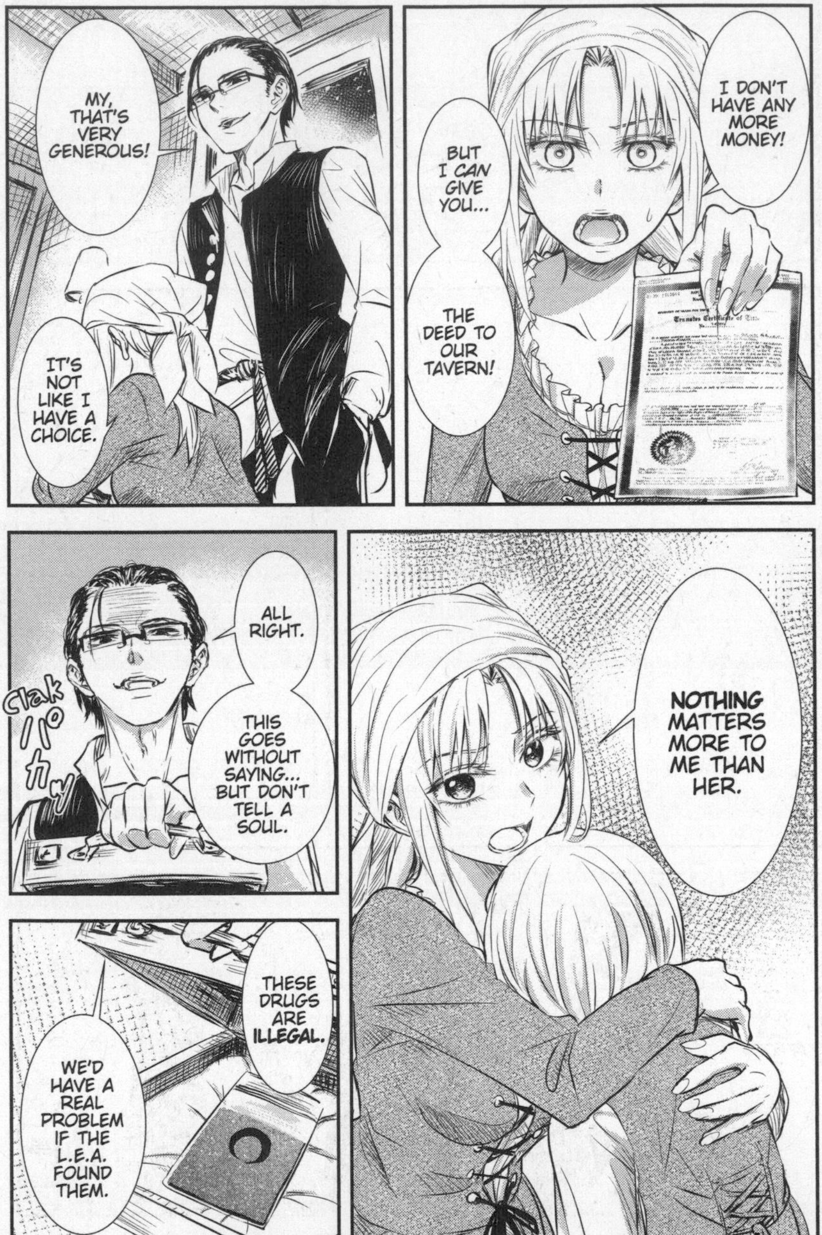
I DON'T HAVE ANY MORE MONEY!
BUT I CAN GIVE YOU...
THE DEED TO OUR TAVERN!
MY, THAT'S VERY GENEROUS!
IT'S NOT LIKE I HAVE A CHOICE.
NOTHING MATTERS MORE TO ME THAN HER.
ALL RIGHT.
THIS GOES WITHOUT SAYING... BUT DON'T TELL A SOUL.
clak パカッ
THESE DRUGS ARE ILLEGAL.
WE'D HAVE A REAL PROBLEM IF THE L.E.A. FOUND THEM.

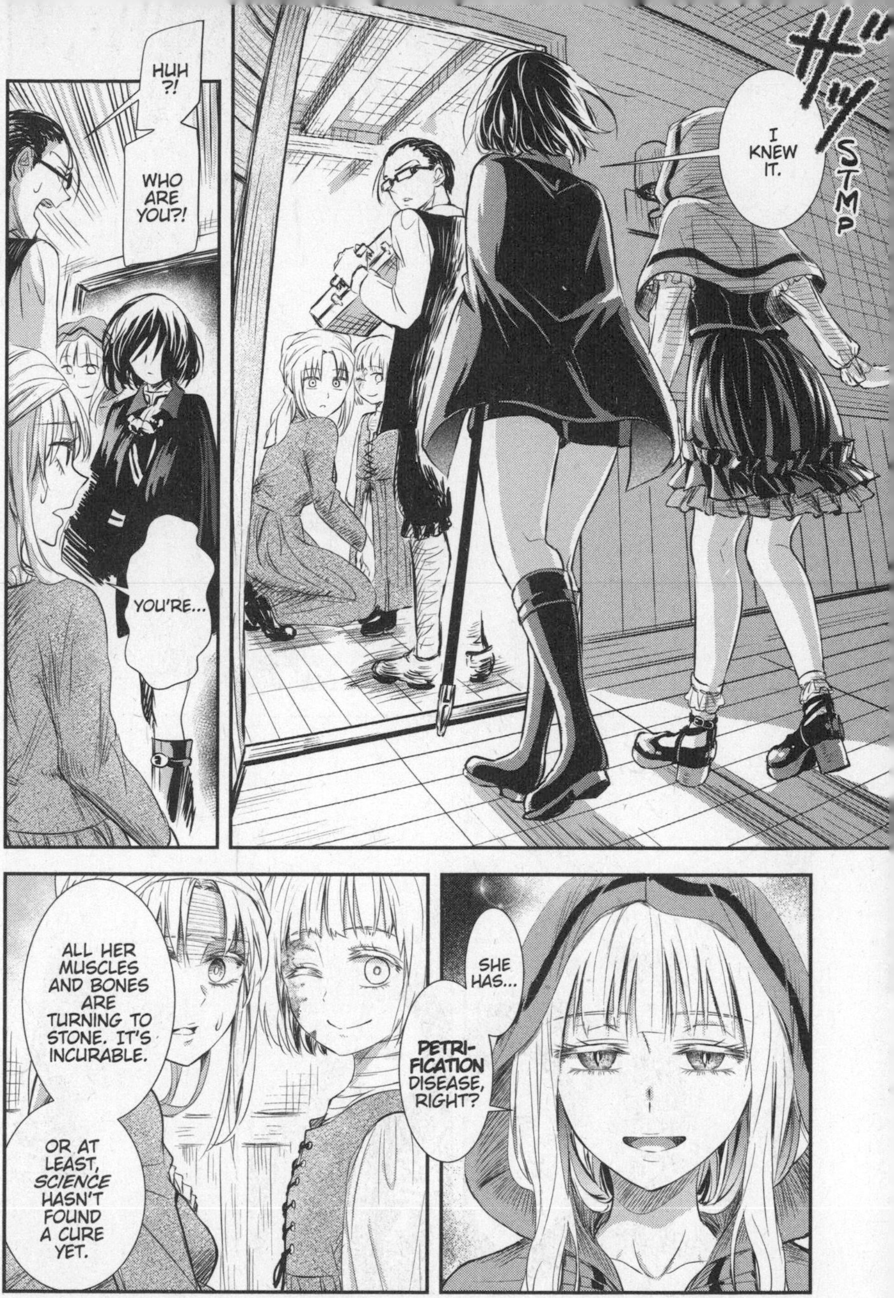
I KNEW IT.
STMP
HUH?!
WHO ARE YOU?!
YOU'RE...
SHE HAS...
PETRIFICATION DISEASE, RIGHT?
ALL HER MUSCLES AND BONES ARE TURNING TO STONE. IT'S INCURABLE.
OR AT LEAST, SCIENCE HASN'T FOUND A CURE YET.

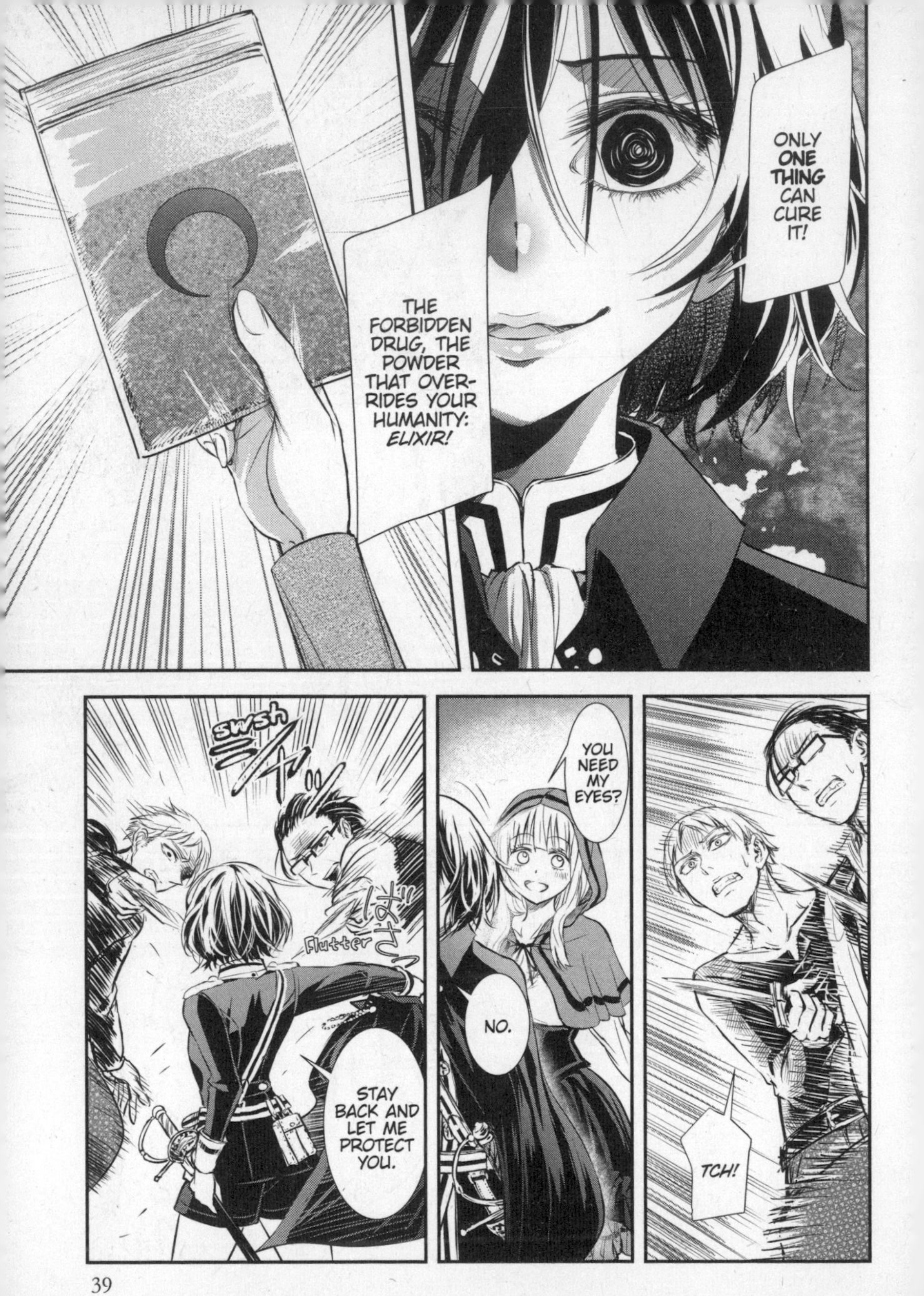
ONLY ONE THING CAN CURE IT!
THE FORBIDDEN DRUG, THE POWDER THAT OVER-RIDES YOUR HUMANITY: *ELIXIR!*
TCH!
YOU NEED MY EYES?
NO.
swsh
Flutter
STAY BACK AND LET ME PROTECT YOU.

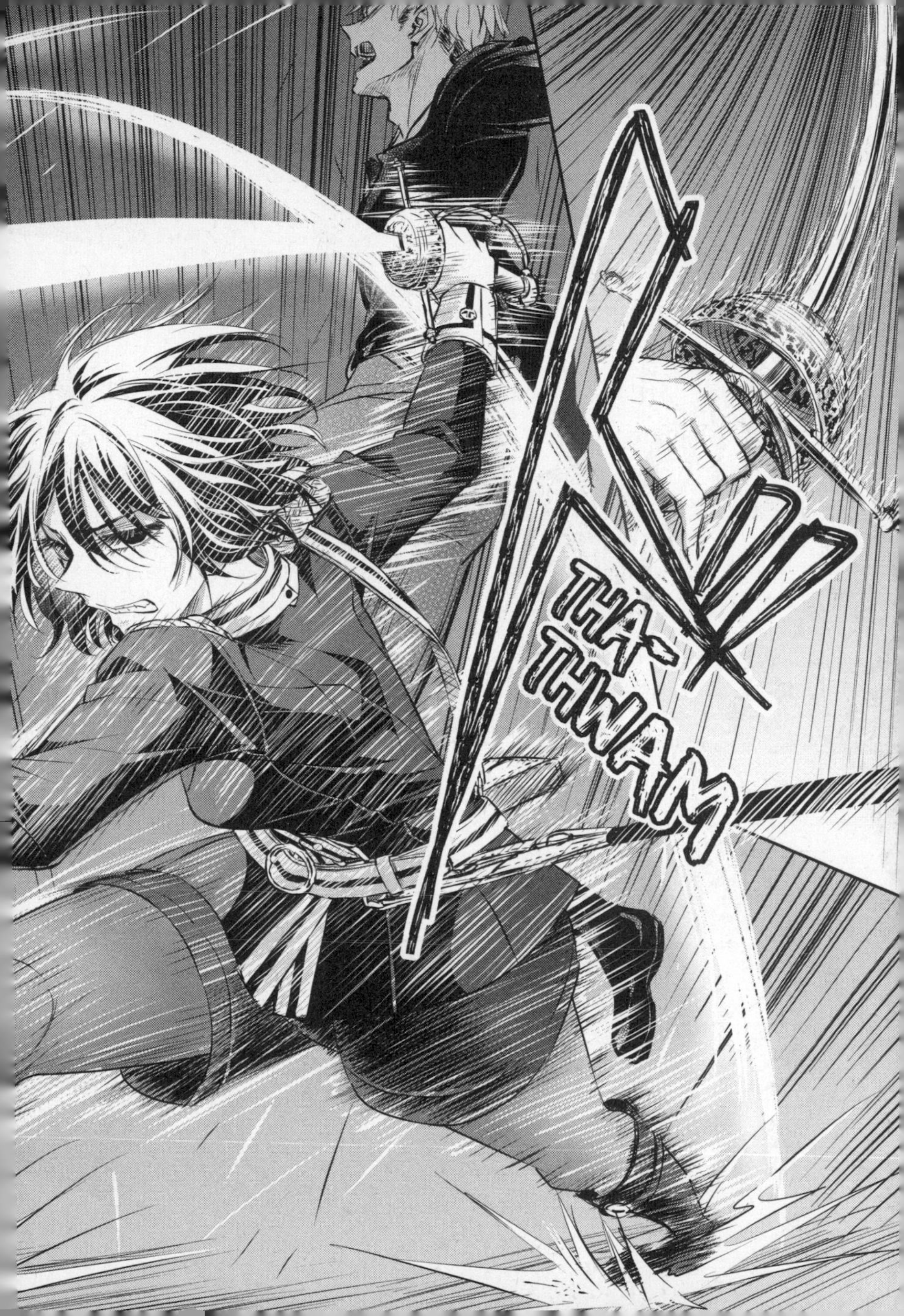
THA-THWAM

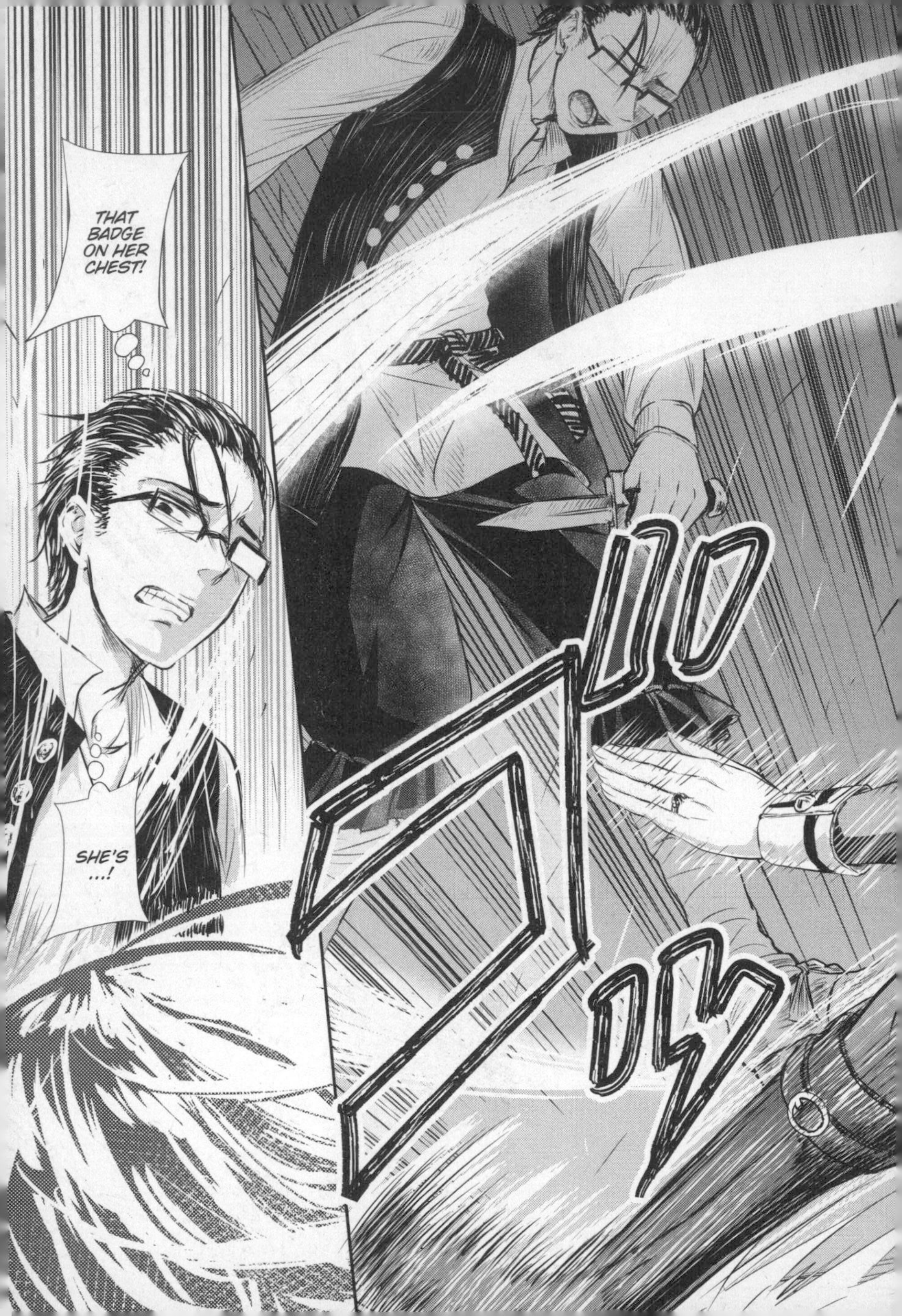
THAT BADGE ON HER CHEST!
SHE'S ...!

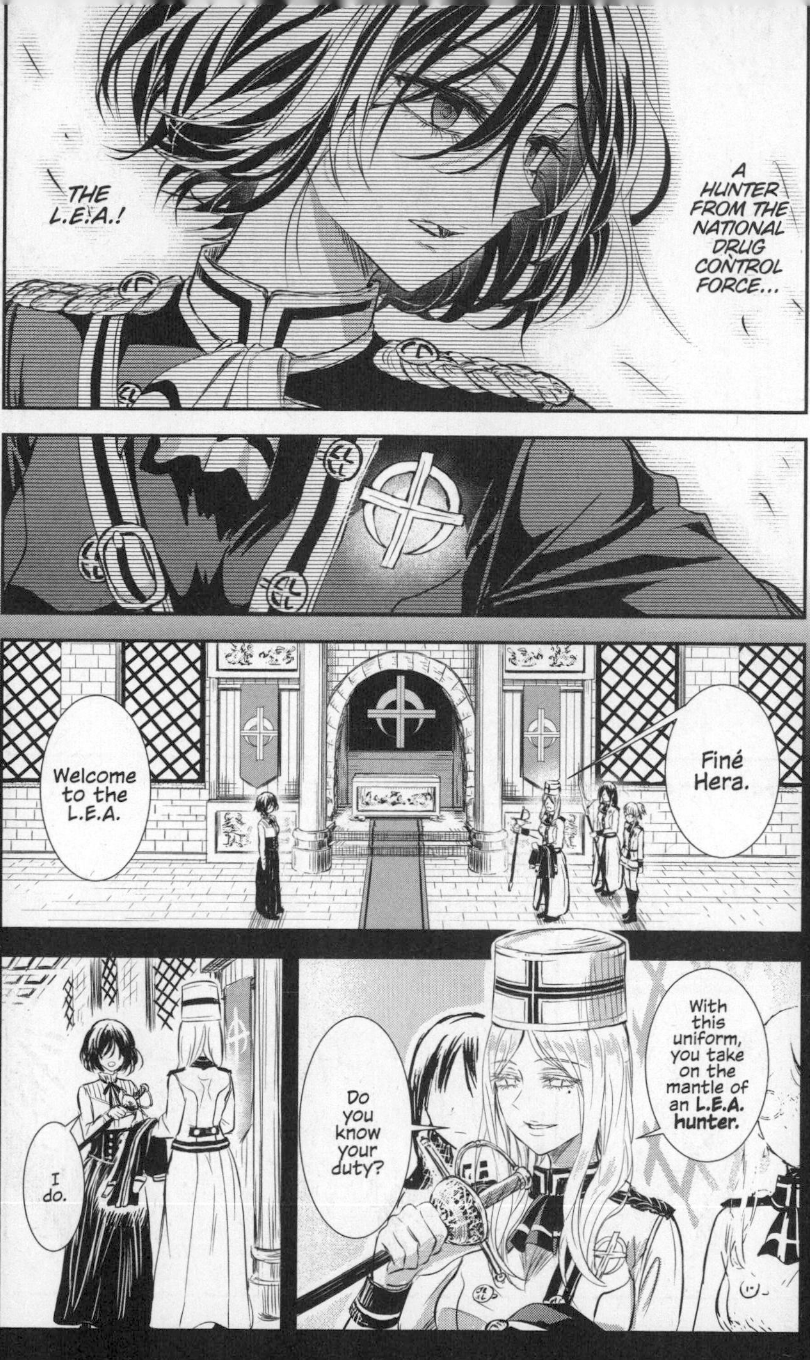
A HUNTER FROM THE NATIONAL DRUG CONTROL FORCE...
THE L.E.A.!
Finé Hera.
Welcome to the L.E.A.
With this uniform, you take on the mantle of an **L.E.A. hunter.**
Do you know your duty?
I do.

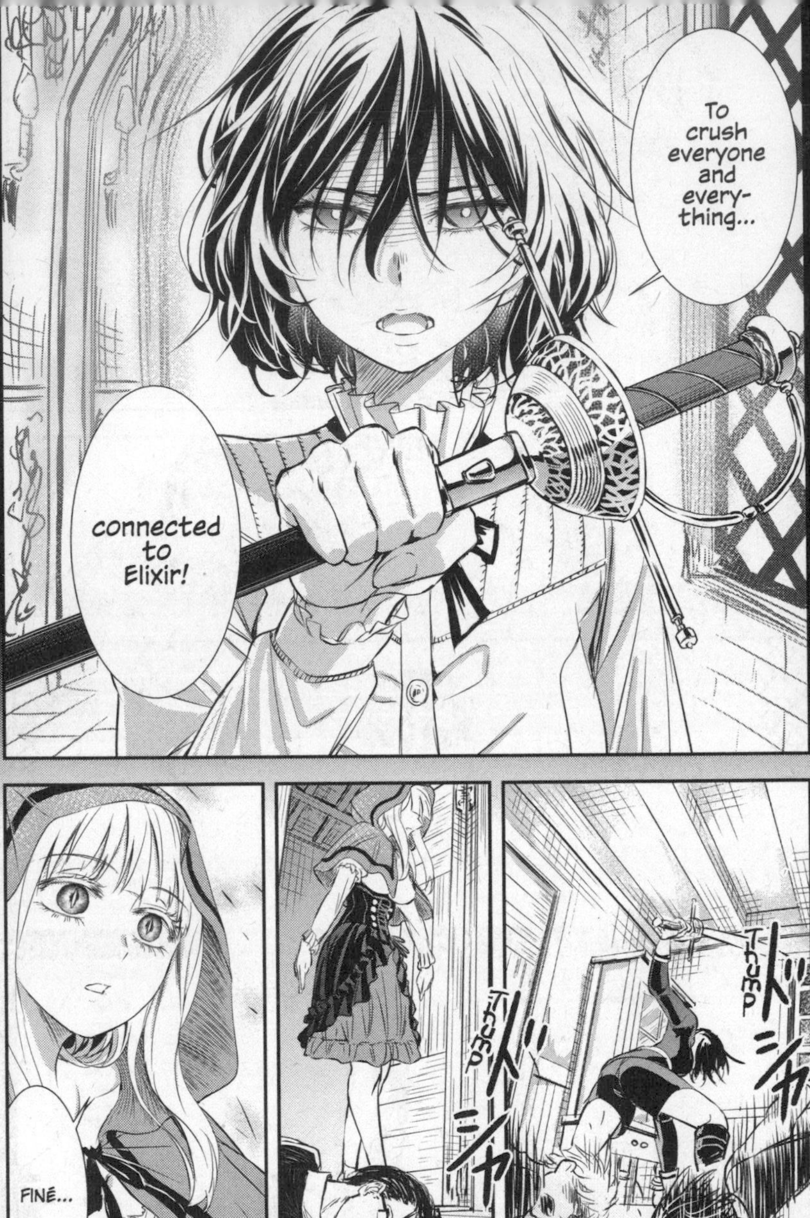
To crush everyone and every-thing...
connected to Elixir!
THUMP
THUMP
FINÉ...

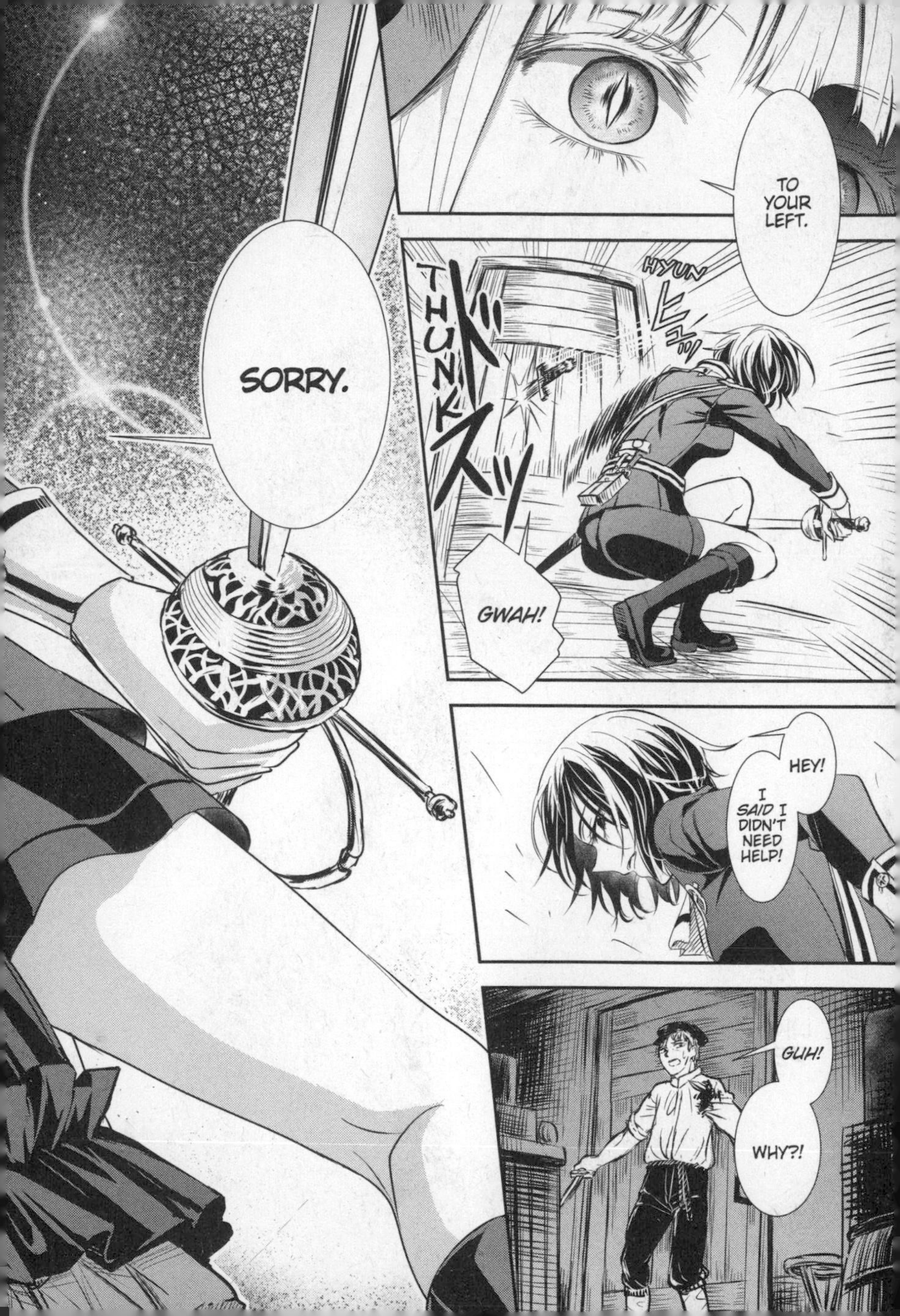
TO YOUR LEFT.
HYUN
THUNK
GWAH!
HEY!
I SAID I DIDN'T NEED HELP!
GUH!
WHY?!
SORRY.

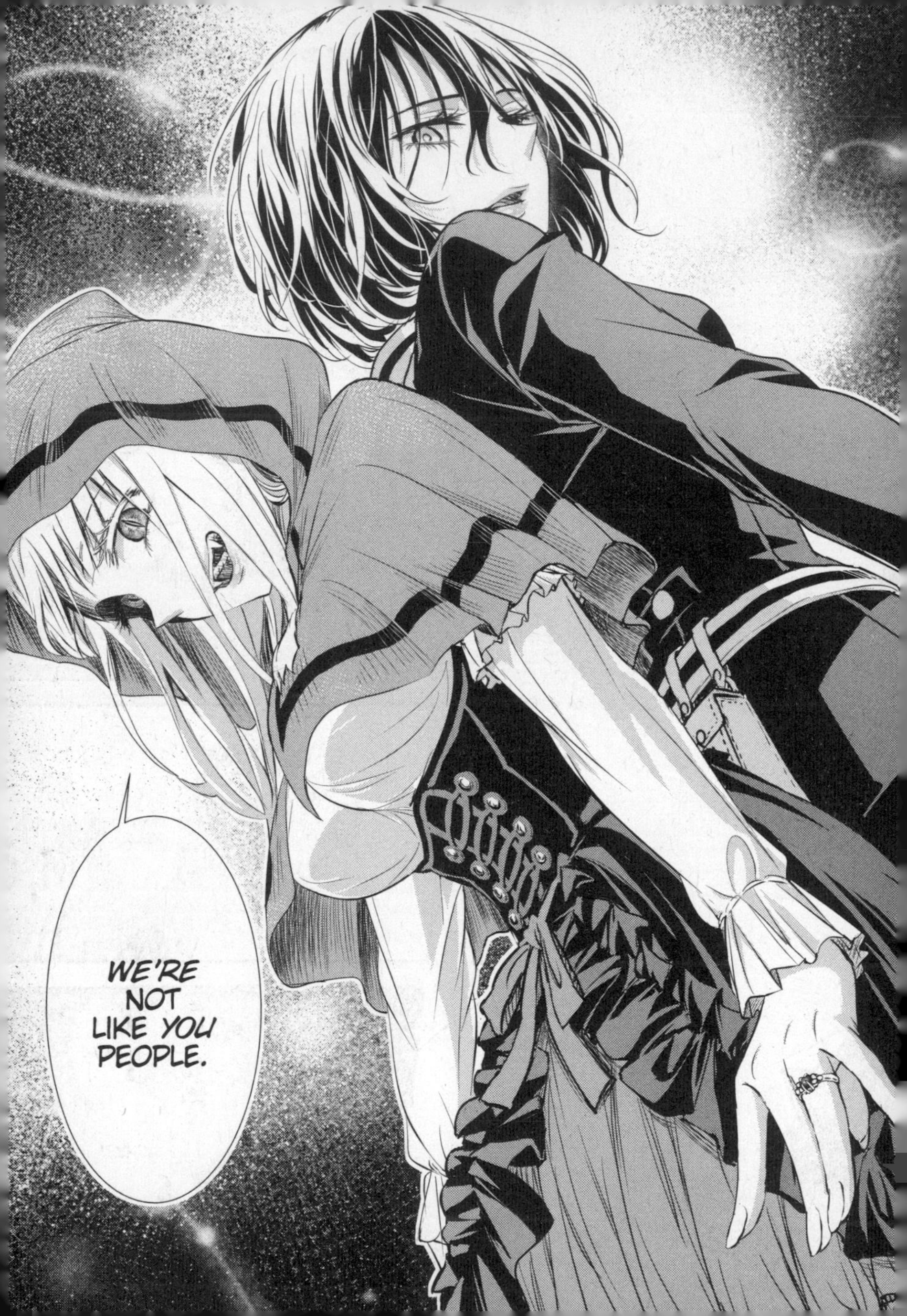
WE'RE NOT LIKE YOU PEOPLE.

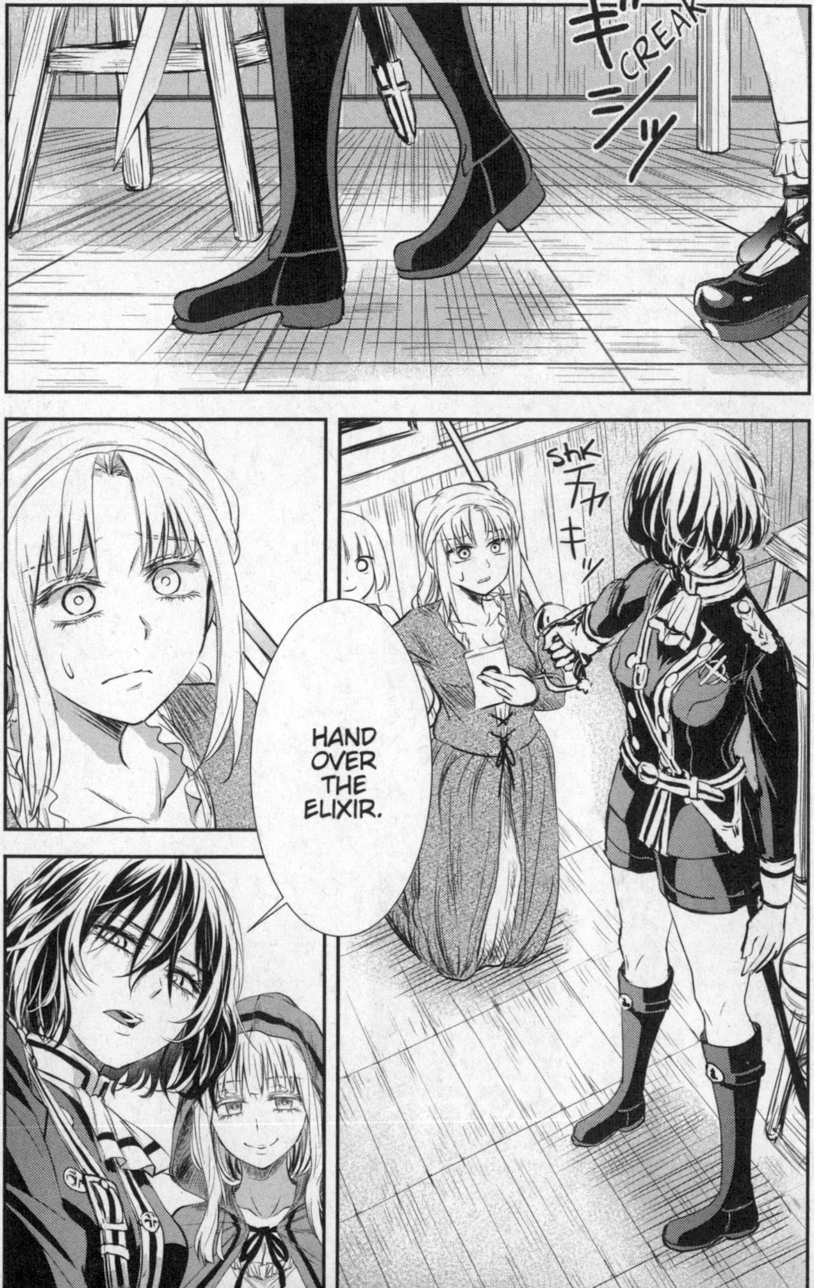

ギシッ
CREAK
ガキッ
Shk
HAND OVER THE ELIXIR.

SCARLET

Finé Hera

【　Name　】Finé Hera
【 Height 】169cm
【　Age　】17 years
【Birthday】October 25th
【　Likes　】Apples
【Dislikes】Hurting people

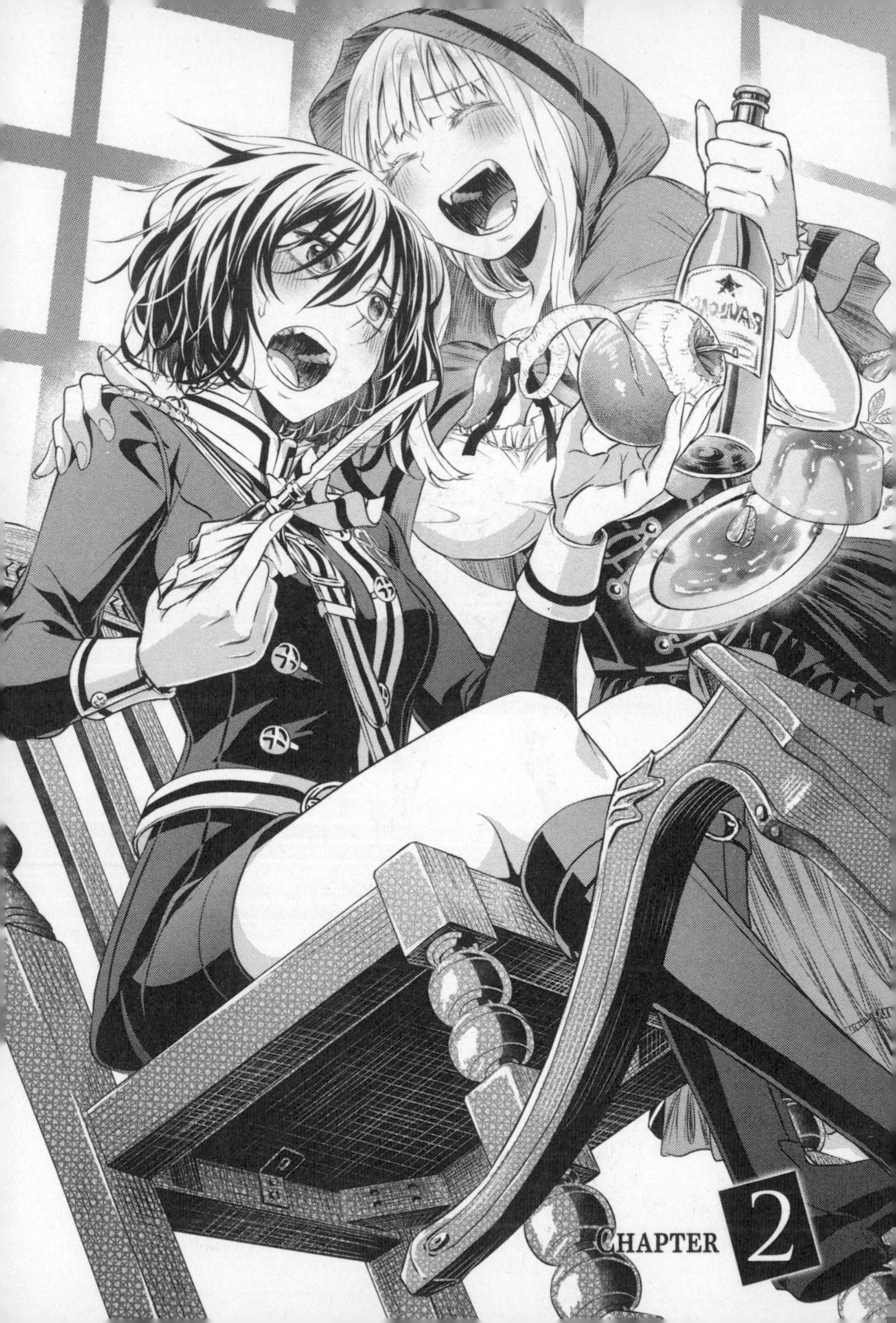
CHAPTER 2

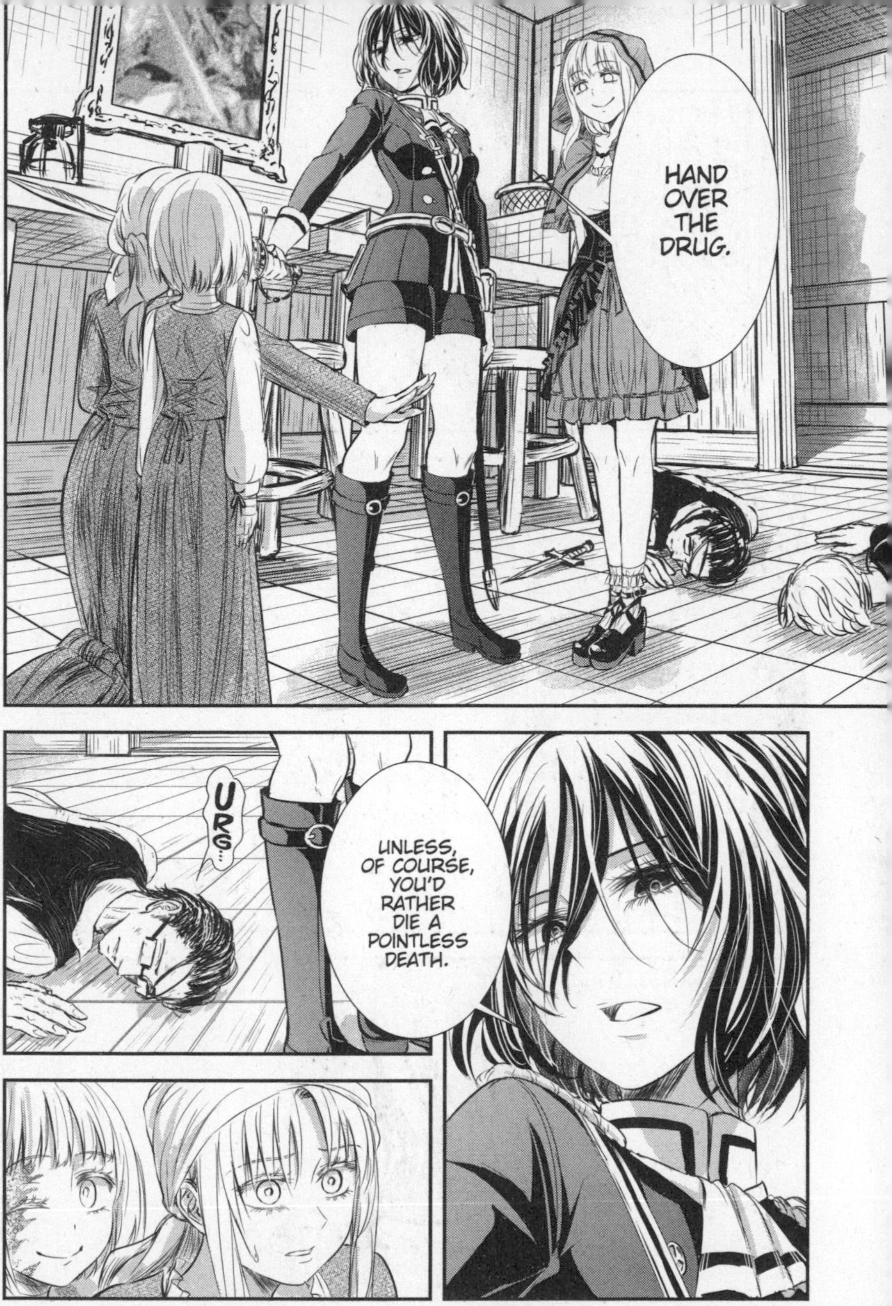
HAND OVER THE DRUG.
UNLESS, OF COURSE, YOU'D RATHER DIE A POINTLESS DEATH.
URG...

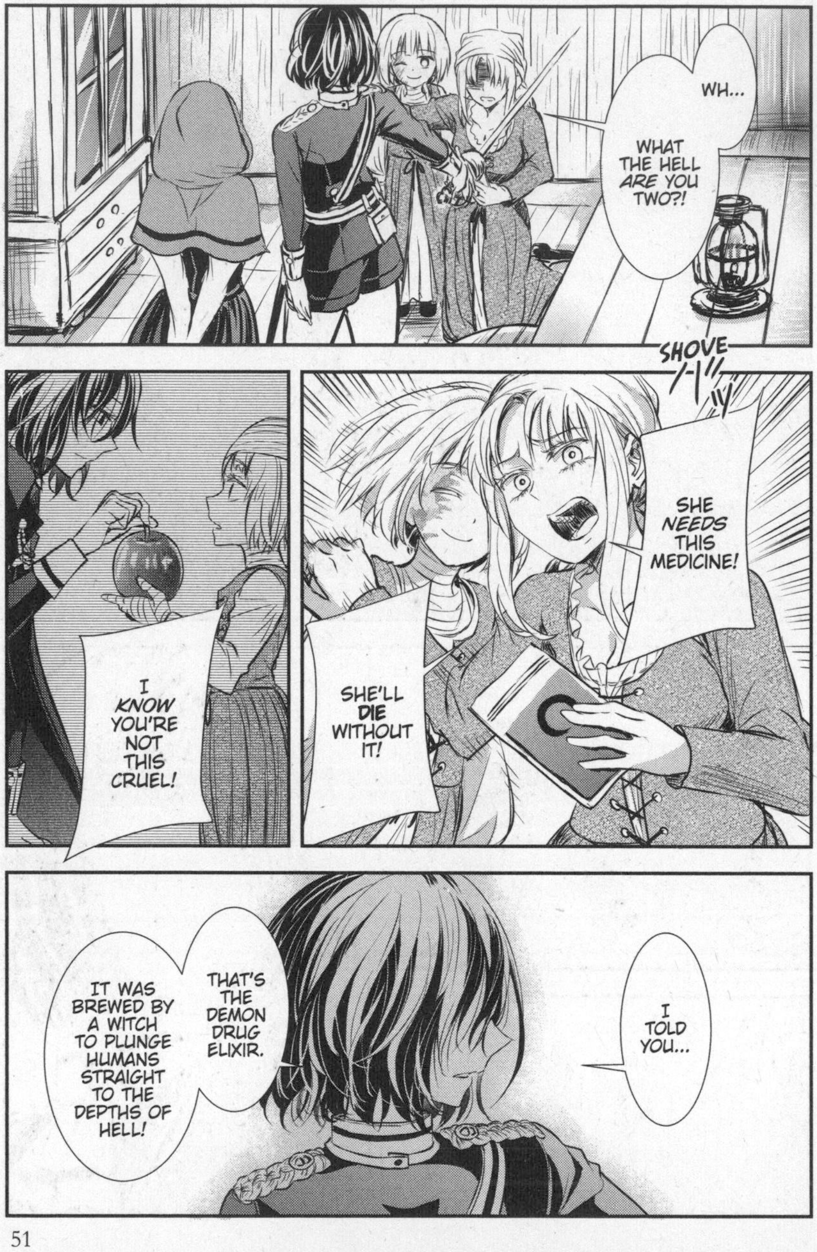
WH...
WHAT THE HELL ARE YOU TWO?!
SHOVE
SHE NEEDS THIS MEDICINE!
SHE'LL DIE WITHOUT IT!
I KNOW YOU'RE NOT THIS CRUEL!
I TOLD YOU...
THAT'S THE DEMON DRUG ELIXIR.
IT WAS BREWED BY A WITCH TO PLUNGE HUMANS STRAIGHT TO THE DEPTHS OF HELL!

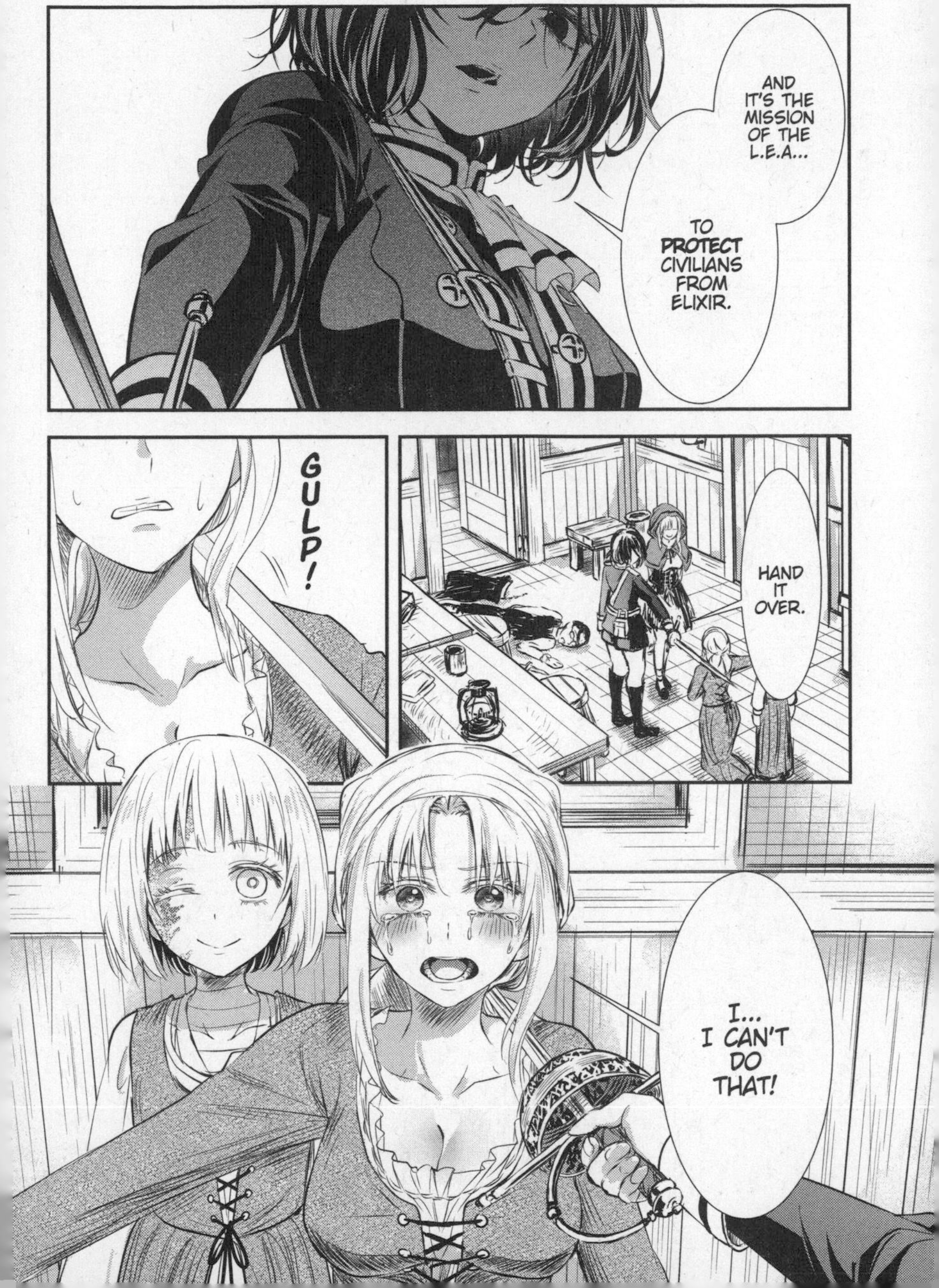
AND IT'S THE MISSION OF THE L.E.A...
TO **PROTECT** CIVILIANS FROM ELIXIR.
HAND IT OVER.
GULP!
I... I CAN'T DO THAT!

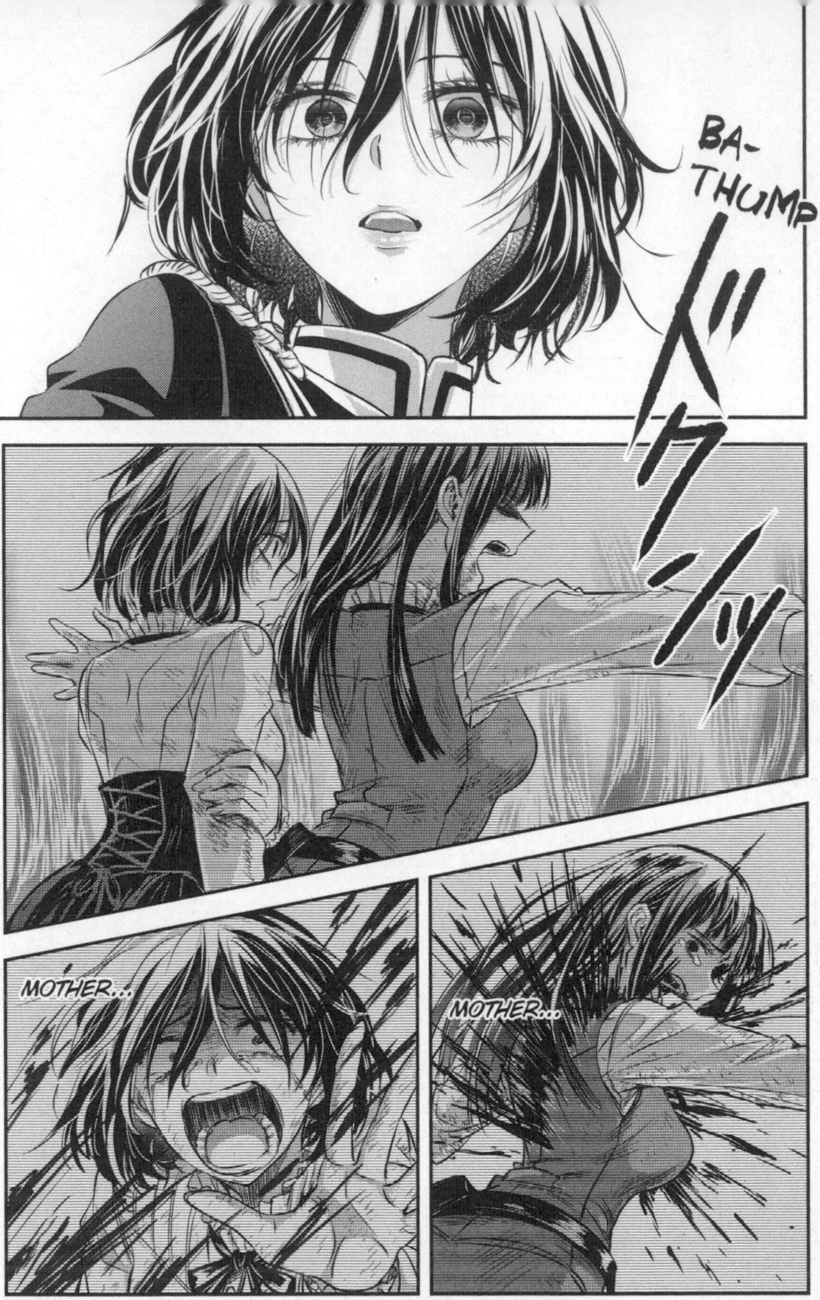
BA-
THUMP
ドクンッ
MOTHER...
MOTHER...

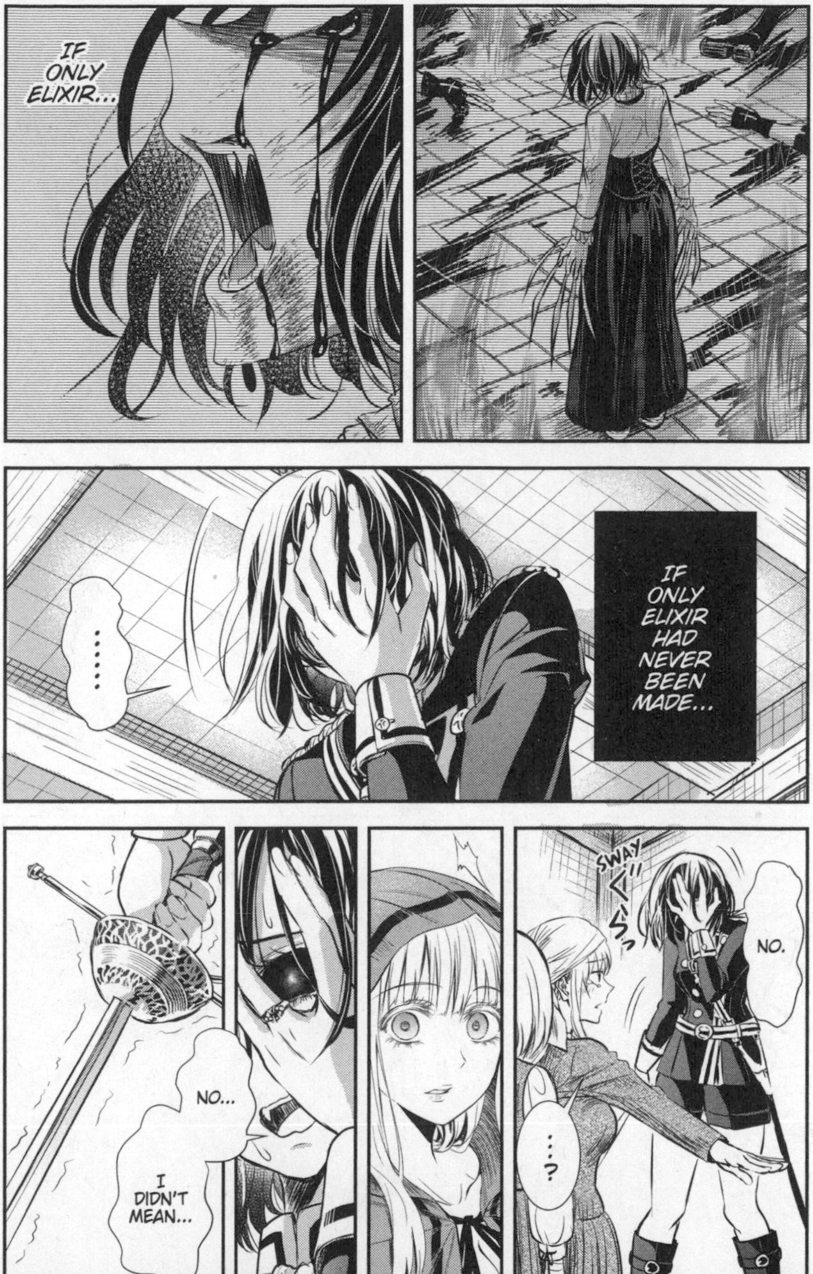
IF ONLY ELIXIR...
IF ONLY ELIXIR HAD NEVER BEEN MADE...
......
SWAY
NO.
...?
NO...
I DIDN'T MEAN...

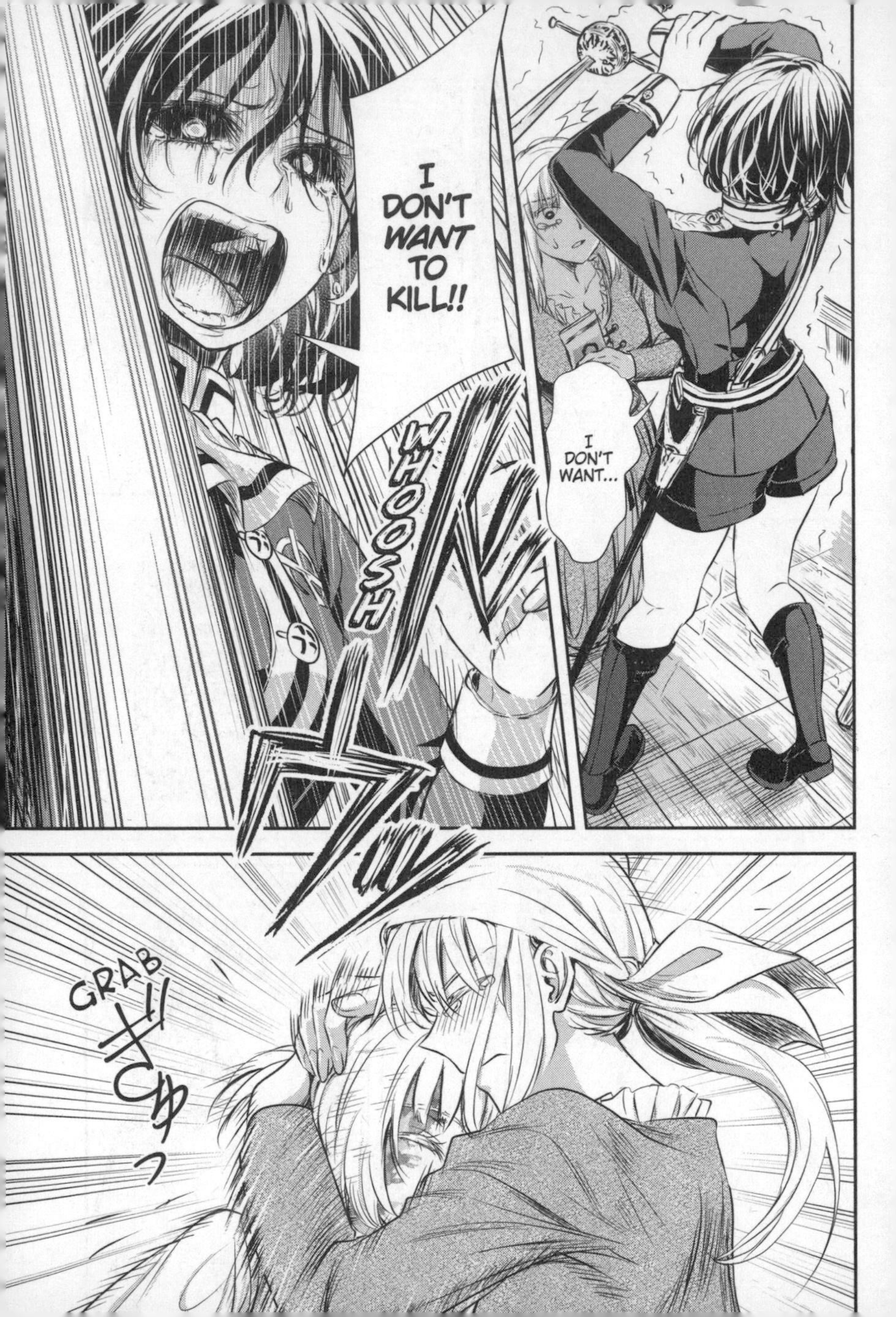
I DON'T WANT...
I DON'T WANT TO KILL!!
WHOOOSH
GRAB

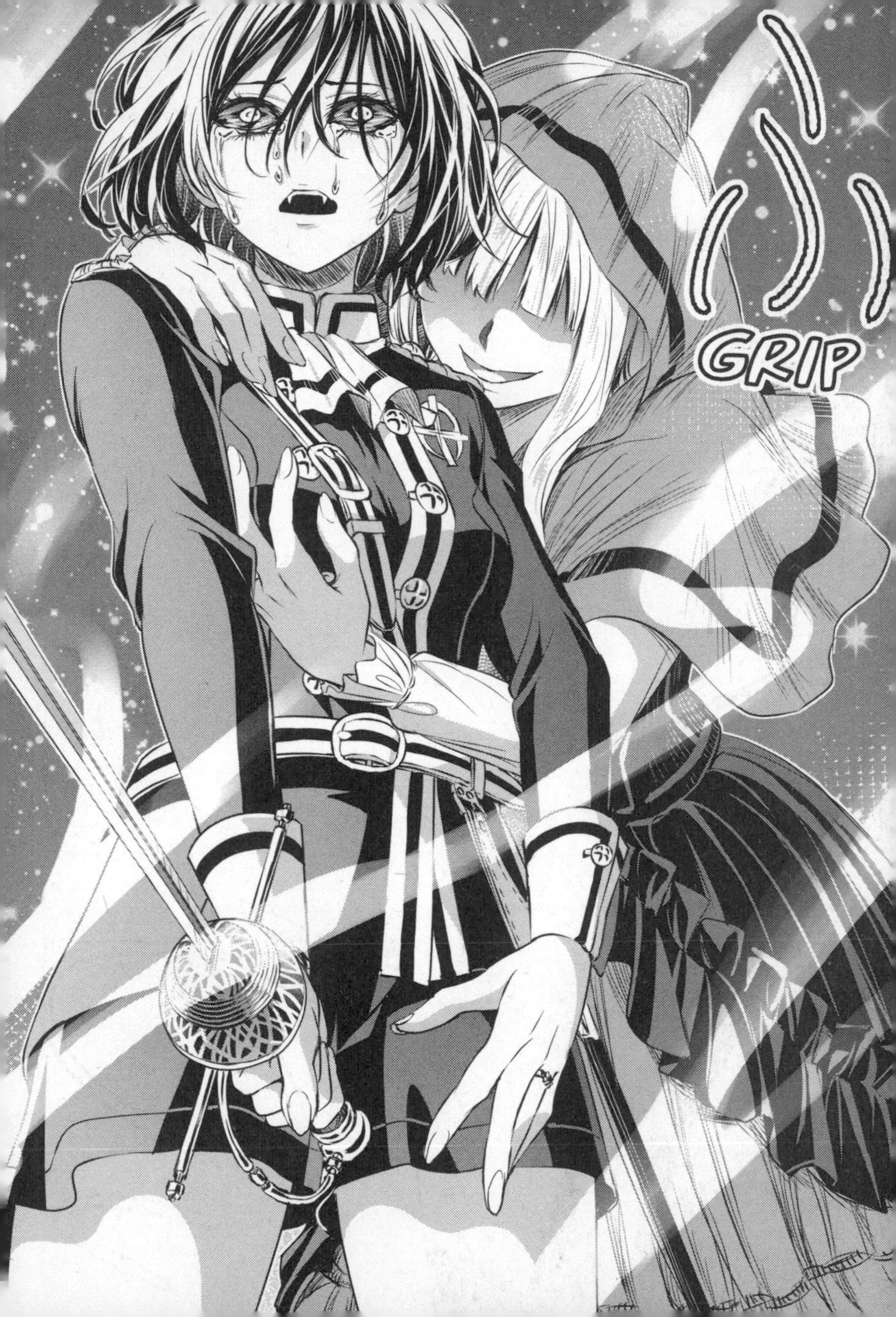
GRIP

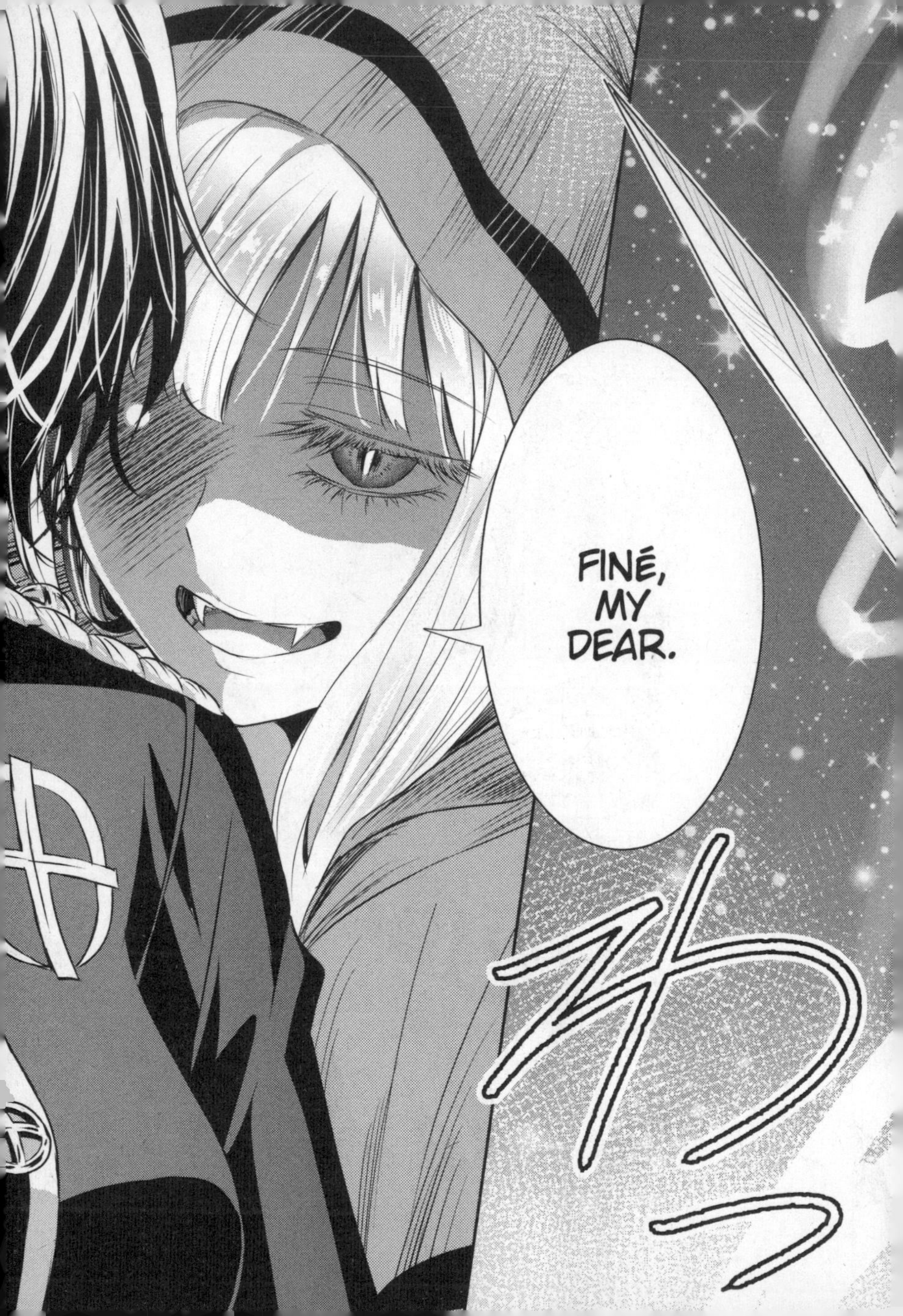
FINÉ, MY DEAR.

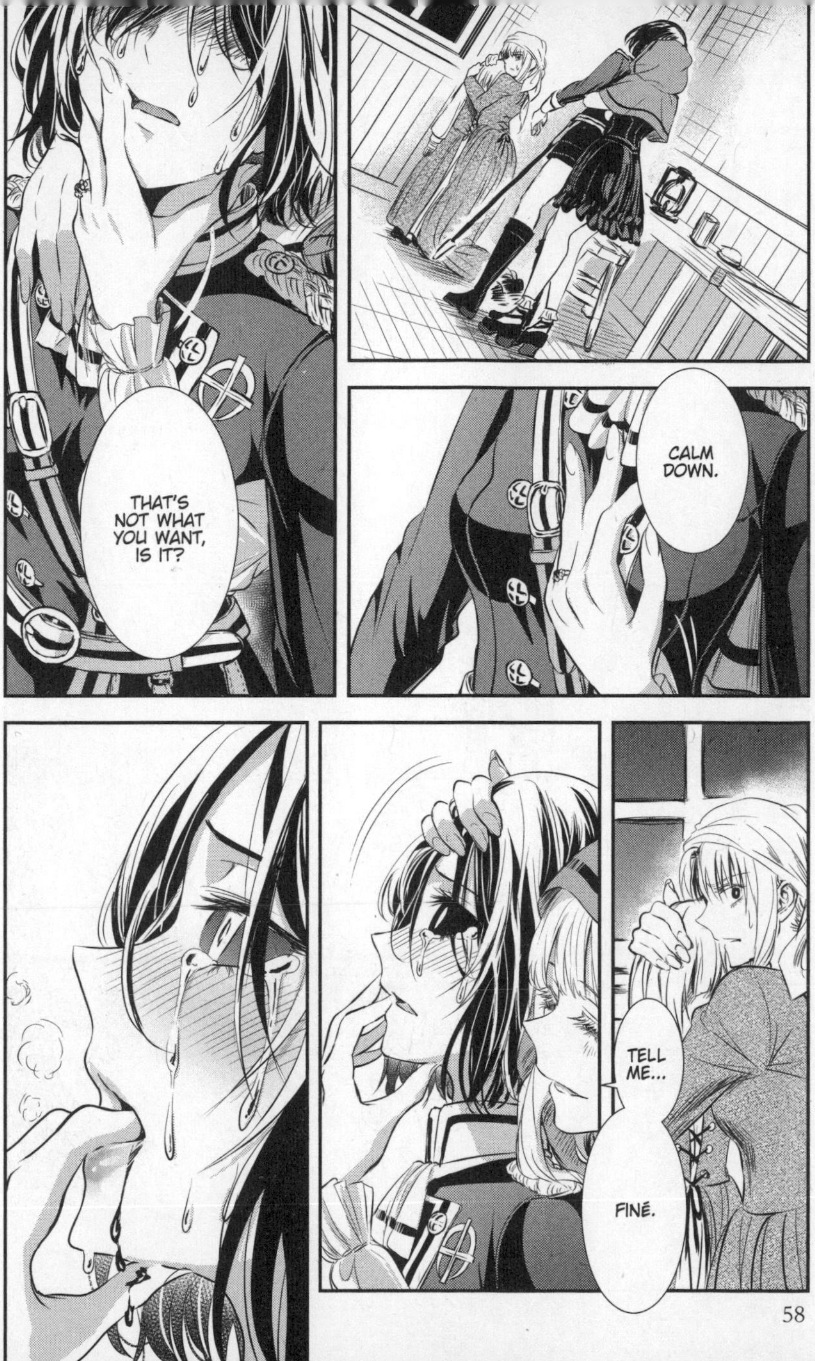
CALM DOWN.
THAT'S NOT WHAT YOU WANT, IS IT?
TELL ME...
FINÉ.

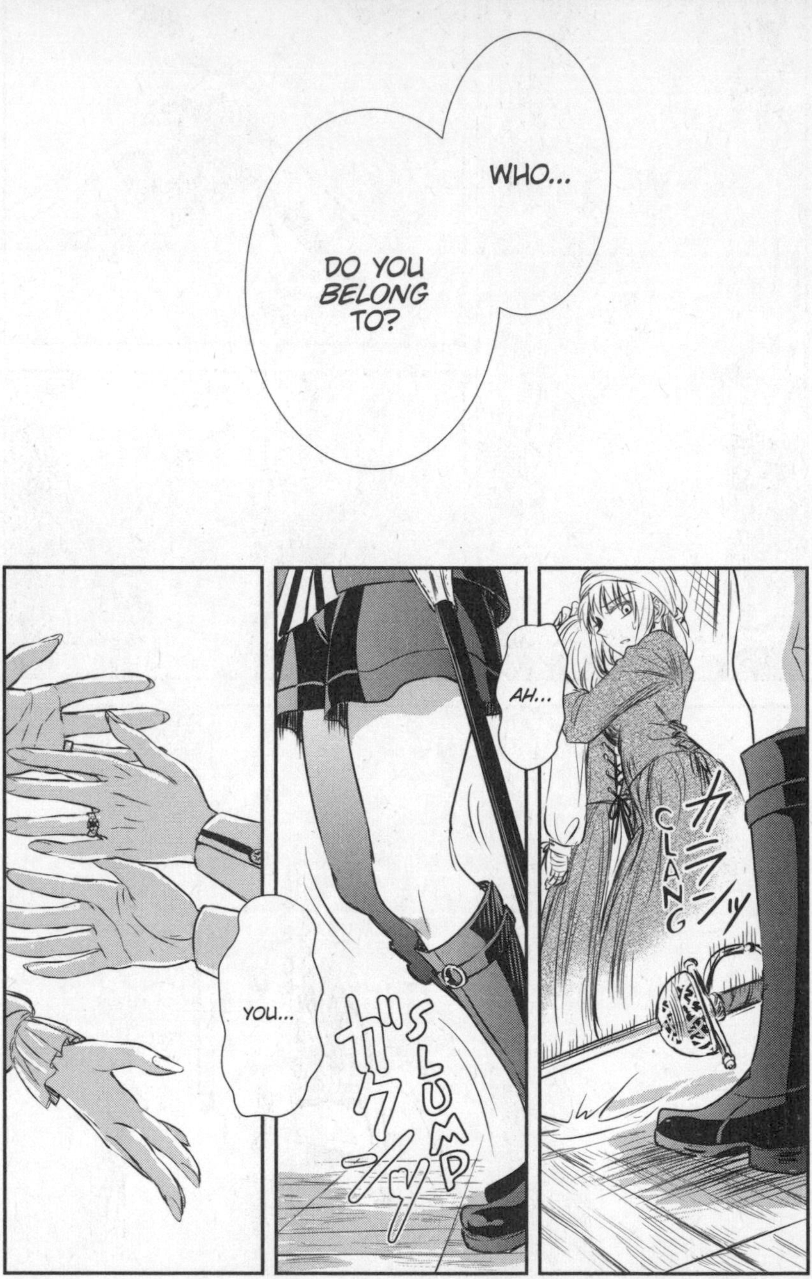
WHO...
DO YOU BELONG TO?
AH...
カラーンッ
CLANG
ガクッ
SLUMP
YOU...

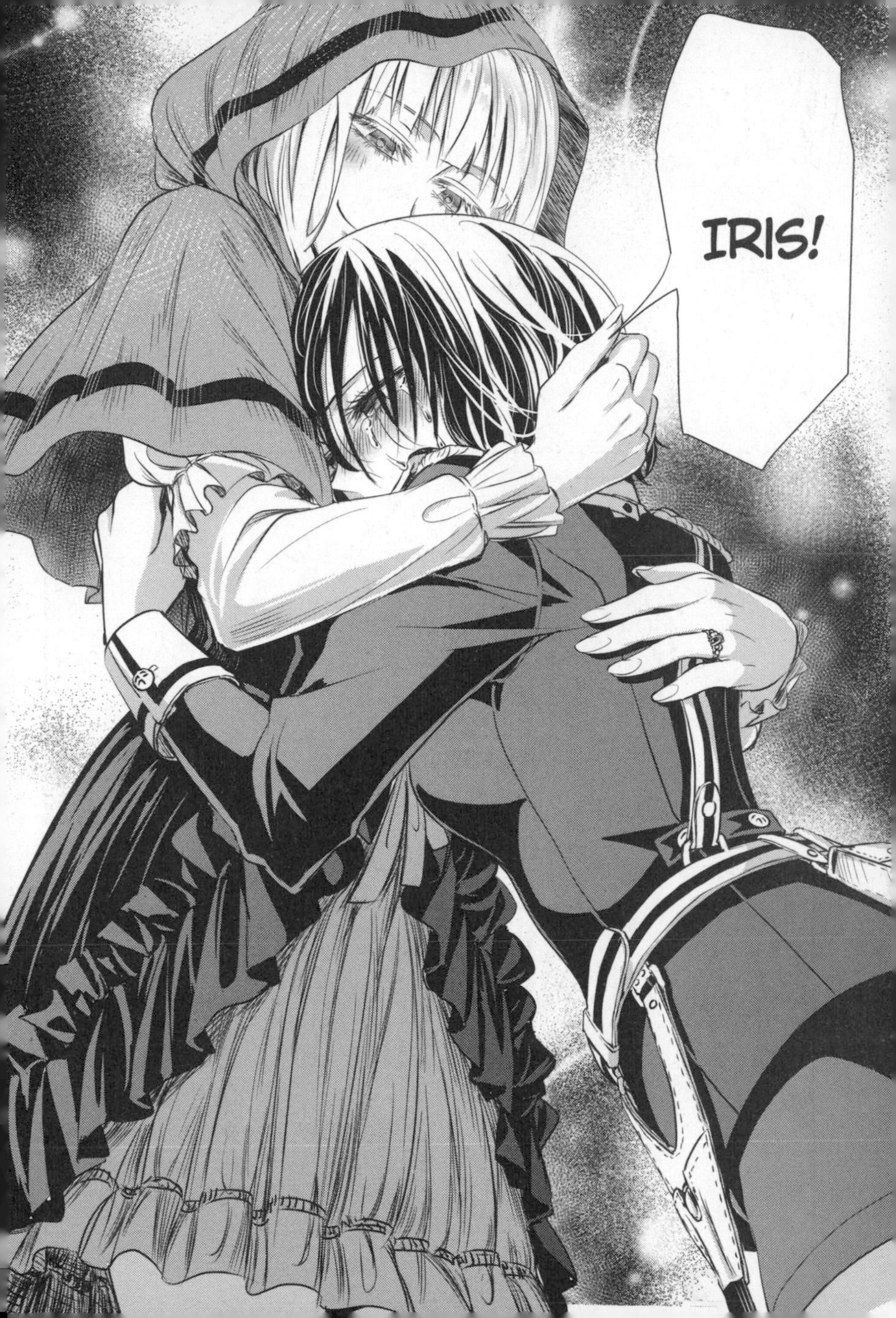
IRIS!

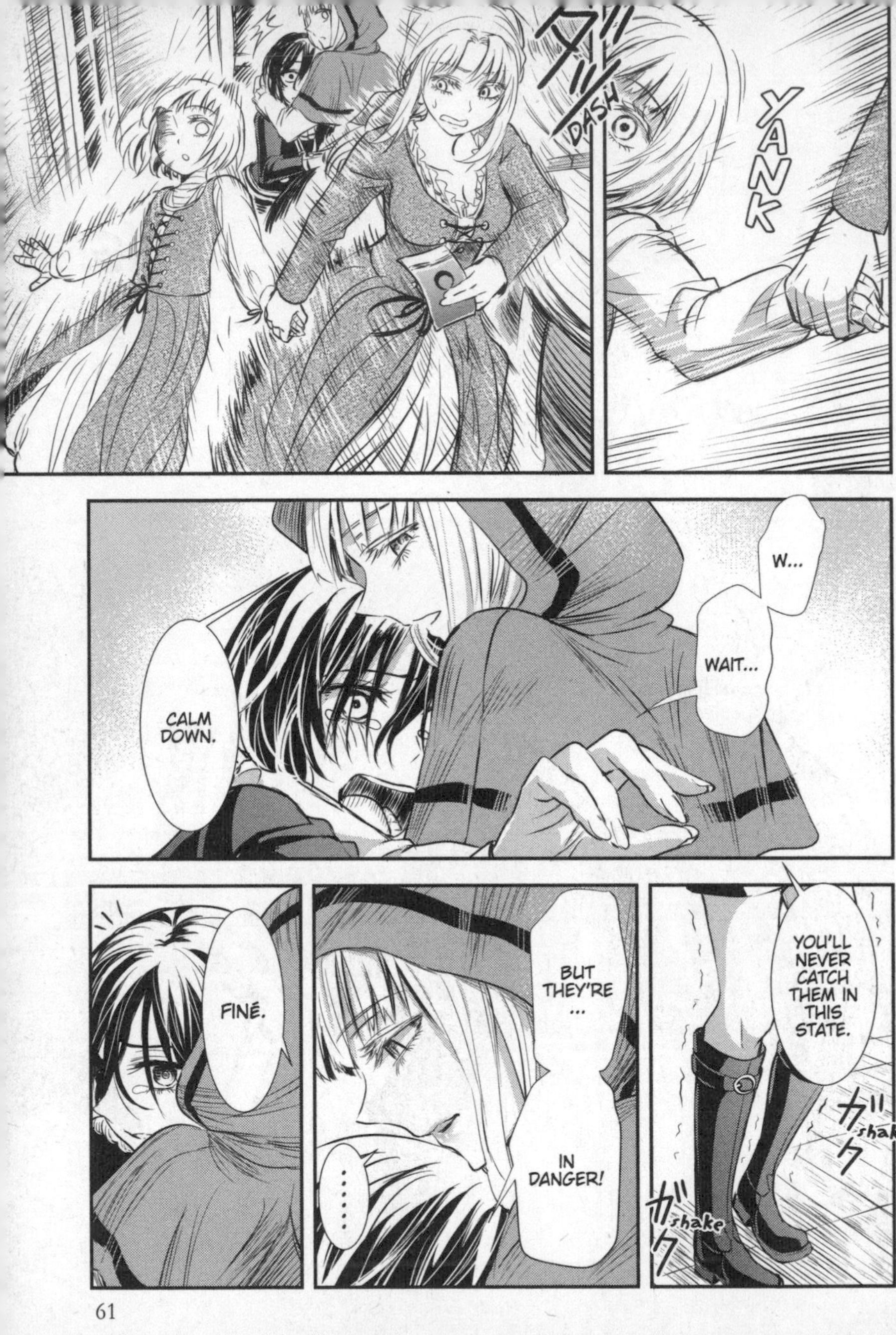
YANK
タッ
DASH
W...
WAIT...
CALM DOWN.
YOU'LL NEVER CATCH THEM IN THIS STATE.
ガク
shake
ガク
shake
BUT THEY'RE ...
IN DANGER!
......
FINÉ.

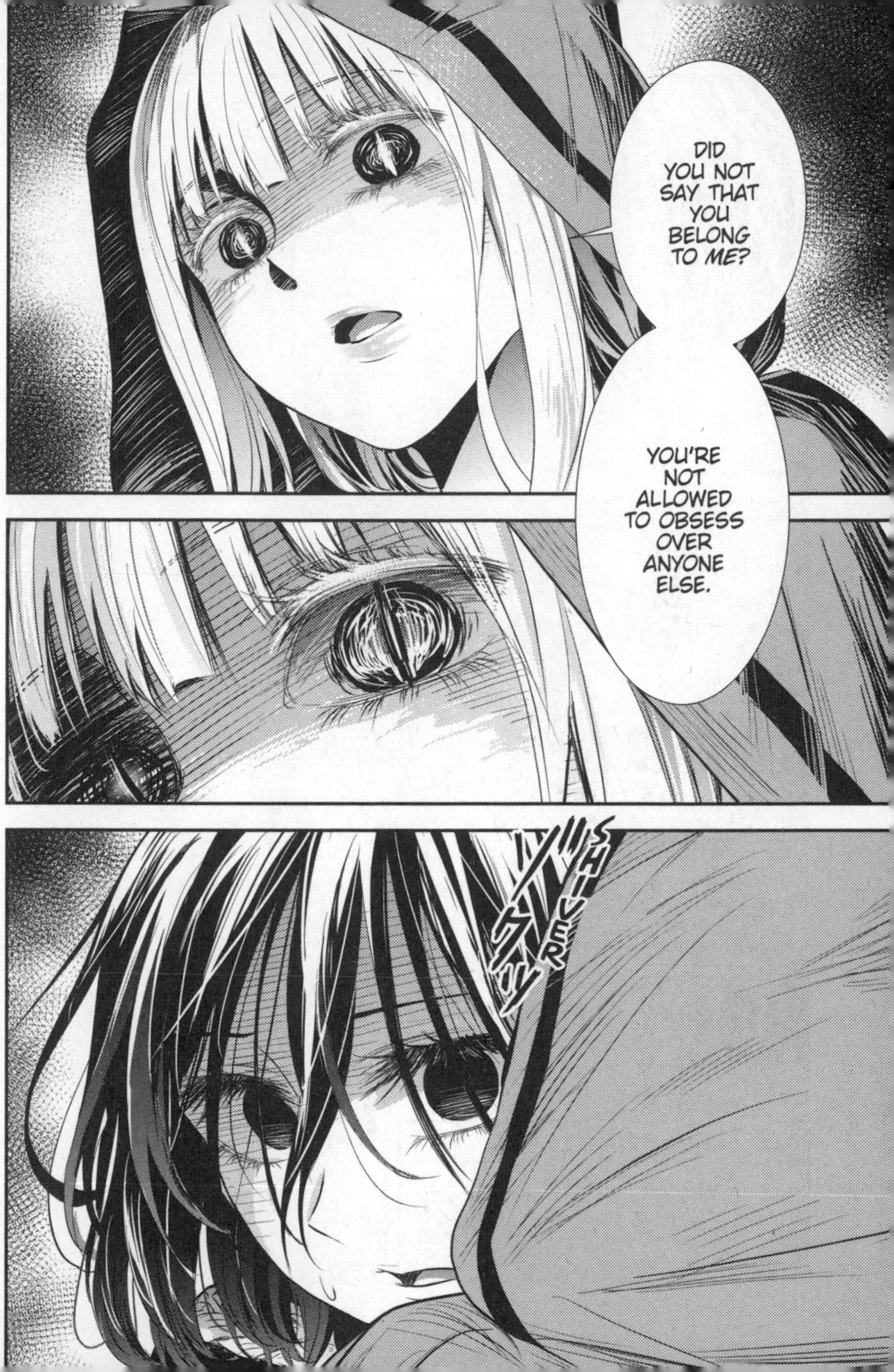
DID YOU NOT SAY THAT YOU BELONG TO ME?
YOU'RE NOT ALLOWED TO OBSESS OVER ANYONE ELSE.
SHIVER

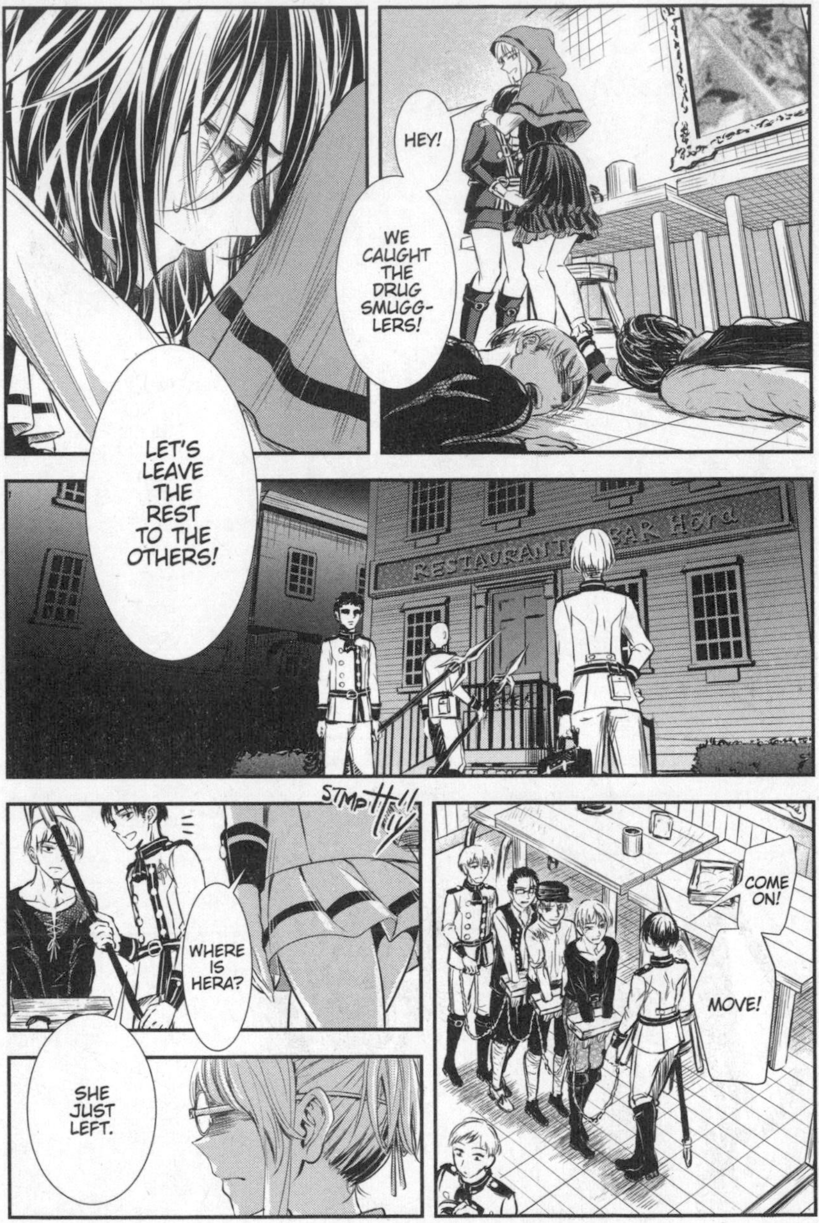
HEY!
WE CAUGHT THE DRUG SMUGG-LERS!
LET'S LEAVE THE REST TO THE OTHERS!
COME ON!
MOVE!
STMP
WHERE IS HERA?
SHE JUST LEFT.

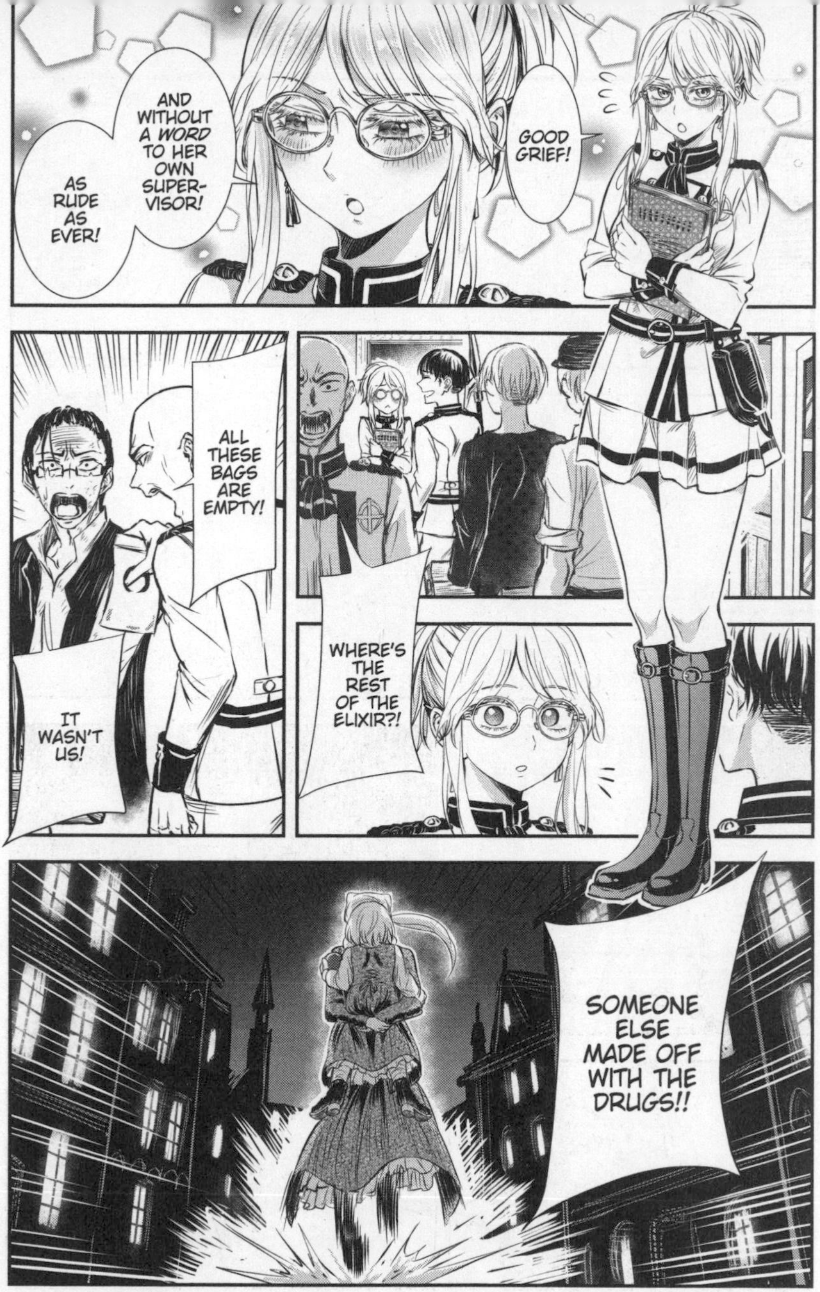
GOOD GRIEF!
AND WITHOUT A *WORD* TO HER OWN SUPER-VISOR!
AS RUDE AS EVER!
ALL THESE BAGS ARE EMPTY!
WHERE'S THE REST OF THE ELIXIR?!
IT WASN'T US!
SOMEONE ELSE MADE OFF WITH THE DRUGS!!

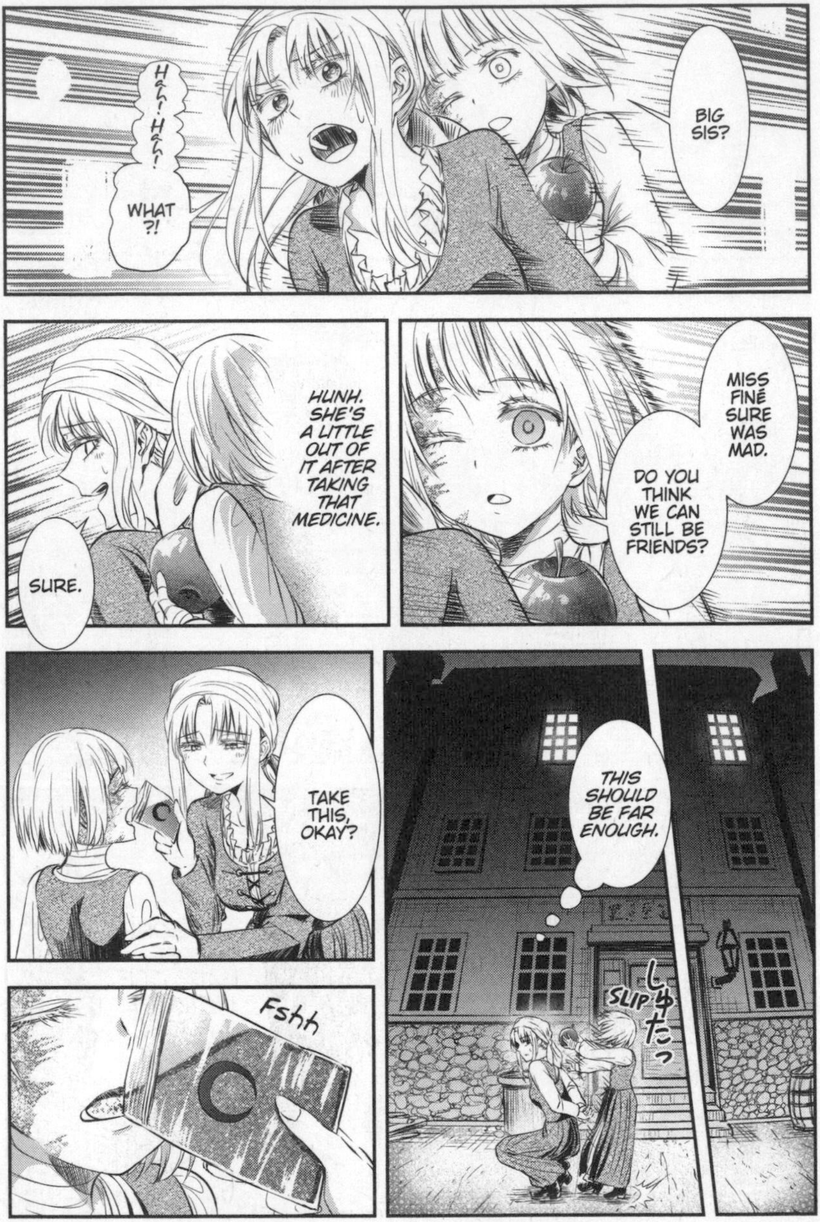
BIG SIS?
Hah! Hah!
WHAT?!
MISS FINÉ SURE WAS MAD.
DO YOU THINK WE CAN STILL BE FRIENDS?
HUNH. SHE'S A LITTLE OUT OF IT AFTER TAKING THAT MEDICINE.
SURE.
THIS SHOULD BE FAR ENOUGH.
しゅたっ
SLIP
TAKE THIS, OKAY?
Fshh

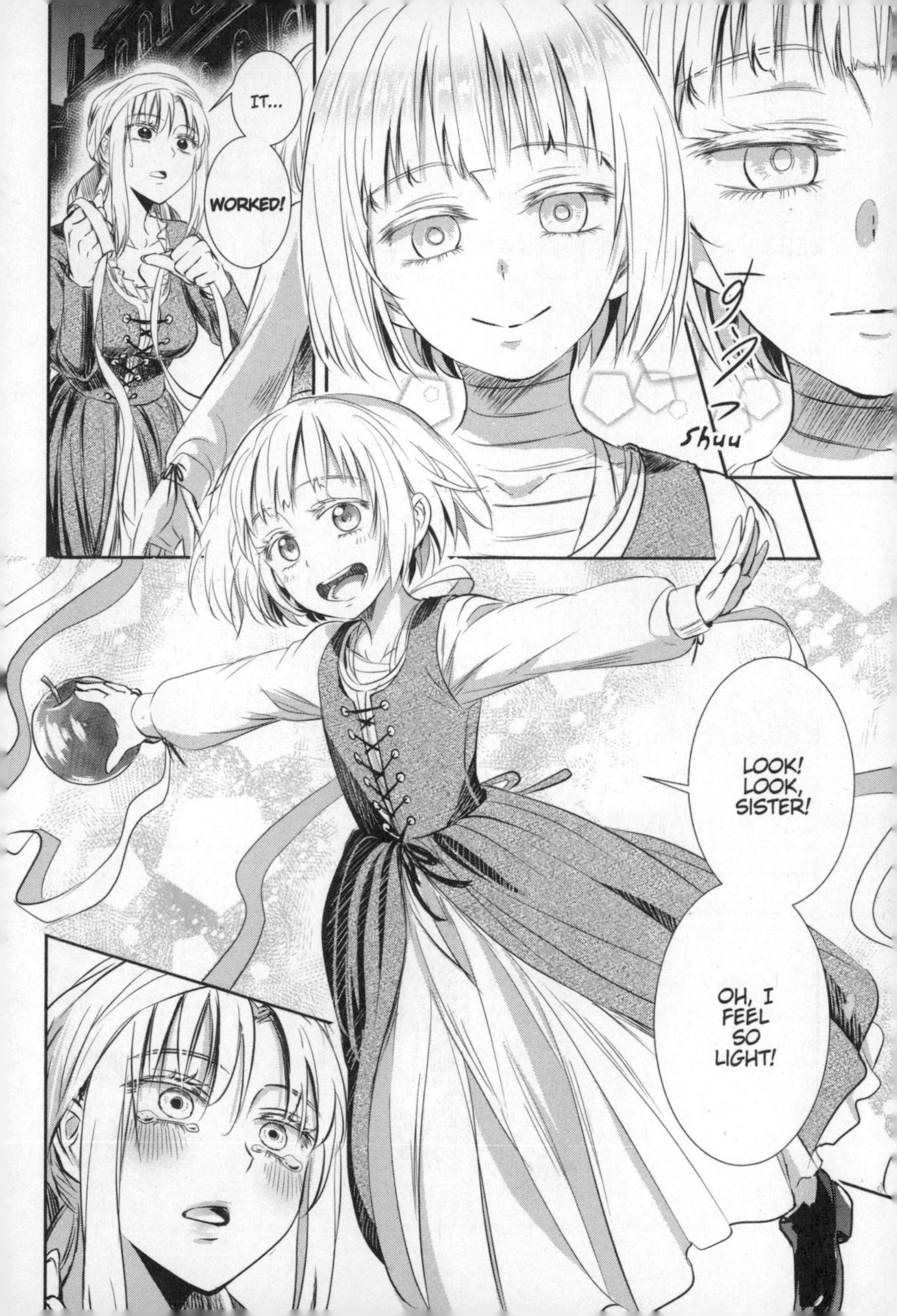
Shuu
IT...
WORKED!
LOOK! LOOK, SISTER!
OH, I FEEL SO LIGHT!

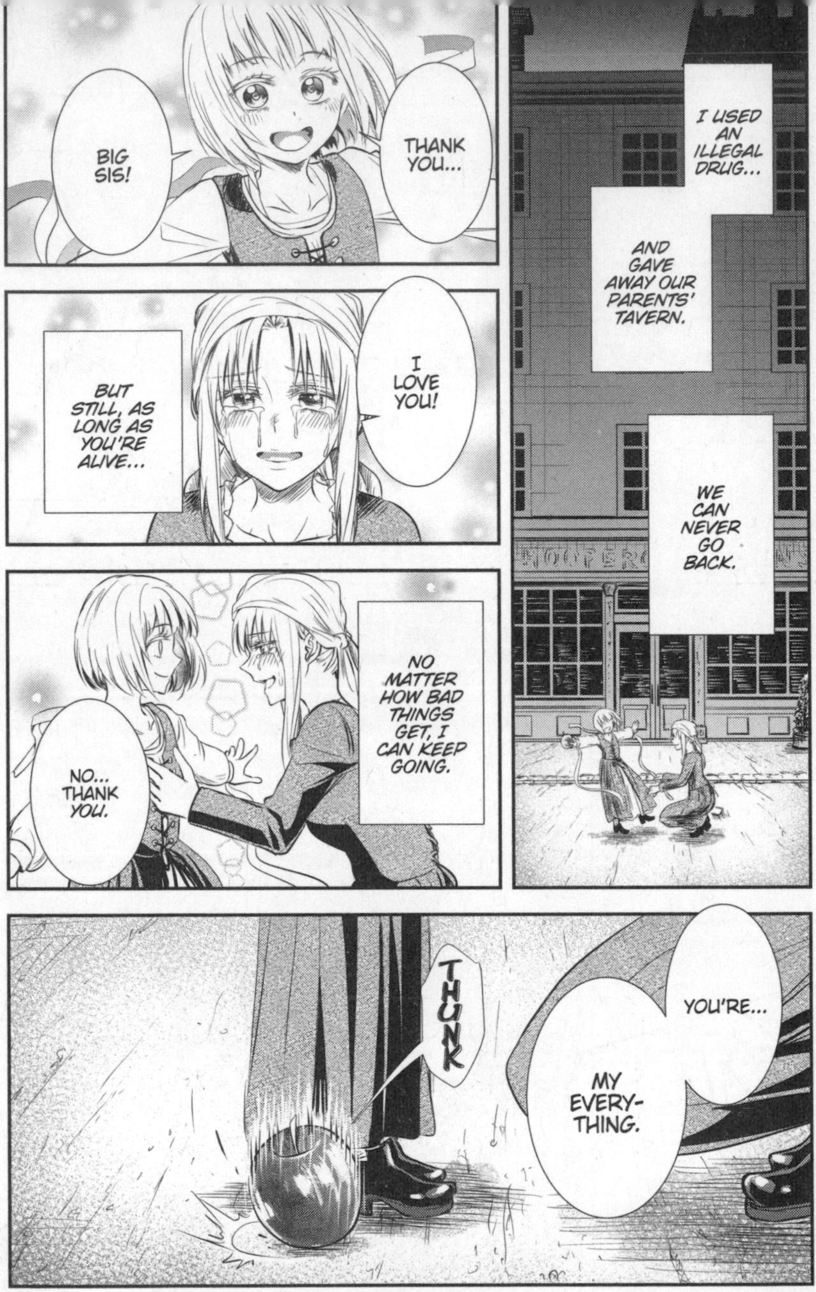
I USED AN ILLEGAL DRUG...
AND GAVE AWAY OUR PARENTS' TAVERN.
WE CAN NEVER GO BACK.
THANK YOU...
BIG SIS!
I LOVE YOU!
BUT STILL, AS LONG AS YOU'RE ALIVE...
NO MATTER HOW BAD THINGS GET, I CAN KEEP GOING.
NO... THANK YOU.
YOU'RE...
MY EVERY-THING.
THUNK

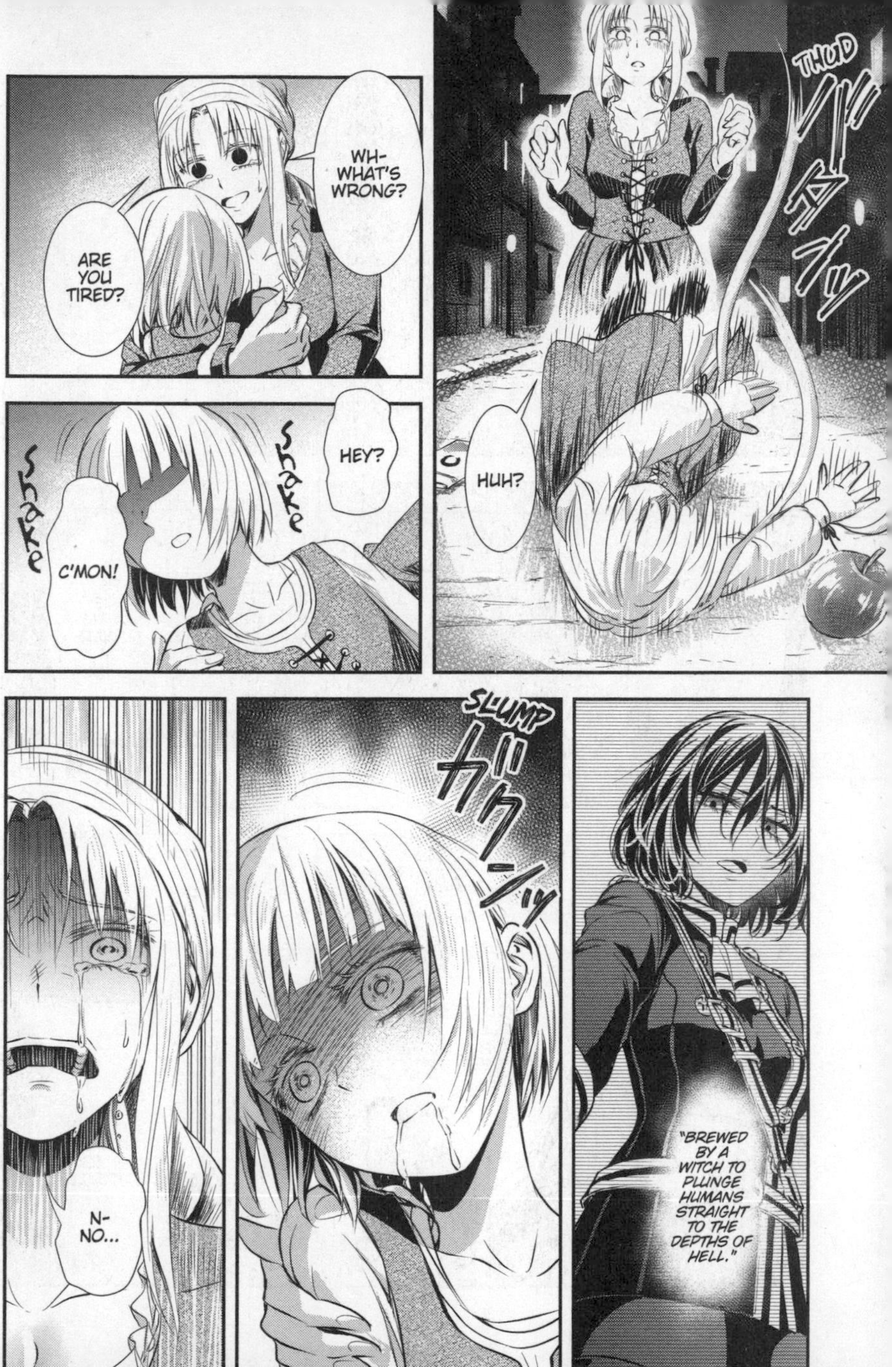
THUD
HUH?
WH- WHAT'S WRONG?
ARE YOU TIRED?
HEY?
shake
C'MON!
shake
"BREWED BY A WITCH TO PLUNGE HUMANS STRAIGHT TO THE DEPTHS OF HELL."
SLUMP
N- NO...

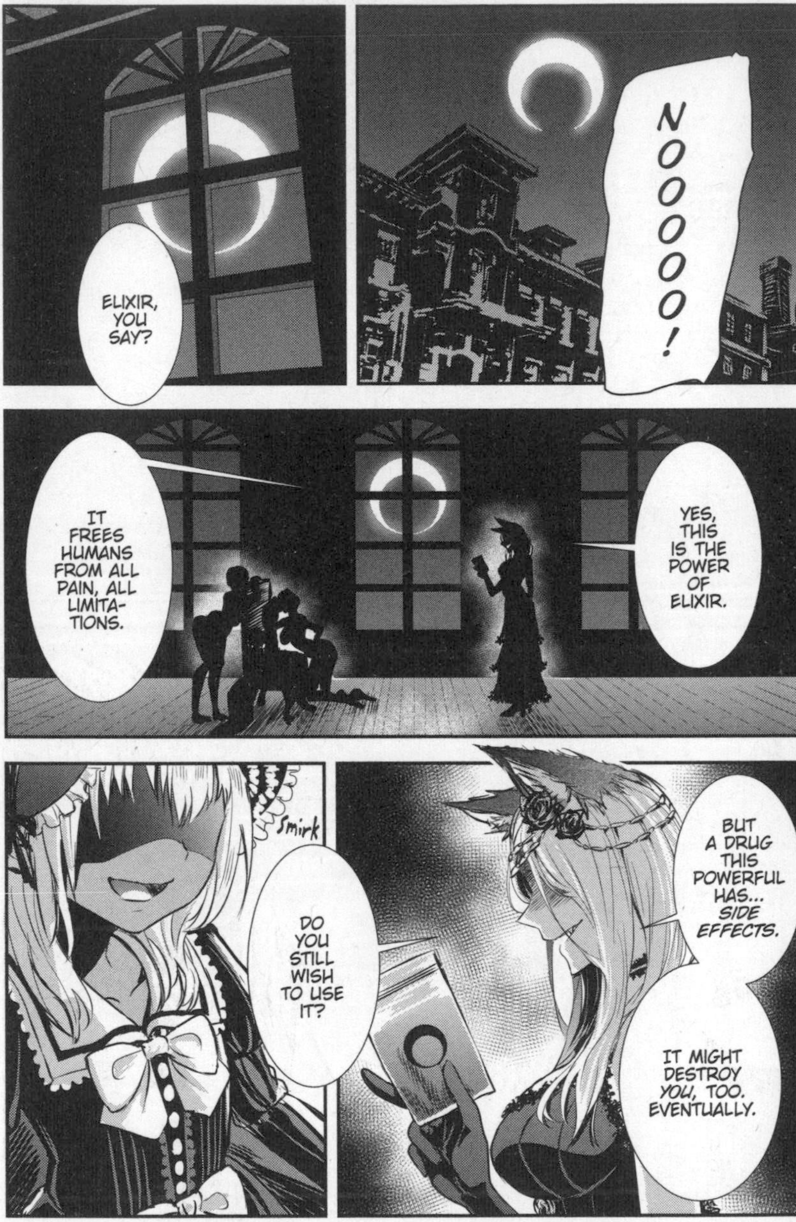
NOOOOOO!
ELIXIR, YOU SAY?
YES, THIS IS THE POWER OF ELIXIR.
IT FREES HUMANS FROM ALL PAIN, ALL LIMITATIONS.
BUT A DRUG THIS POWERFUL HAS... SIDE EFFECTS.
IT MIGHT DESTROY YOU, TOO. EVENTUALLY.
Smirk
DO YOU STILL WISH TO USE IT?

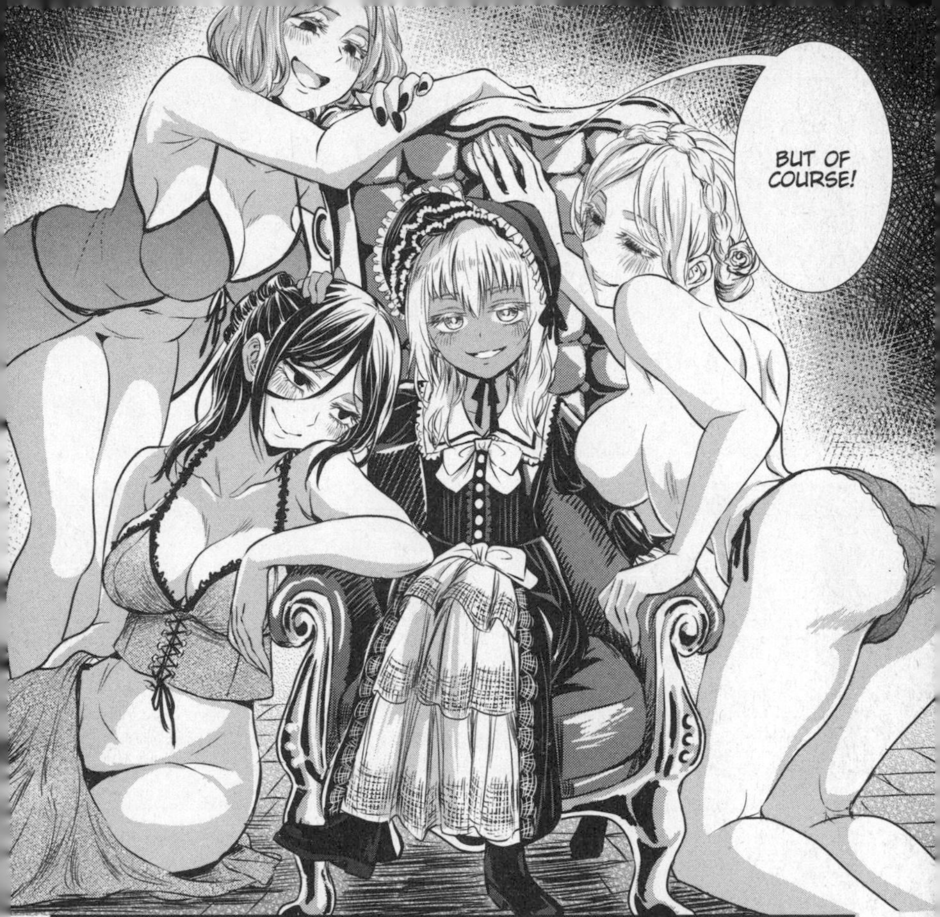
BUT OF COURSE!

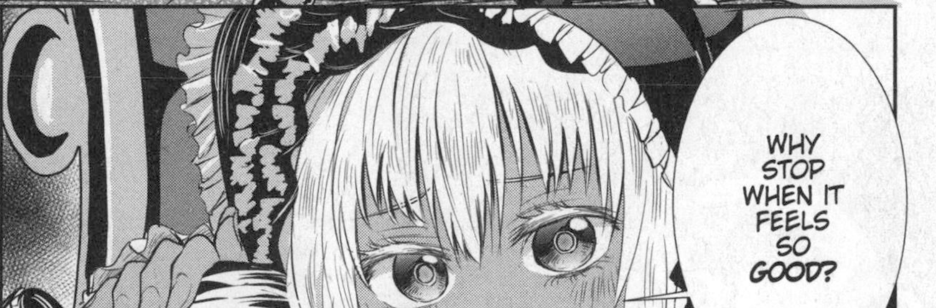
WHY STOP WHEN IT FEELS SO GOOD?

SCARLET

Iris Redhood

【 Name 】 Iris Redhood

【 Height 】 155cm

【 Age 】 Presumably over 100

【Birthday】 June 25th

【 Likes 】 Finé, booze

【Dislikes】 Silver, anything that gets
in the way of her goals

CHAPTER 3

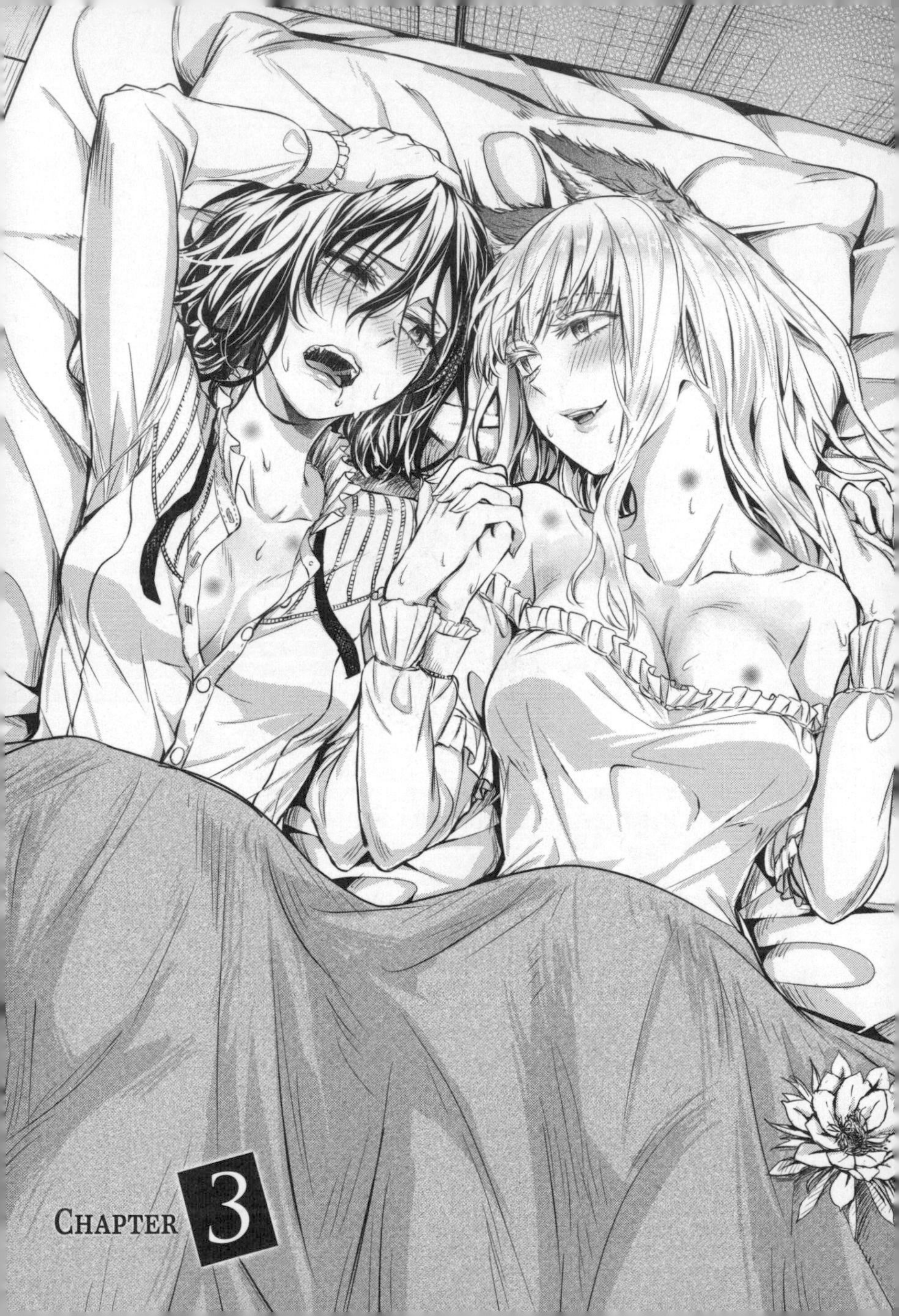

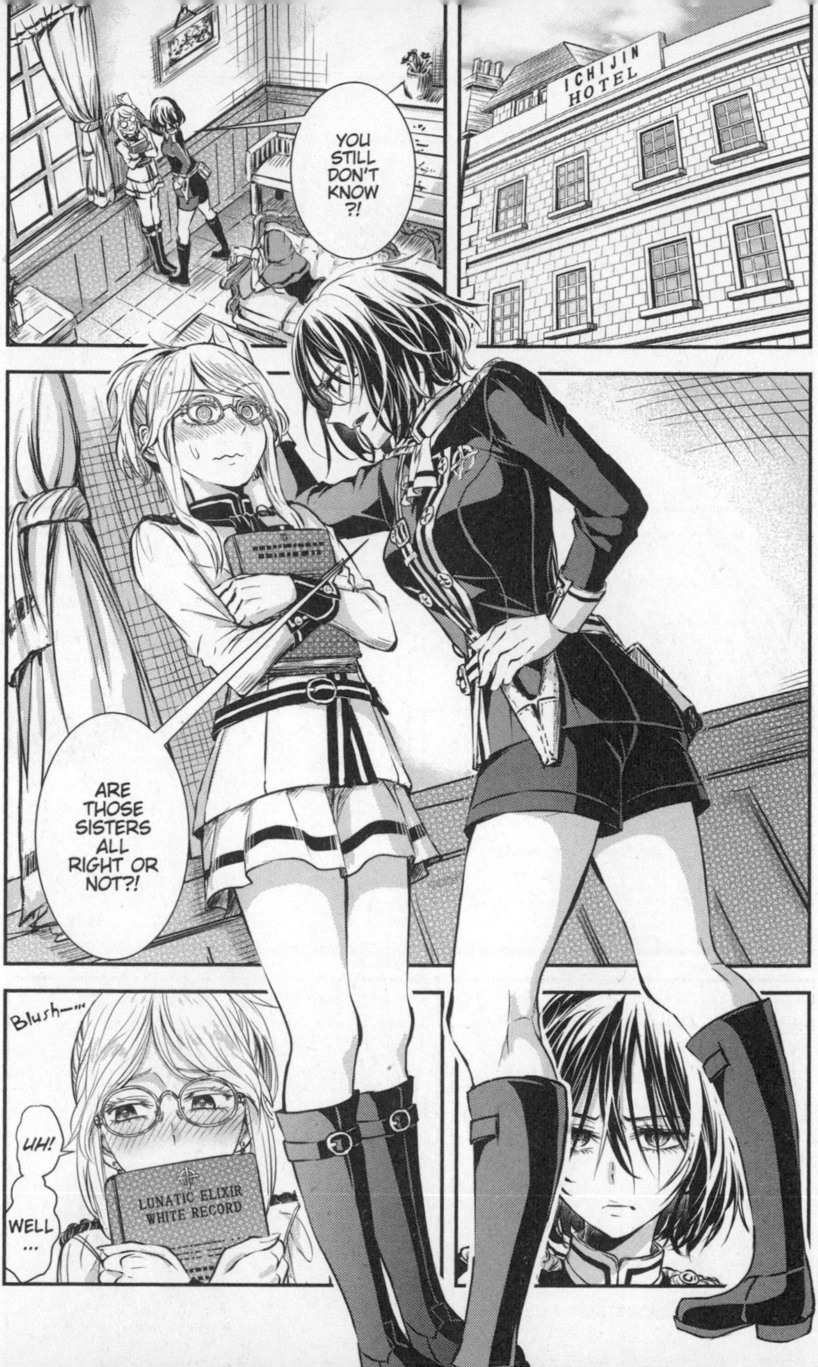
ICHIJIN HOTEL
YOU STILL DON'T KNOW?!
ARE THOSE SISTERS ALL RIGHT OR NOT?!
Blush—...
UH!
WELL ...
LUNATIC ELIXIR WHITE RECORD

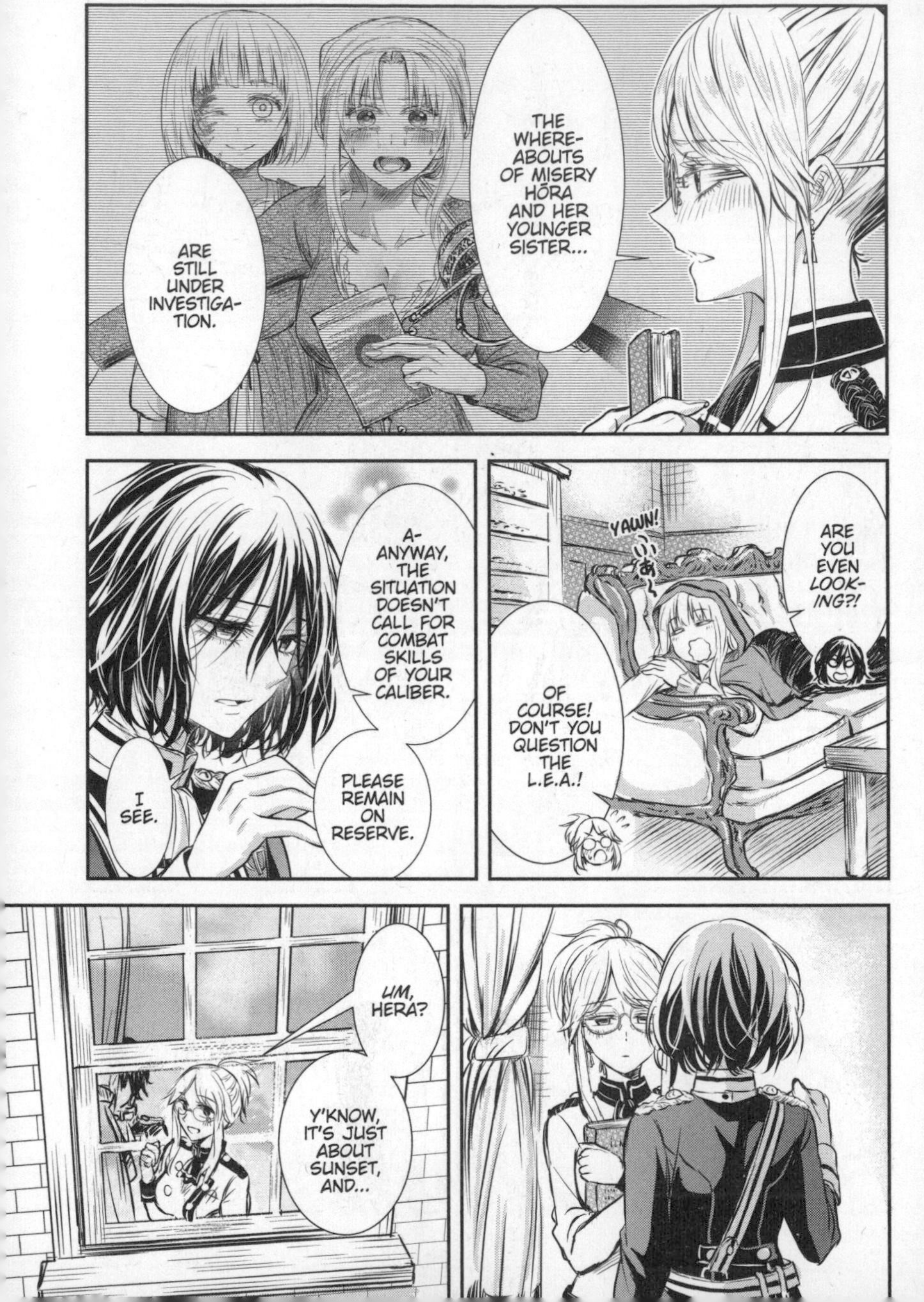
THE WHERE-ABOUTS OF MISERY HŌRA AND HER YOUNGER SISTER...
ARE STILL UNDER INVESTIGA-TION.
ARE YOU EVEN LOOKING?!
YAWN!
OF COURSE! DON'T YOU QUESTION THE L.E.A.!
A-ANYWAY, THE SITUATION DOESN'T CALL FOR COMBAT SKILLS OF YOUR CALIBER.
PLEASE REMAIN ON RESERVE.
I SEE.
UM, HERA?
Y'KNOW, IT'S JUST ABOUT SUNSET, AND...

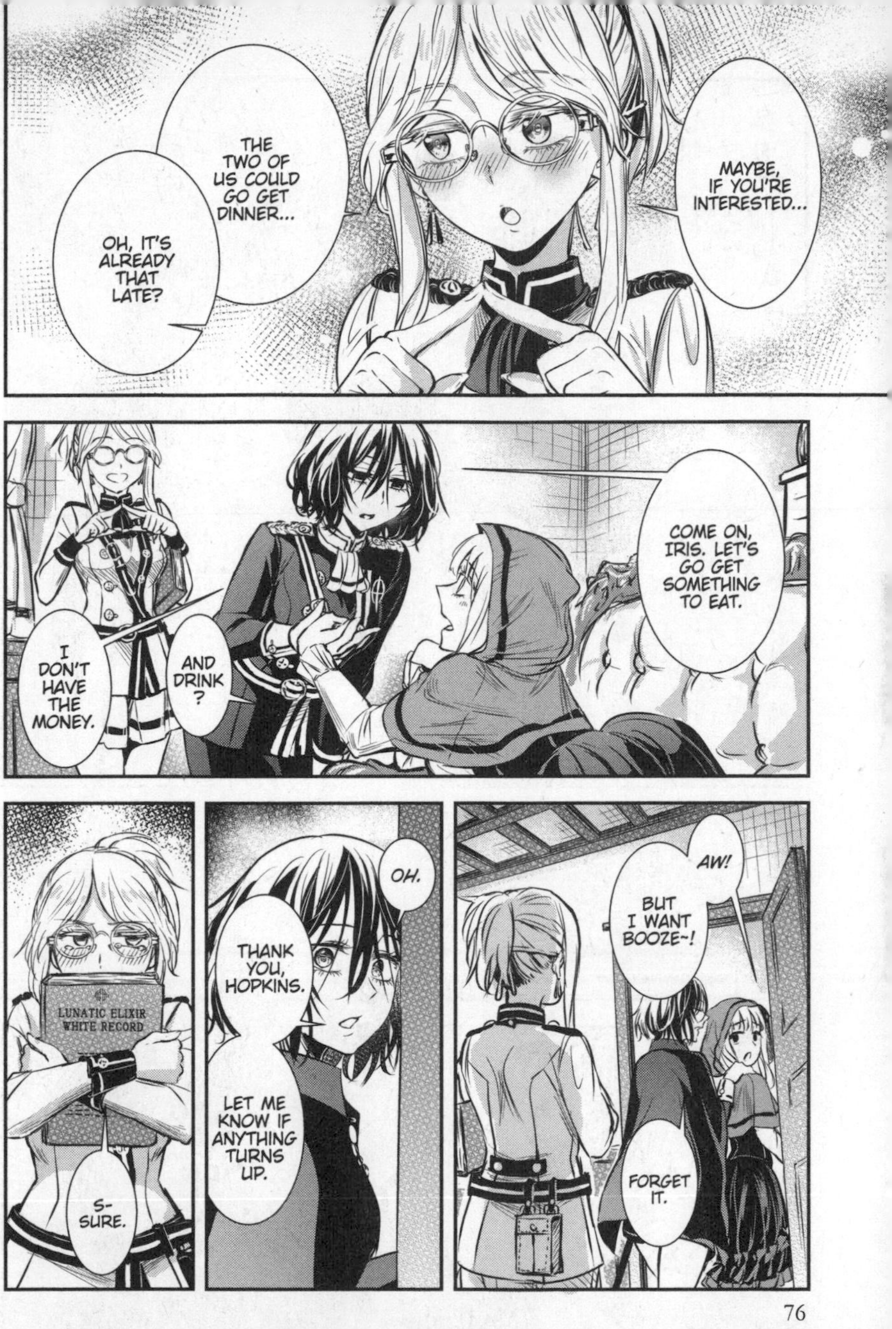
MAYBE, IF YOU'RE INTERESTED...
THE TWO OF US COULD GO GET DINNER...
OH, IT'S ALREADY THAT LATE?
COME ON, IRIS. LET'S GO GET SOMETHING TO EAT.
AND DRINK?
I DON'T HAVE THE MONEY.
AW!
BUT I WANT BOOZE~!
FORGET IT.
OH.
THANK YOU, HOPKINS.
LET ME KNOW IF ANYTHING TURNS UP.
LUNATIC ELIXIR WHITE RECORD
S- SURE.

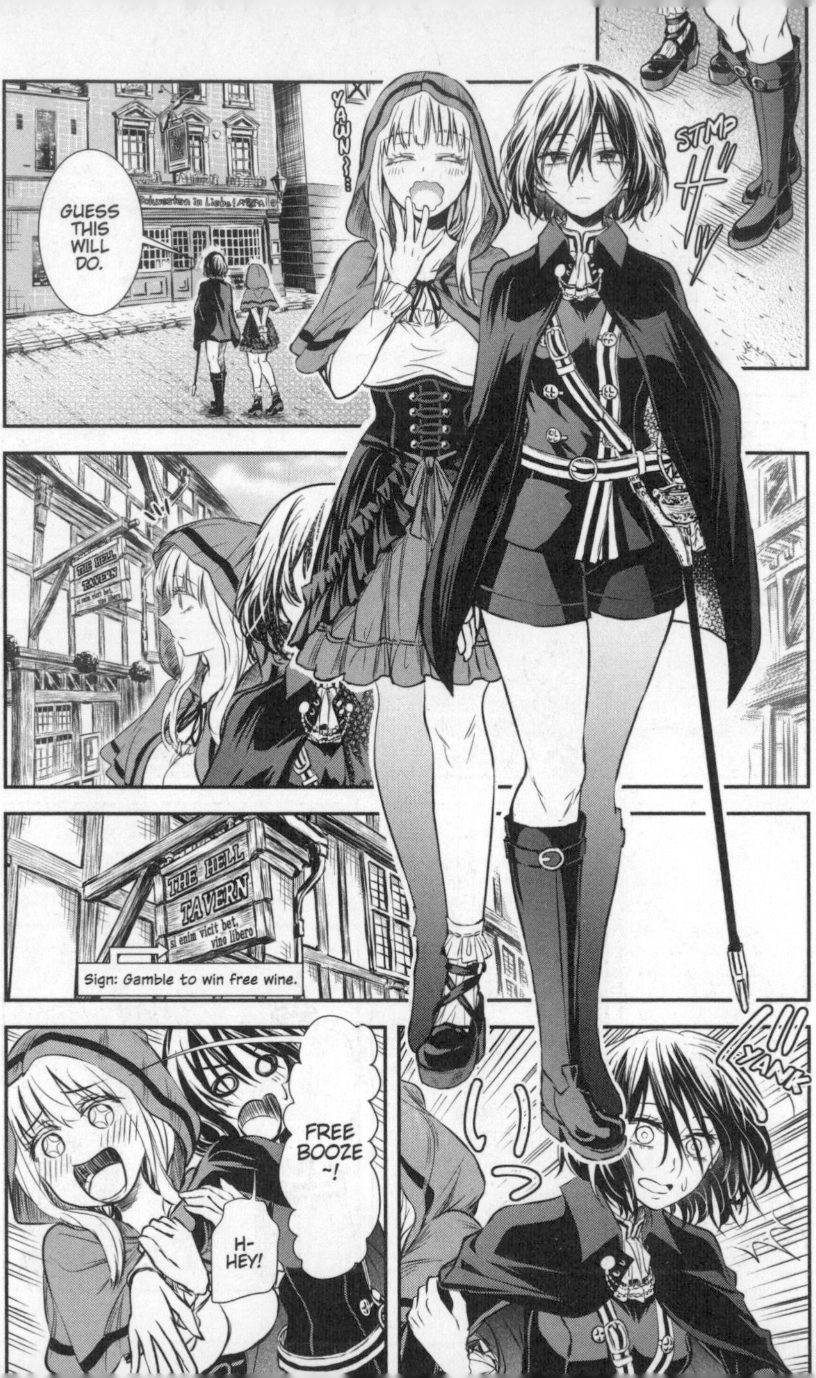
STMP
YAWN~~!
GUESS THIS WILL DO.
THE HELL TAVERN
si enim vicit bet, vino libero
THE HELL TAVERN
si enim vicit bet, vino libero
Sign: Gamble to win free wine.
YANK
FREE BOOZE~!
H-HEY!

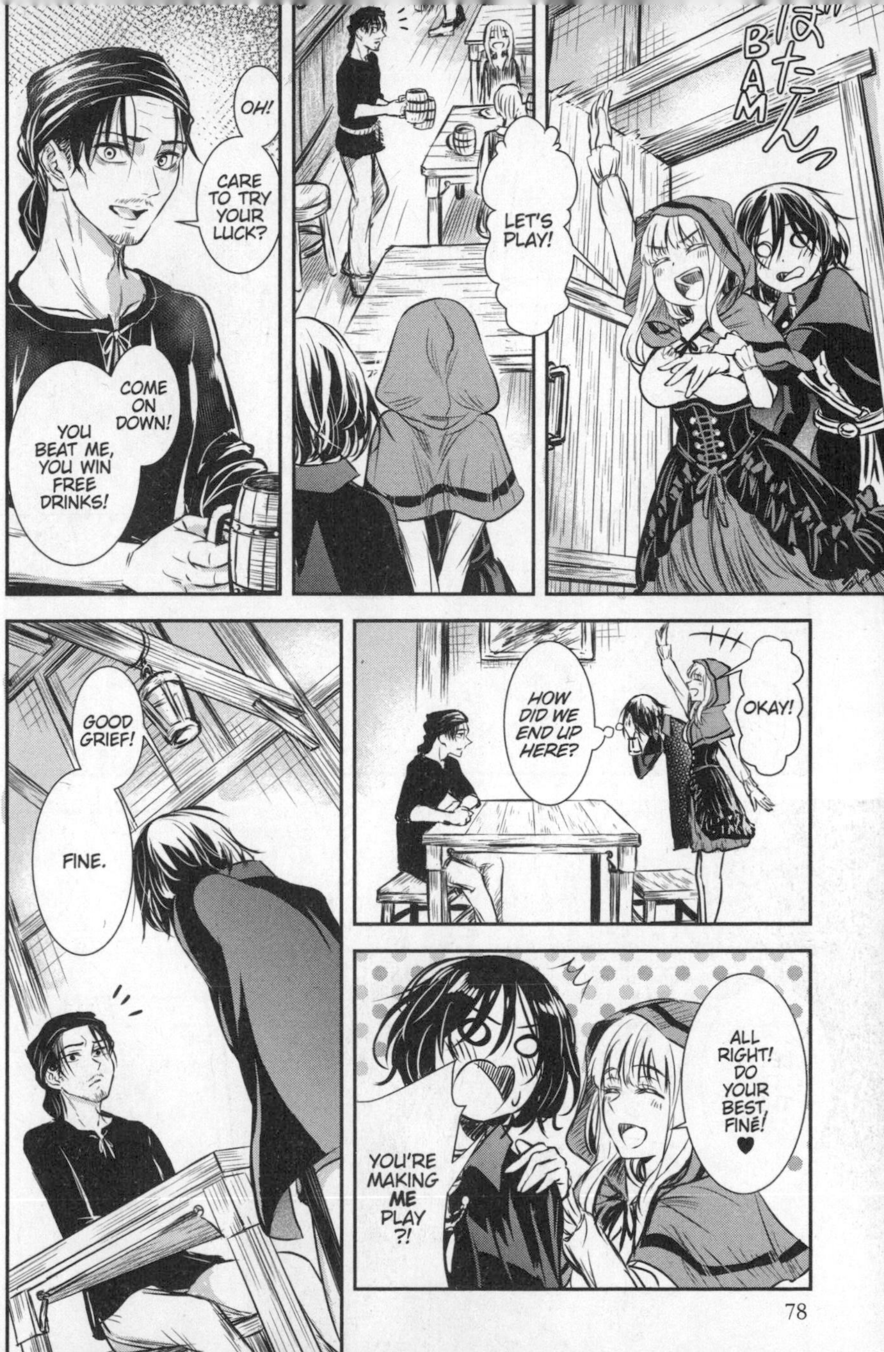
ばたーんっ
BAM
LET'S PLAY!
OH!
CARE TO TRY YOUR LUCK?
COME ON DOWN!
YOU BEAT ME, YOU WIN FREE DRINKS!
OKAY!
HOW DID WE END UP HERE?
ALL RIGHT! DO YOUR BEST, FINÉ! ♥
YOU'RE MAKING ME PLAY ?!
GOOD GRIEF!
FINE.

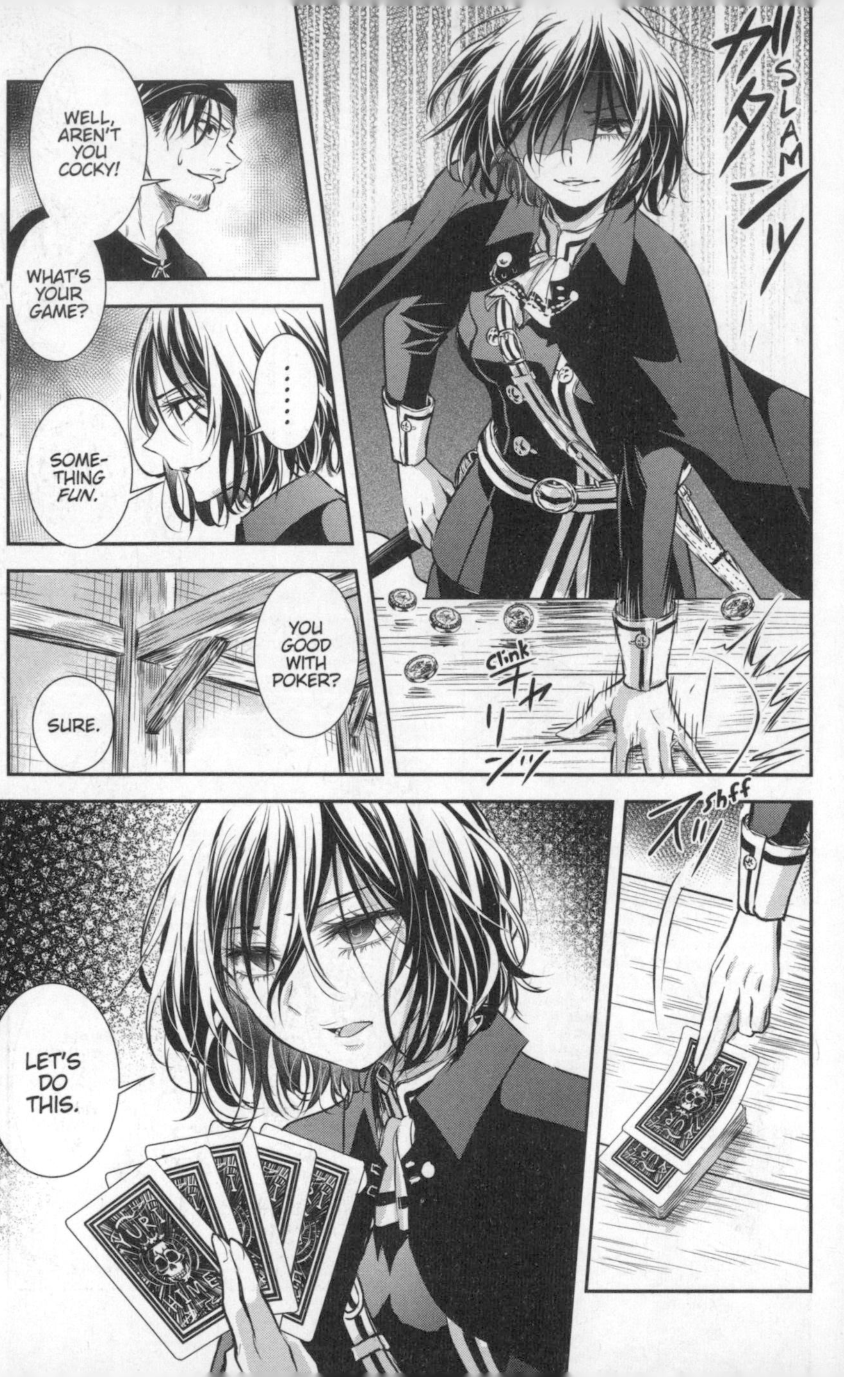

ガタンッ
SLAM
WELL, AREN'T YOU COCKY!
WHAT'S YOUR GAME?
......
SOME-THING FUN.
clink
チャリーンッ
YOU GOOD WITH POKER?
SURE.
スッ
shff
LET'S DO THIS.

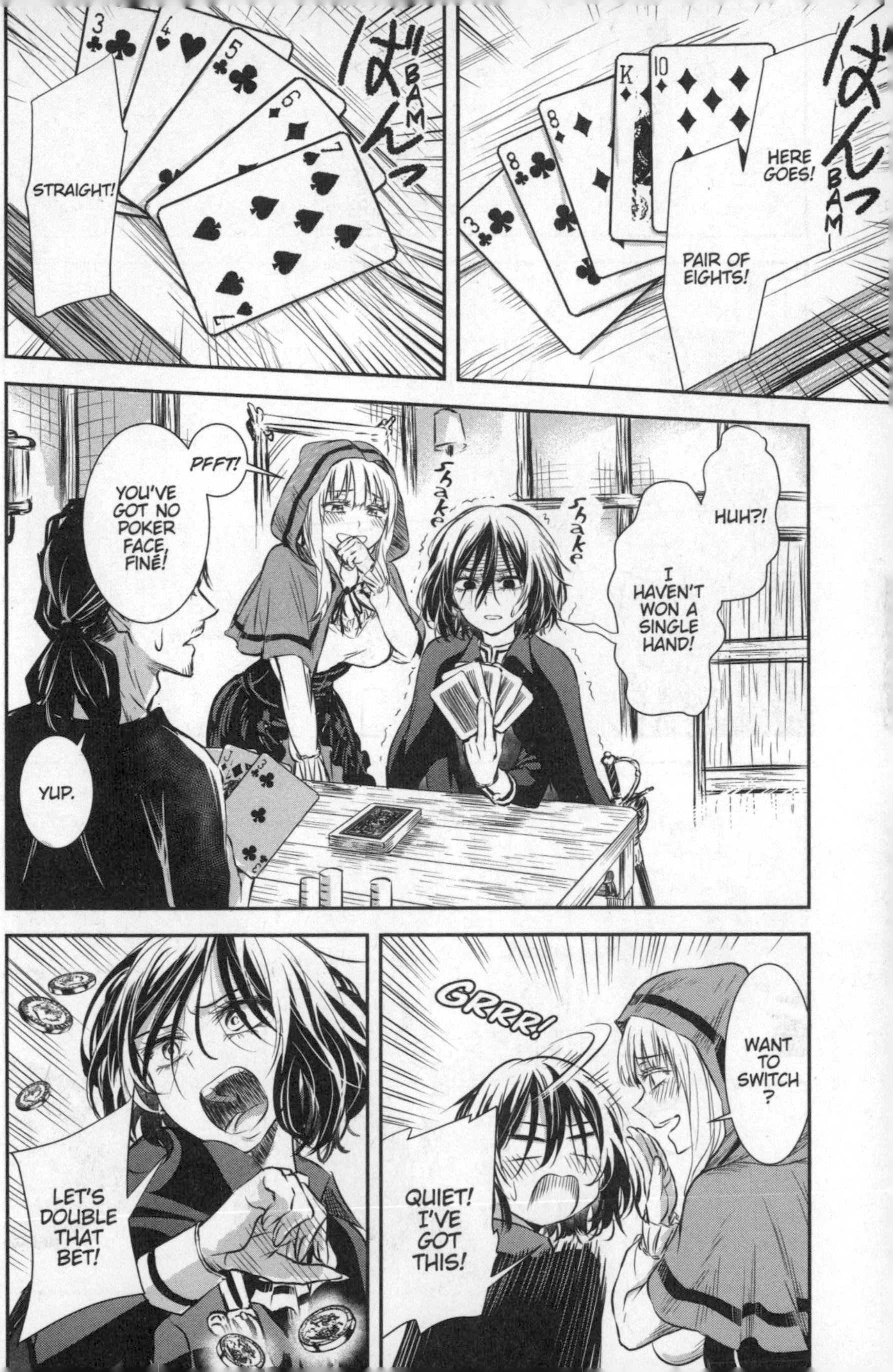
ぱんっ
BAM
HERE GOES!
PAIR OF EIGHTS!
ばんっ
BAM
STRAIGHT!
HUH?!
I HAVEN'T WON A SINGLE HAND!
Shake
Shake
PFFT!
YOU'VE GOT NO POKER FACE, FINE!
YUP.
WANT TO SWITCH?
GRRR!
QUIET! I'VE GOT THIS!
LET'S DOUBLE THAT BET!

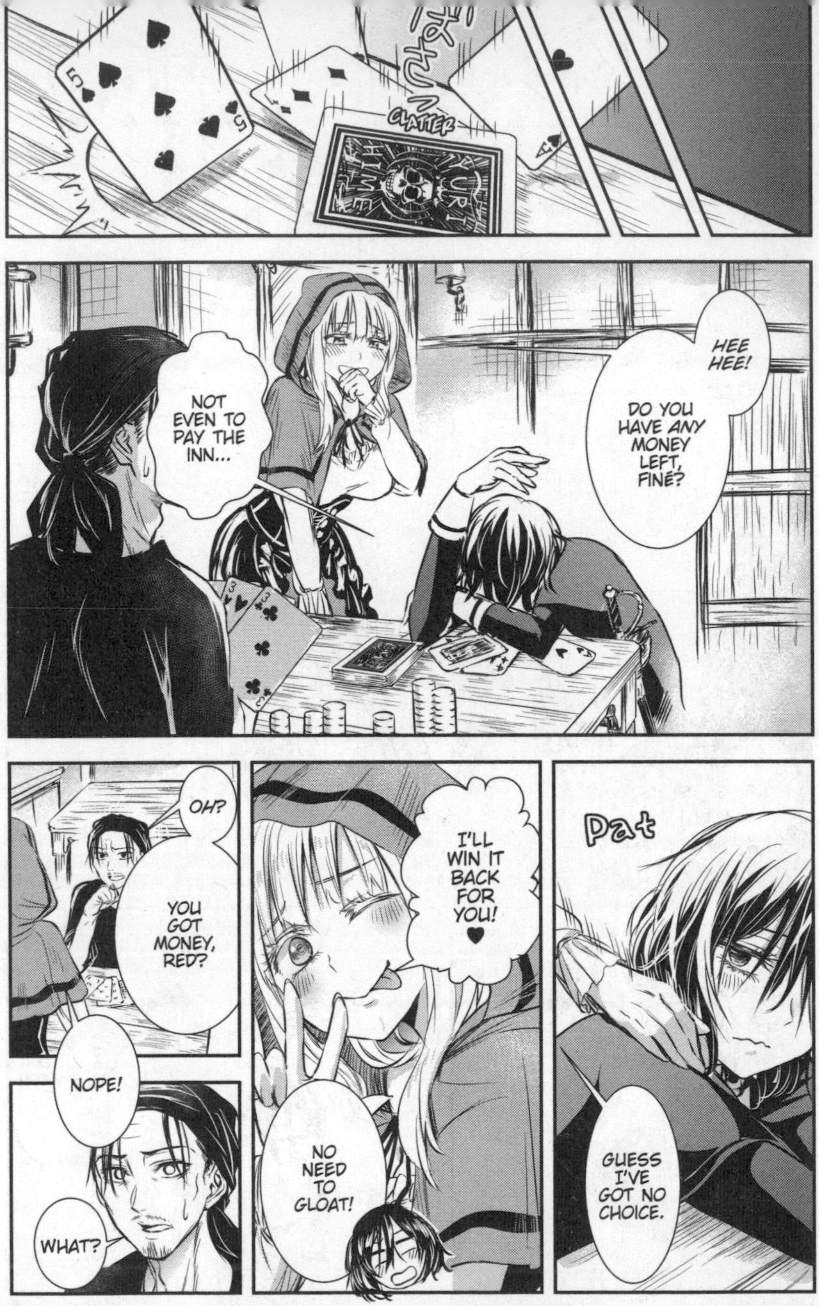
ばさっ
CLATTER
YURI HIME
HEE HEE!
DO YOU HAVE ANY MONEY LEFT, FINE?
NOT EVEN TO PAY THE INN...
Pat
GUESS I'VE GOT NO CHOICE.
I'LL WIN IT BACK FOR YOU! ♥
NO NEED TO GLOAT!
OH?
YOU GOT MONEY, RED?
NOPE!
WHAT?

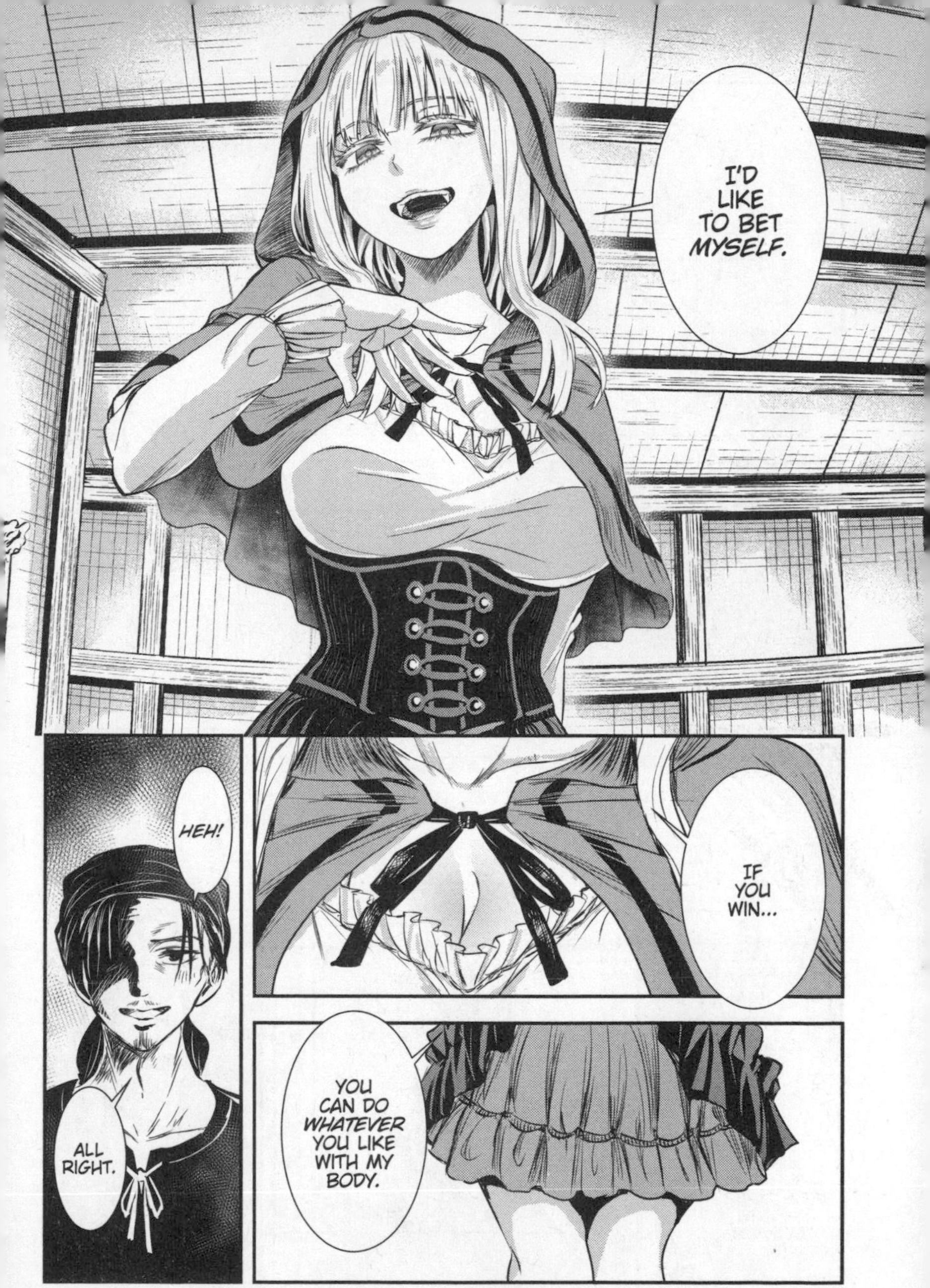
I'D LIKE TO BET *MYSELF.*
IF YOU WIN...
YOU CAN DO *WHATEVER* YOU LIKE WITH MY BODY.
HEH!
ALL RIGHT.

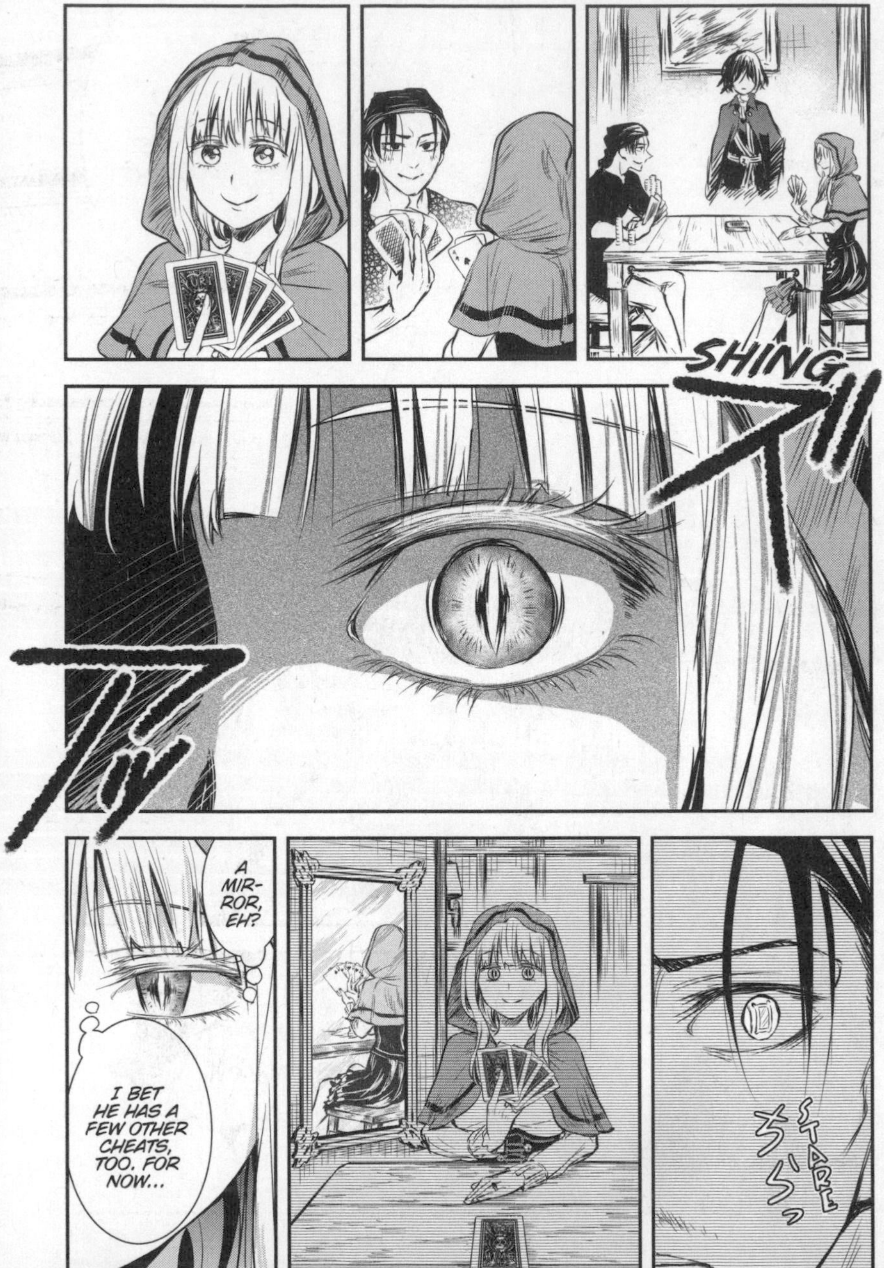
SHING
STARE
A MIRROR, EH?
I BET HE HAS A FEW OTHER CHEATS, TOO. FOR NOW...

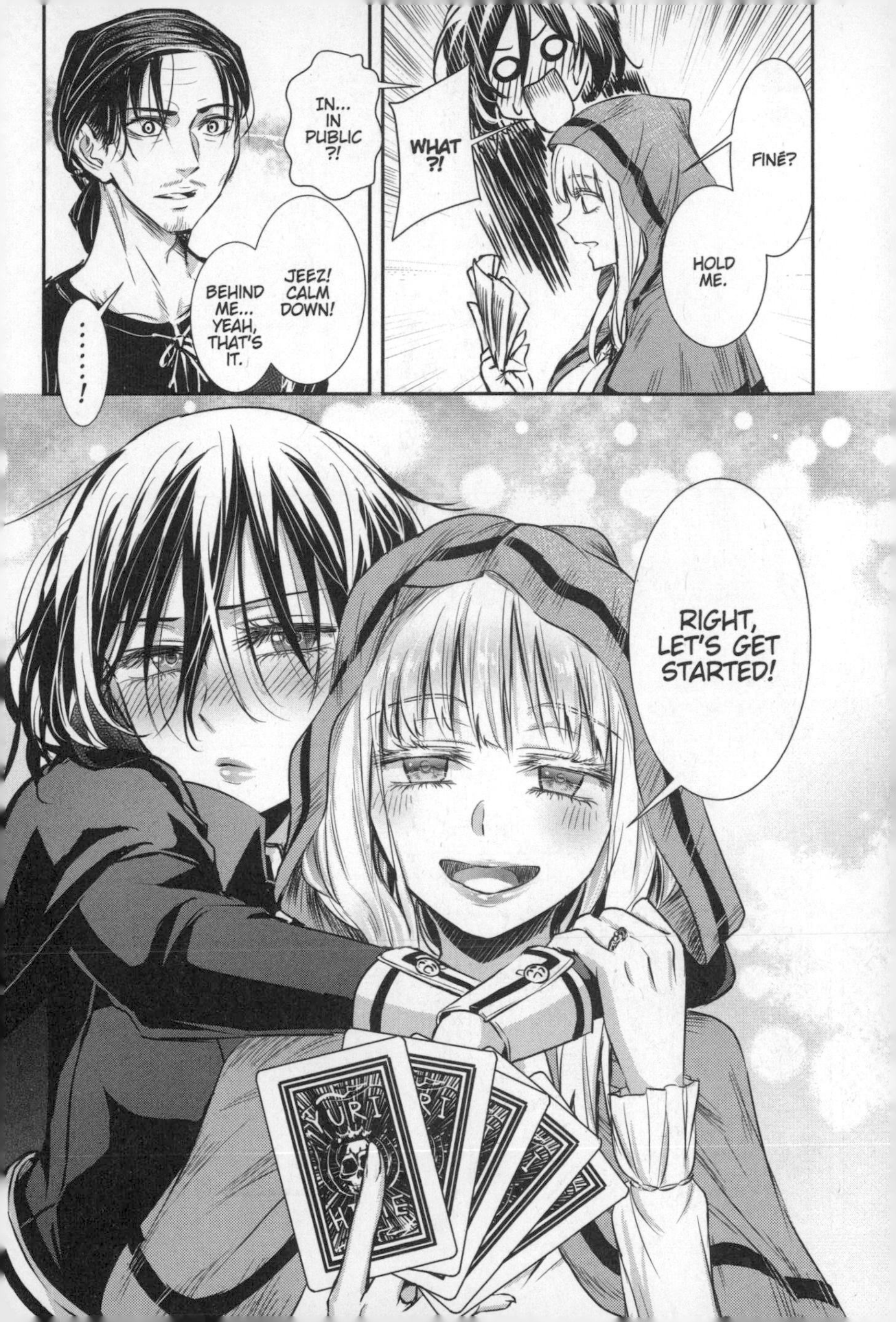
FINE? HOLD ME.
WHAT?!
IN... IN PUBLIC?!
JEEZ! CALM DOWN! BEHIND ME... YEAH, THAT'S IT.
......!
RIGHT, LET'S GET STARTED!

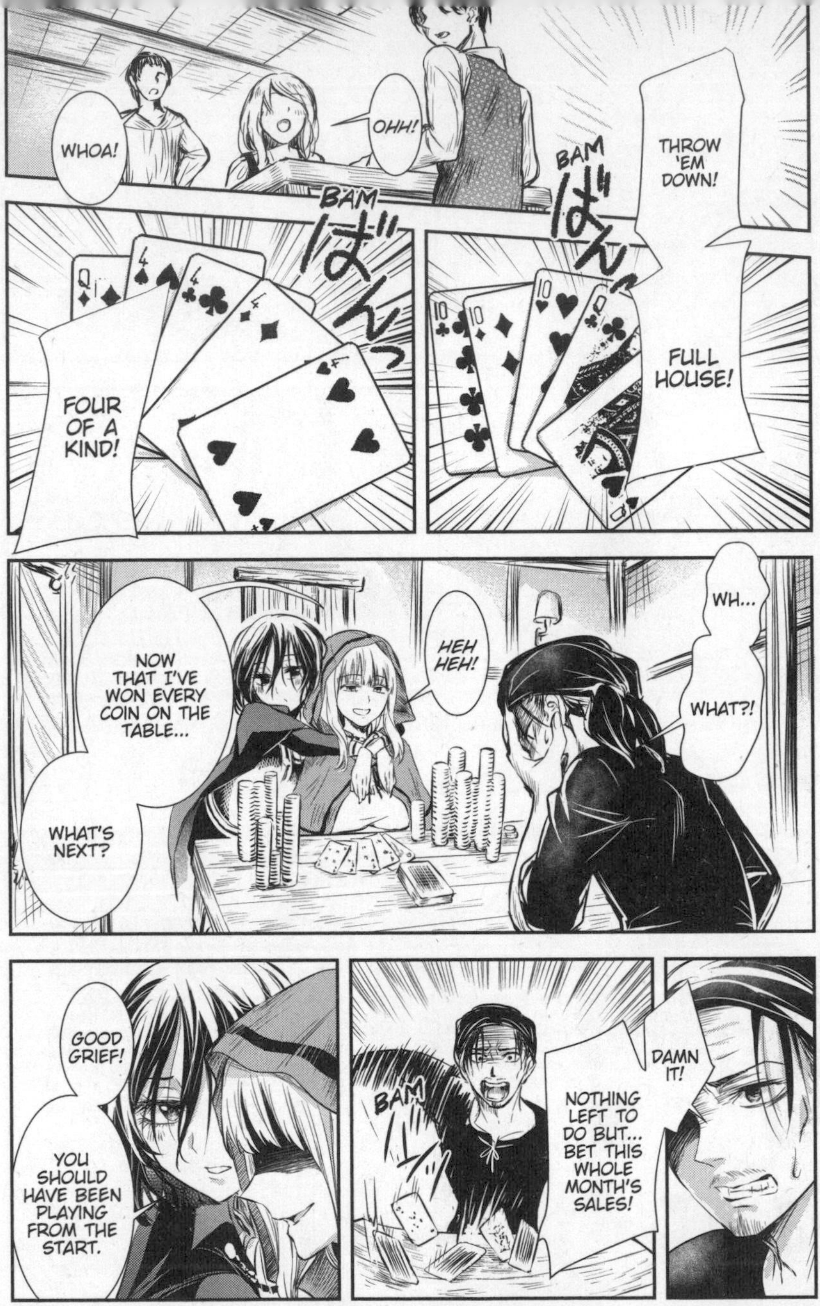
THROW 'EM DOWN!
OHH!
WHOA!
BAM
ばんっ
FULL HOUSE!
BAM
ばんっ
FOUR OF A KIND!
WH... WHAT?!
HEH HEH!
NOW THAT I'VE WON EVERY COIN ON THE TABLE...
WHAT'S NEXT?
DAMN IT!
NOTHING LEFT TO DO BUT... BET THIS WHOLE MONTH'S SALES!
BAM
GOOD GRIEF!
YOU SHOULD HAVE BEEN PLAYING FROM THE START.

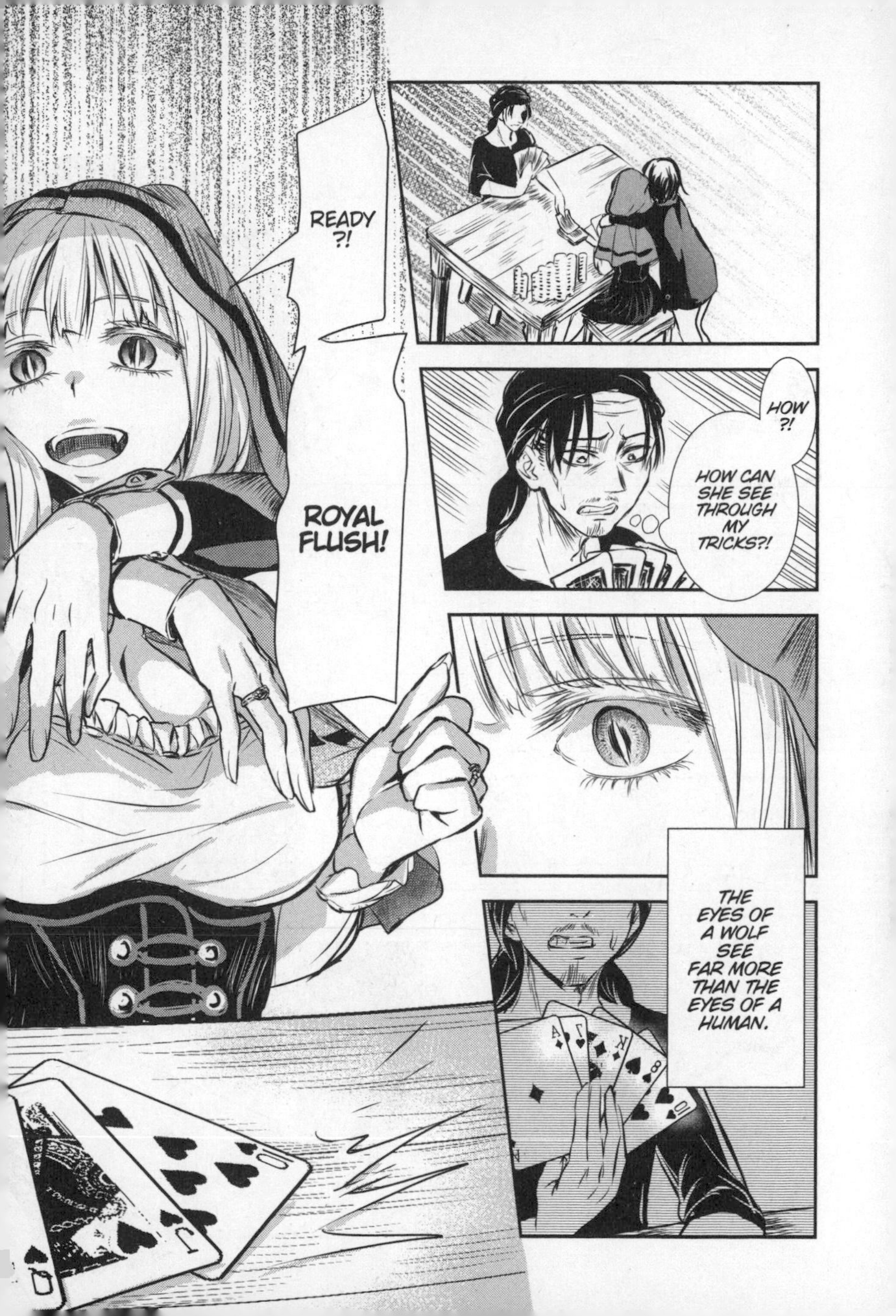
HOW ?!
HOW CAN SHE SEE THROUGH MY TRICKS?!
THE EYES OF A WOLF SEE FAR MORE THAN THE EYES OF A HUMAN.
READY ?!
ROYAL FLUSH!

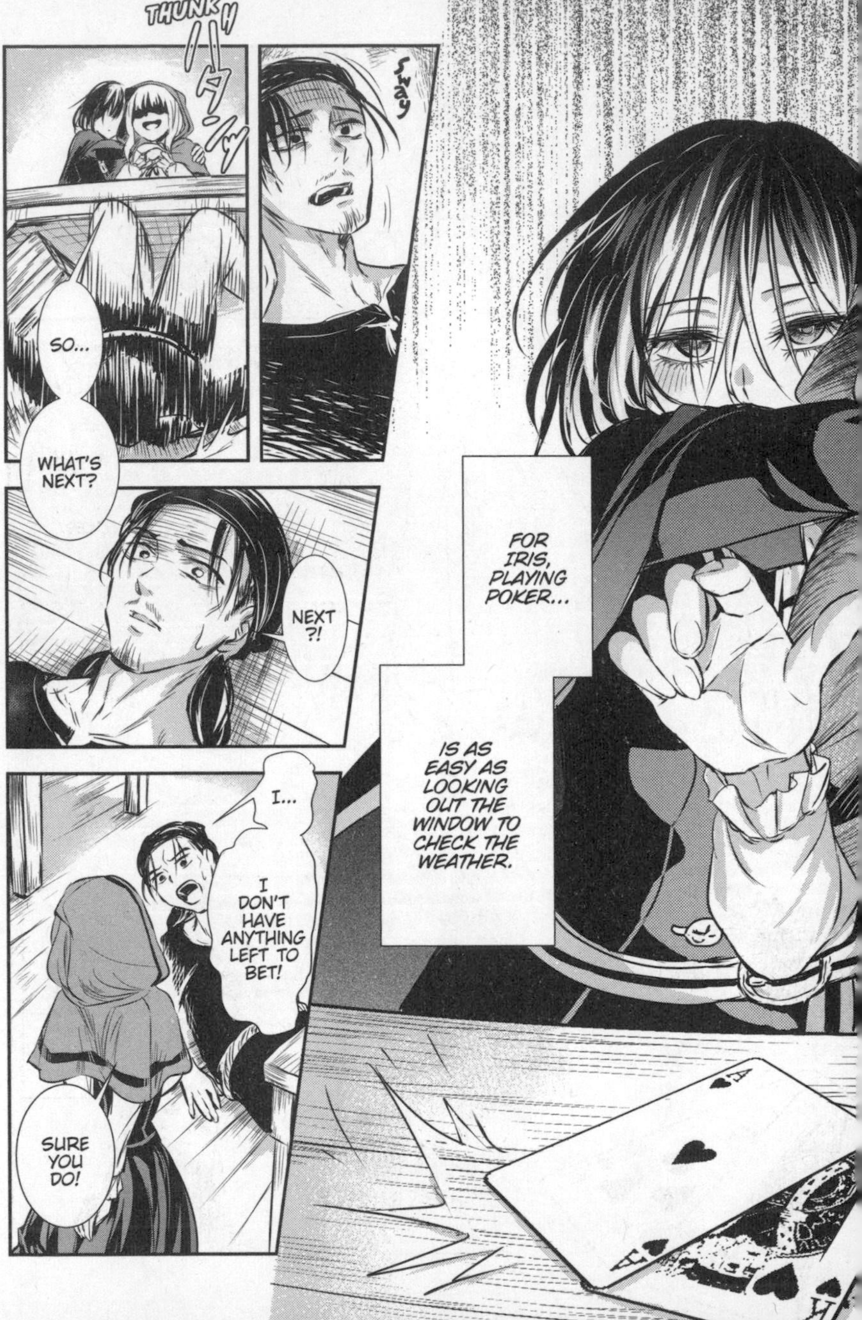
FOR IRIS, PLAYING POKER...
IS AS EASY AS LOOKING OUT THE WINDOW TO CHECK THE WEATHER.
sway
THUNK
SO...
WHAT'S NEXT?
NEXT?!
I...
I DON'T HAVE ANYTHING LEFT TO BET!
SURE YOU DO!

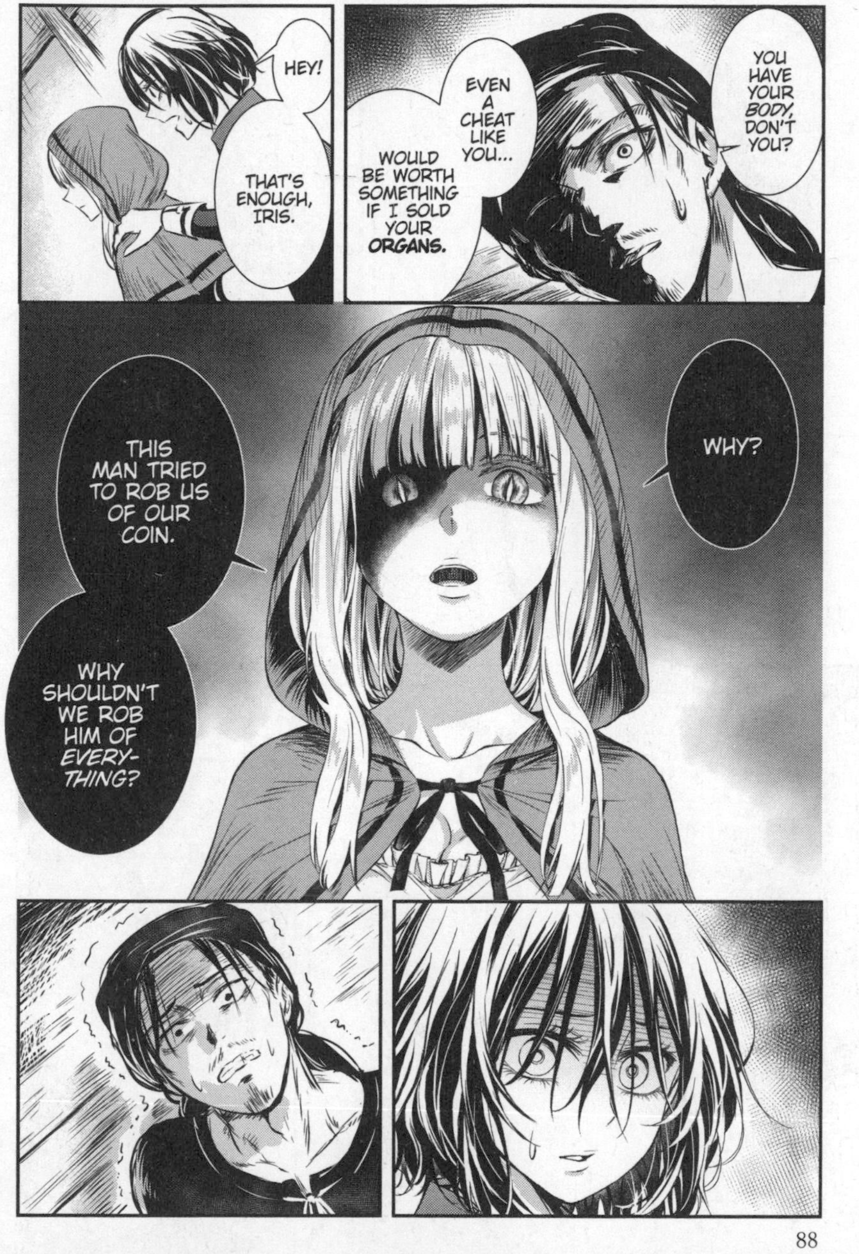
YOU HAVE YOUR BODY, DON'T YOU?
EVEN A CHEAT LIKE YOU...
WOULD BE WORTH SOMETHING IF I SOLD YOUR **ORGANS.**
HEY!
THAT'S ENOUGH, IRIS.
WHY?
THIS MAN TRIED TO ROB US OF OUR COIN.
WHY SHOULDN'T WE ROB HIM OF *EVERY-THING?*

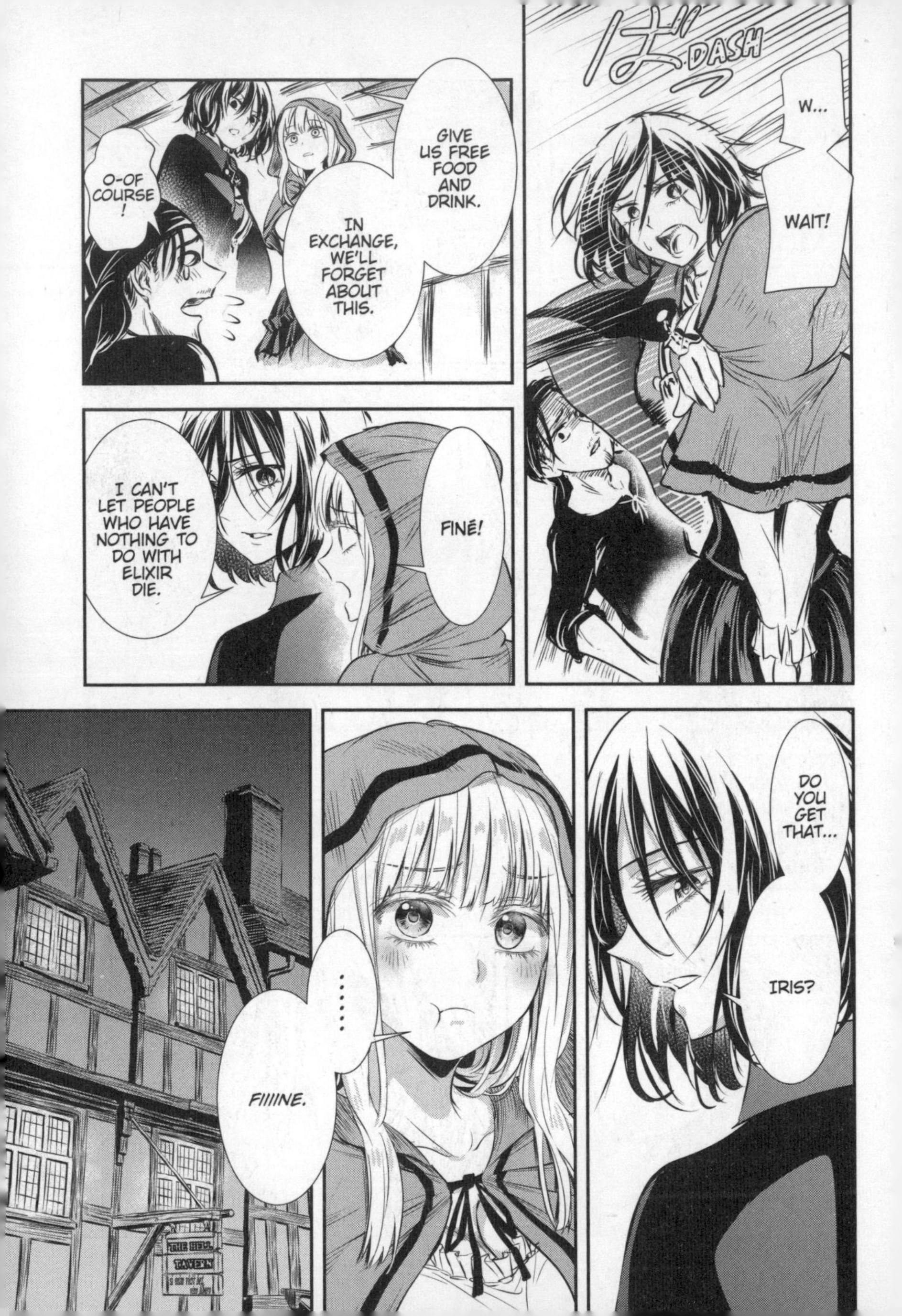
ぱ DASH
W...
WAIT!
GIVE US FREE FOOD AND DRINK.
IN EXCHANGE, WE'LL FORGET ABOUT THIS.
O-OF COURSE!
I CAN'T LET PEOPLE WHO HAVE NOTHING TO DO WITH ELIXIR DIE.
FINÉ!
DO YOU GET THAT...
IRIS?
......
FIIIINE.
THE HELL TAVERN

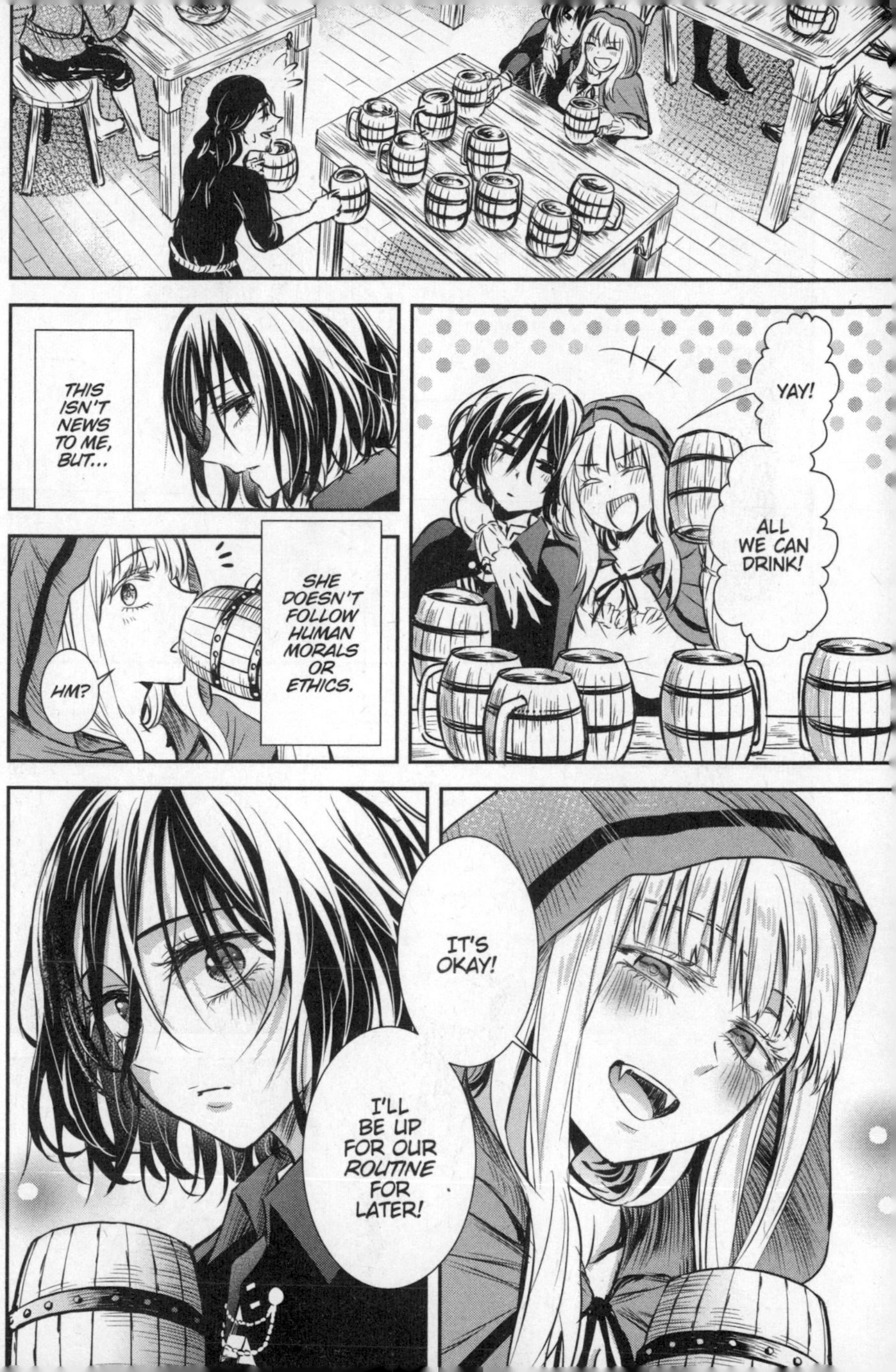
YAY!
ALL WE CAN DRINK!
THIS ISN'T NEWS TO ME, BUT...
SHE DOESN'T FOLLOW HUMAN MORALS OR ETHICS.
HM?
IT'S OKAY!
I'LL BE UP FOR OUR ROUTINE FOR LATER!

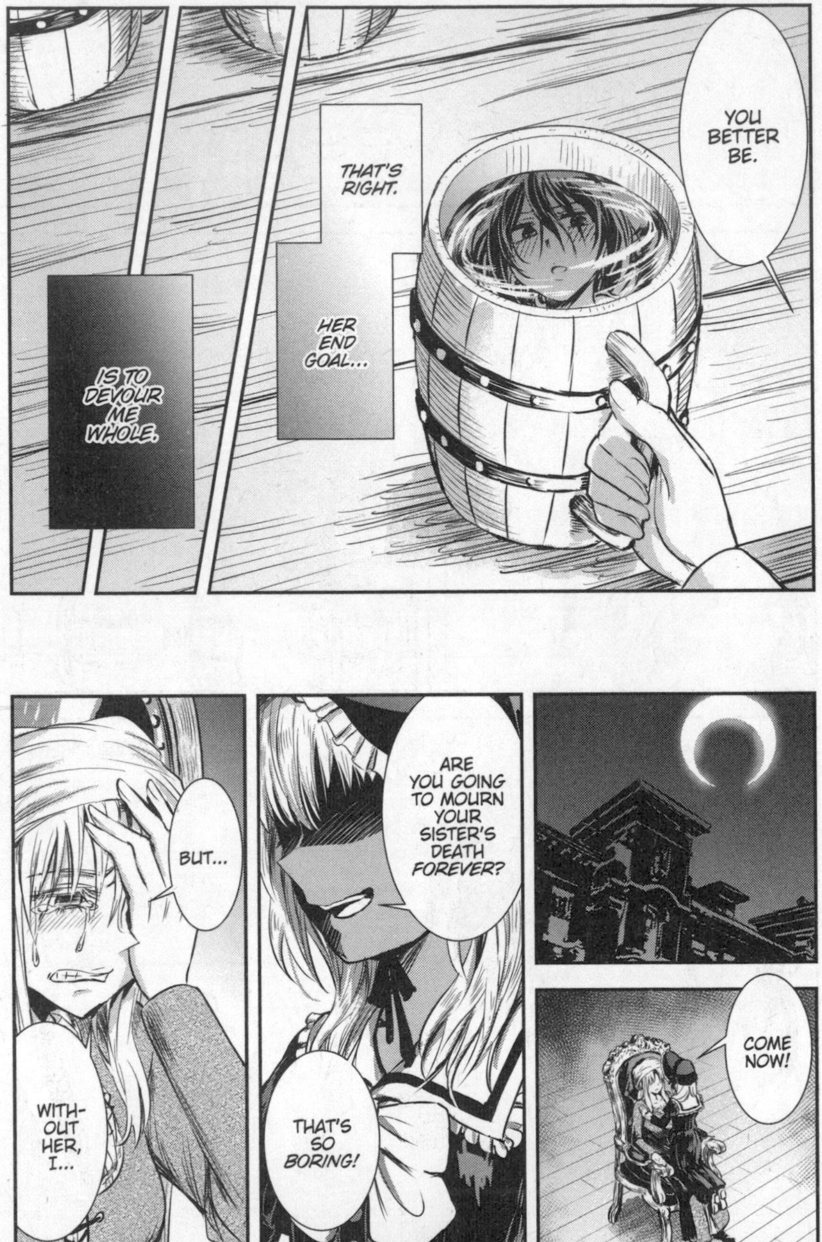
YOU BETTER BE.
THAT'S RIGHT.
HER END GOAL...
IS TO DEVOUR ME WHOLE.
COME NOW!
ARE YOU GOING TO MOURN YOUR SISTER'S DEATH FOREVER?
THAT'S SO BORING!
BUT...
WITH-OUT HER, I...

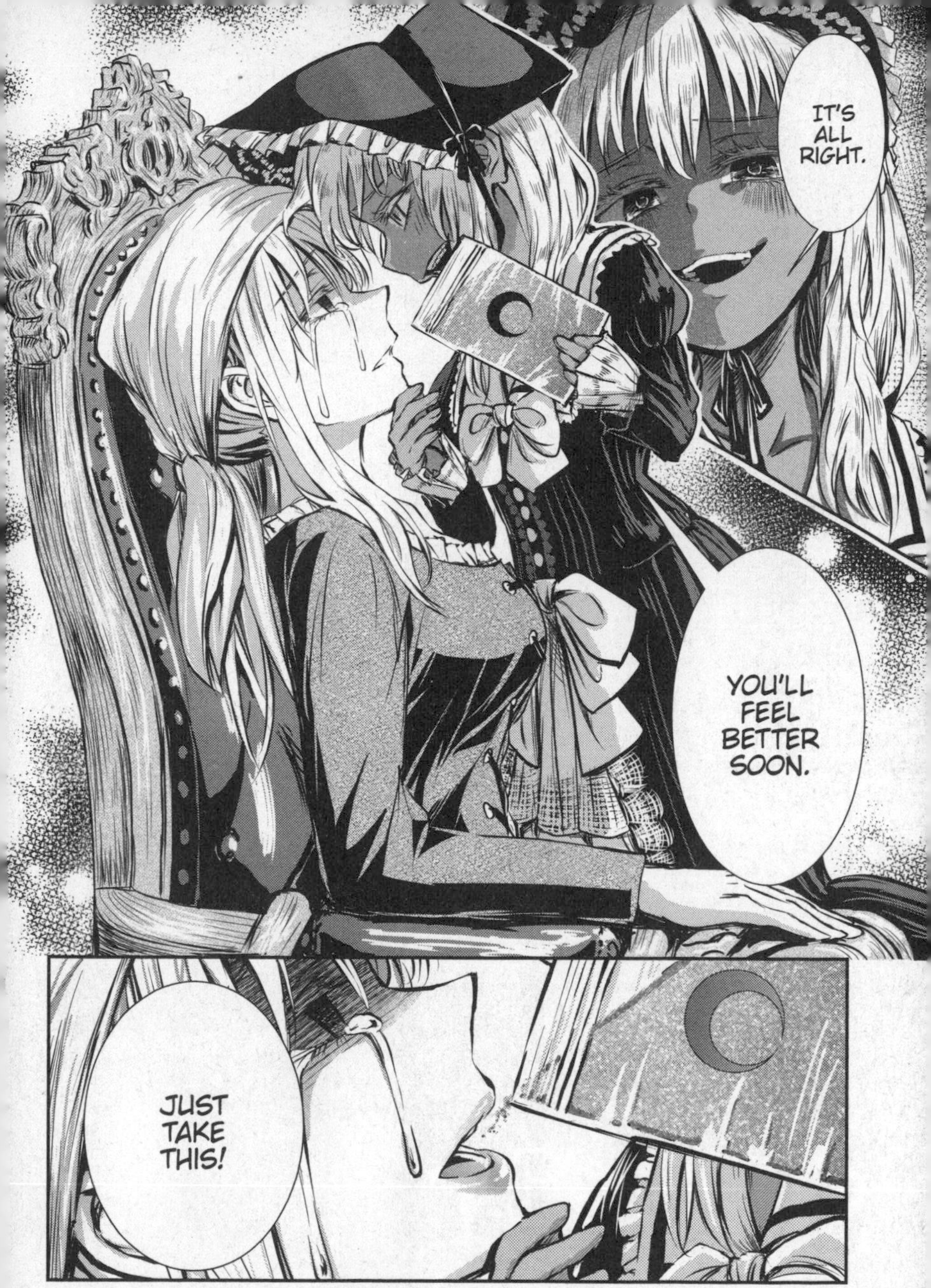
IT'S ALL RIGHT.
YOU'LL FEEL BETTER SOON.
JUST TAKE THIS!

SCARLET

Misery Hōra

- 【 Name 】 Misery Hōra
- 【 Height 】 161cm
- 【 Age 】 19
- 【Birthday】 December 23rd
- 【 Likes 】 Cooking, looking after her household
- 【Dislikes】 Conflict

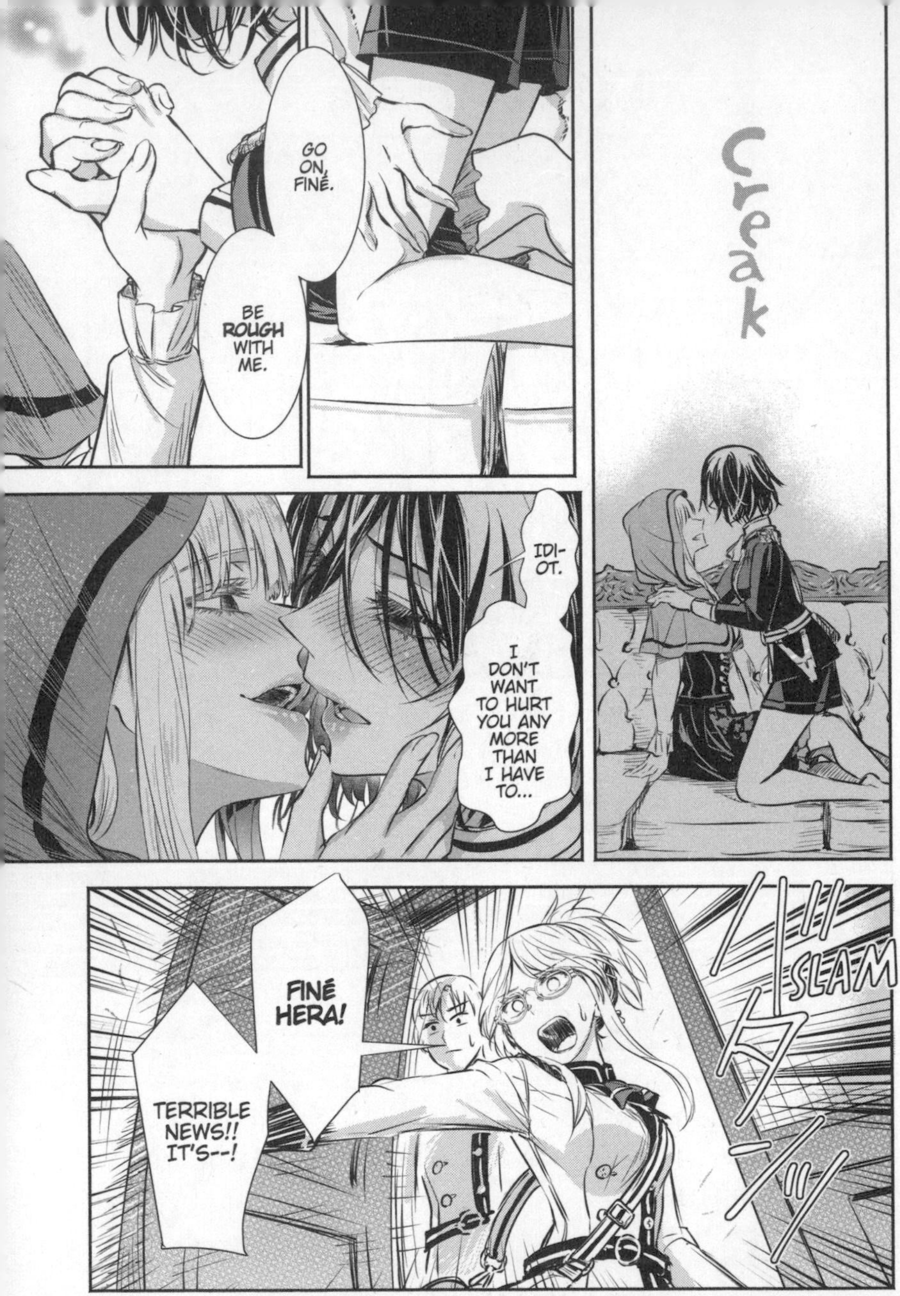
Creak
GO ON, FINÉ.
BE ROUGH WITH ME.
IDI-OT.
I DON'T WANT TO HURT YOU ANY MORE THAN I HAVE TO...
SLAM
FINÉ HERA!
TERRIBLE NEWS!! IT'S--!

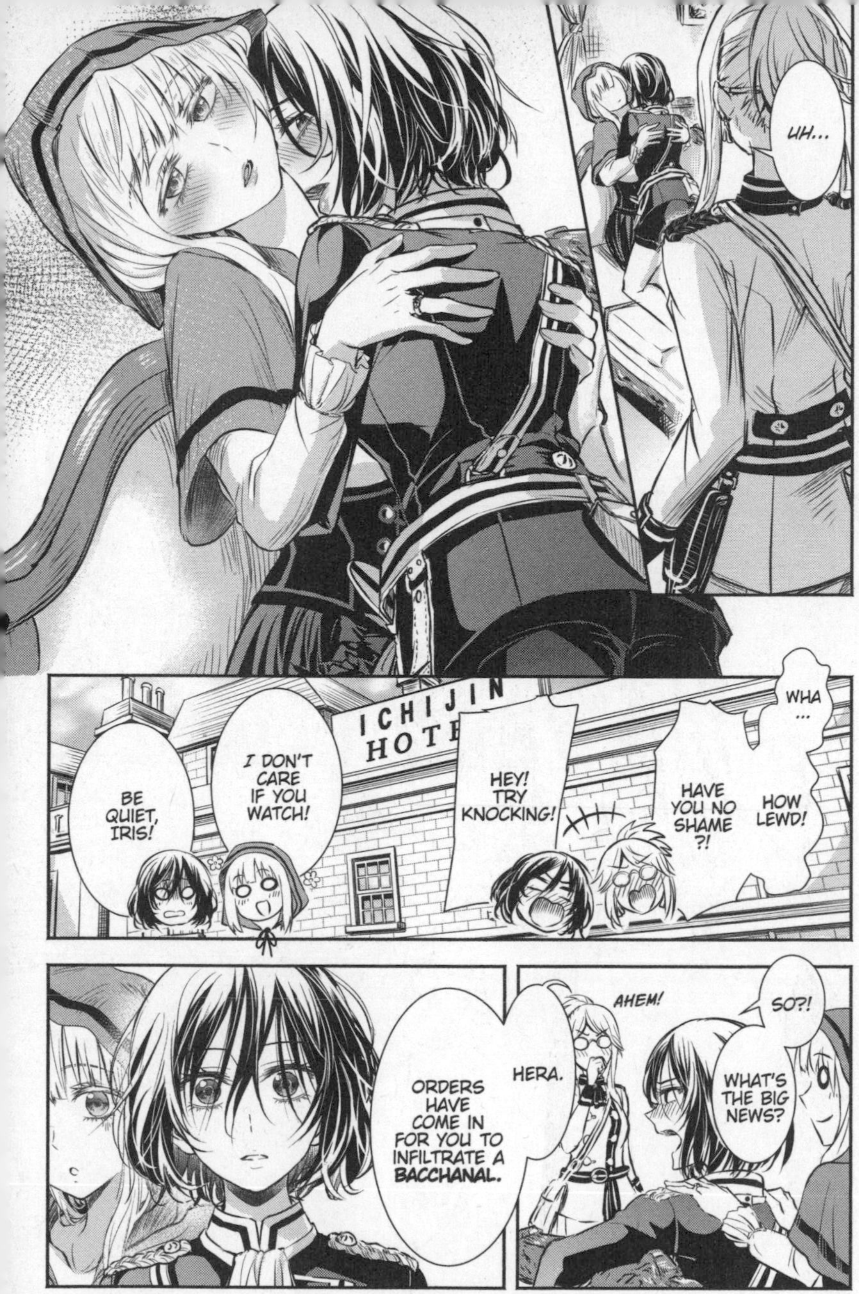
UH...
ICHIJIN HOTE
WHA ... HOW LEWD!
HAVE YOU NO SHAME ?!
HEY! TRY KNOCKING!
I DON'T CARE IF YOU WATCH!
BE QUIET, IRIS!
SO?!
WHAT'S THE BIG NEWS?
AHEM!
HERA.
ORDERS HAVE COME IN FOR YOU TO INFILTRATE A **BACCHANAL.**

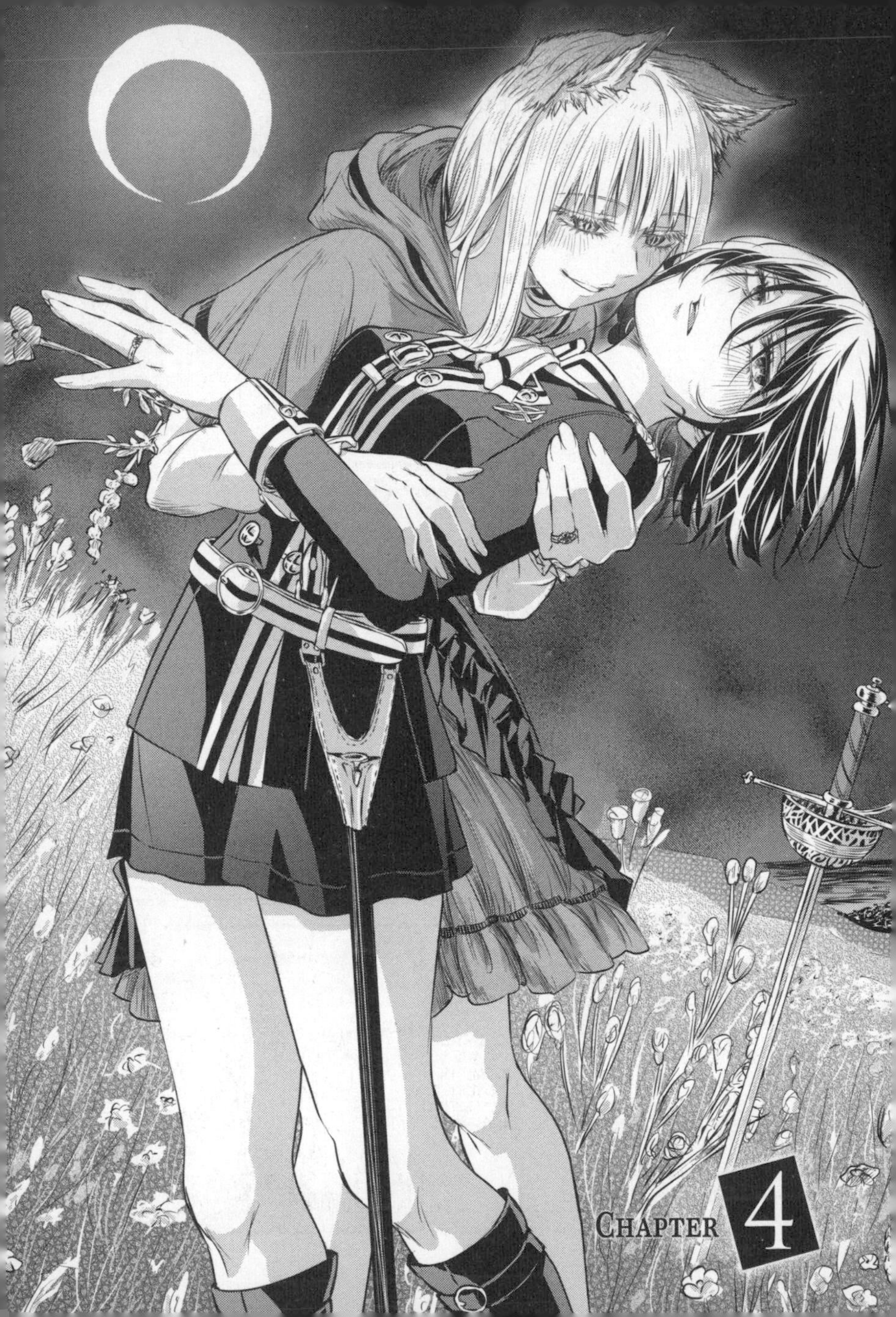
CHAPTER 4

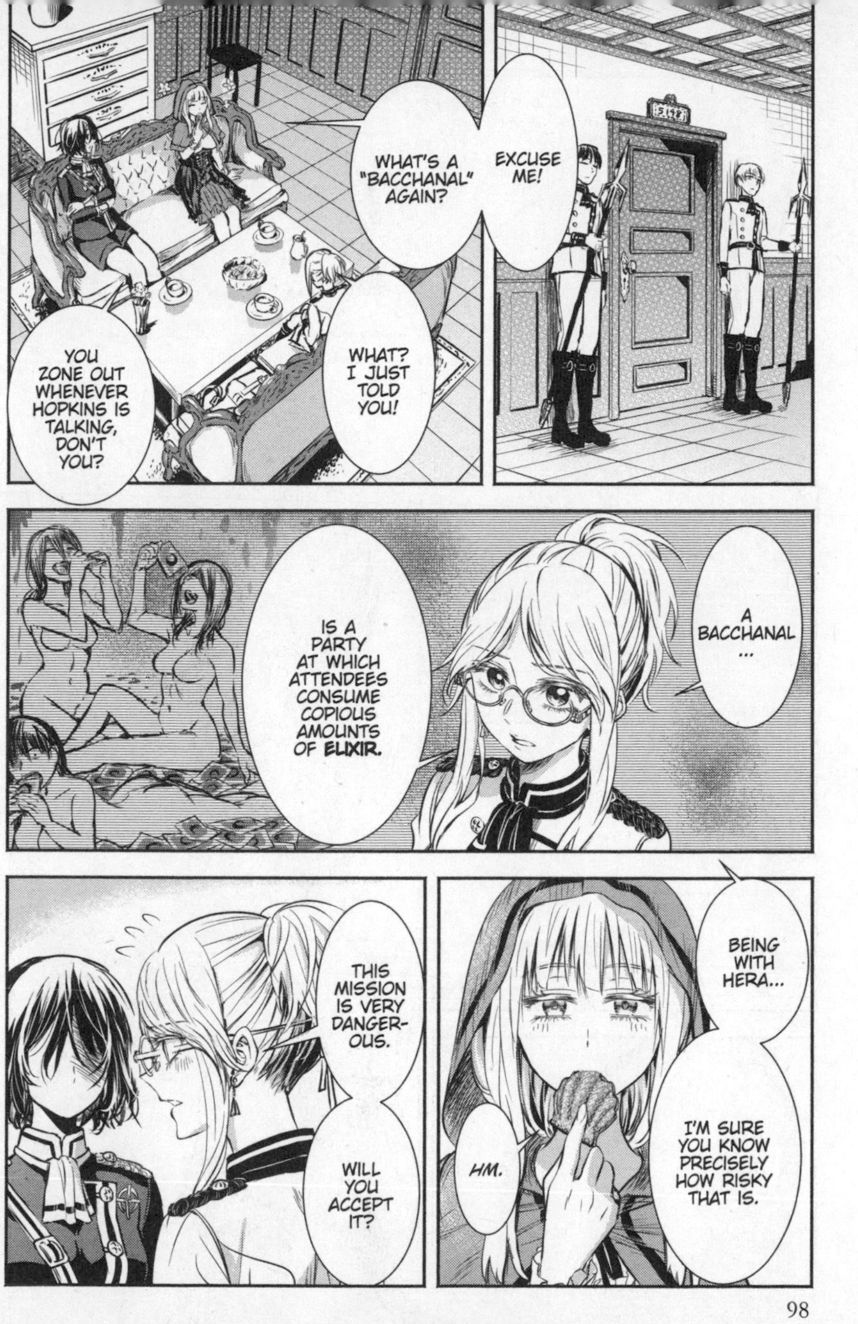
EXCUSE ME!
WHAT'S A "BACCHANAL" AGAIN?
WHAT? I JUST TOLD YOU!
YOU ZONE OUT WHENEVER HOPKINS IS TALKING, DON'T YOU?
A BACCHANAL ...
IS A PARTY AT WHICH ATTENDEES CONSUME COPIOUS AMOUNTS OF **ELIXIR.**
BEING WITH HERA...
I'M SURE YOU KNOW PRECISELY HOW RISKY THAT IS.
HM.
THIS MISSION IS VERY DANGEROUS.
WILL YOU ACCEPT IT?

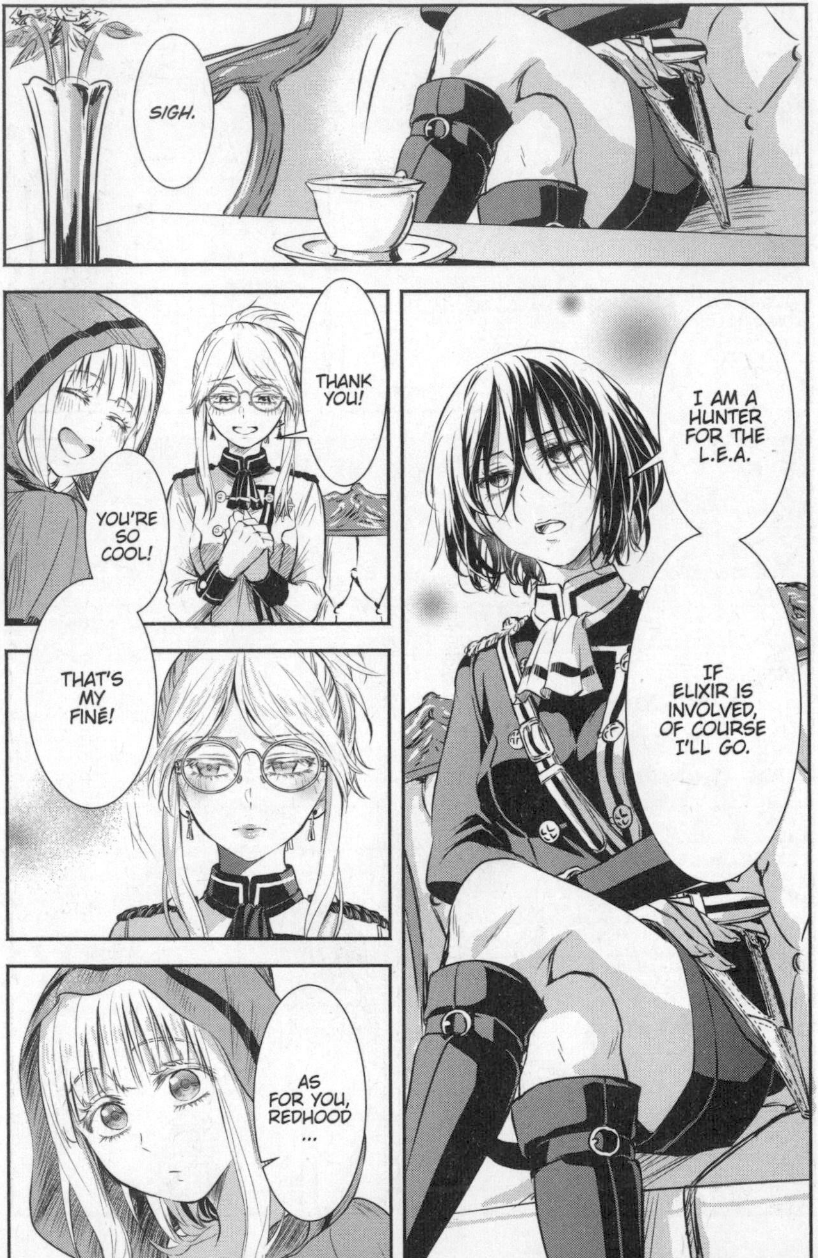
SIGH.
I AM A HUNTER FOR THE L.E.A.
IF ELIXIR IS INVOLVED, OF COURSE I'LL GO.
THANK YOU!
YOU'RE SO COOL!
THAT'S MY FINÉ!
AS FOR YOU, REDHOOD ...

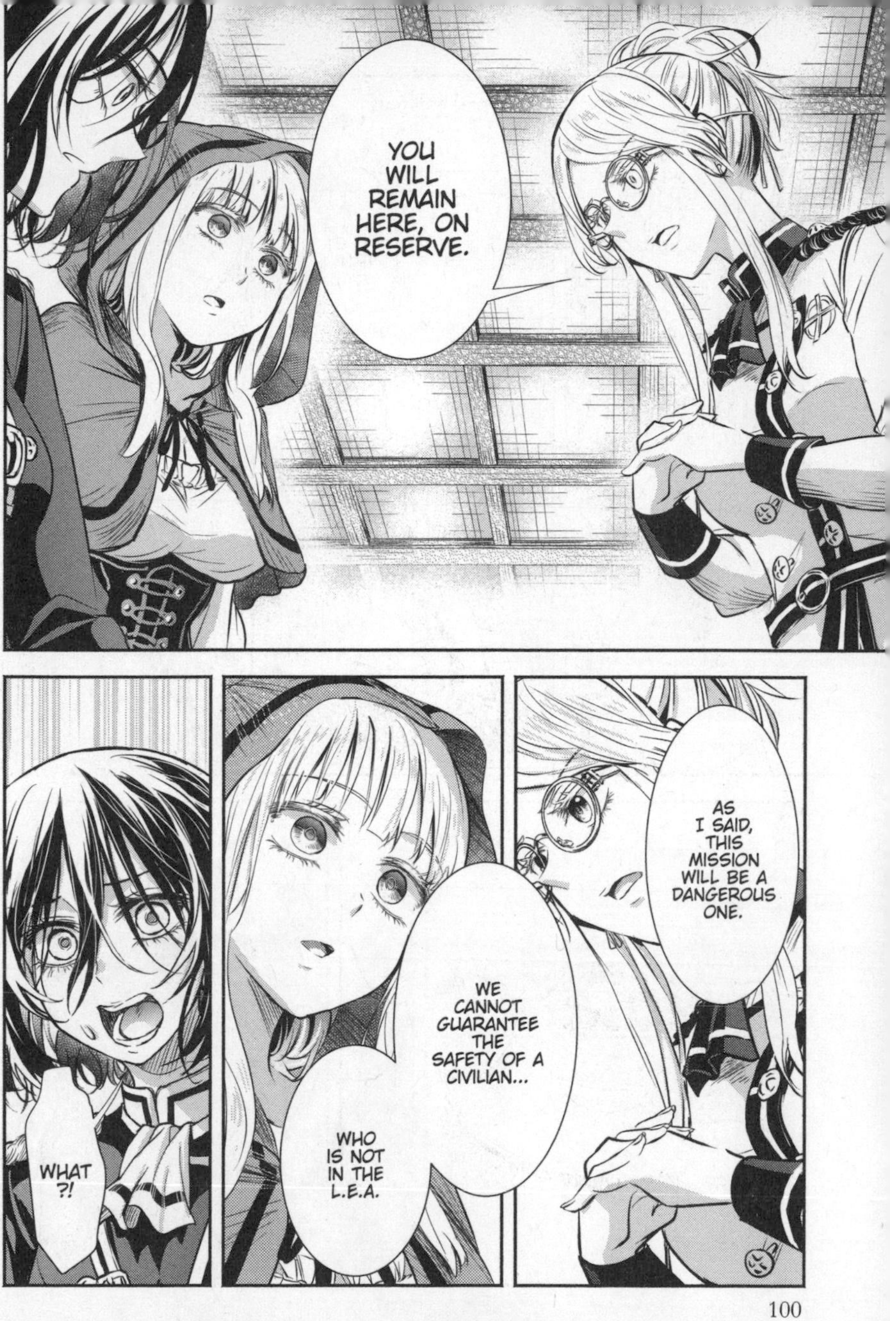
YOU WILL REMAIN HERE, ON RESERVE.
AS I SAID, THIS MISSION WILL BE A DANGEROUS ONE.
WE CANNOT GUARANTEE THE SAFETY OF A CIVILIAN...
WHO IS NOT IN THE L.E.A.
WHAT?!

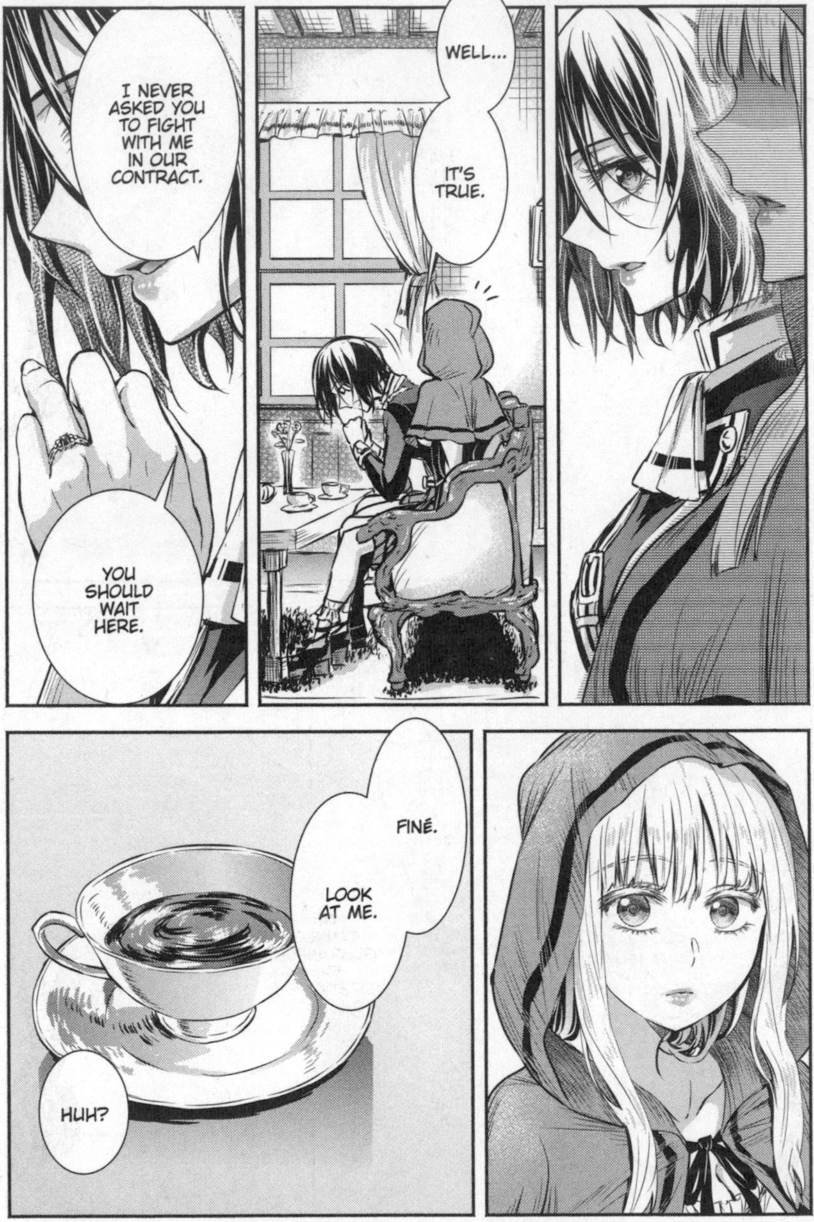
WELL...
IT'S TRUE.
I NEVER ASKED YOU TO FIGHT WITH ME IN OUR CONTRACT.
YOU SHOULD WAIT HERE.
FINE.
LOOK AT ME.
HUH?

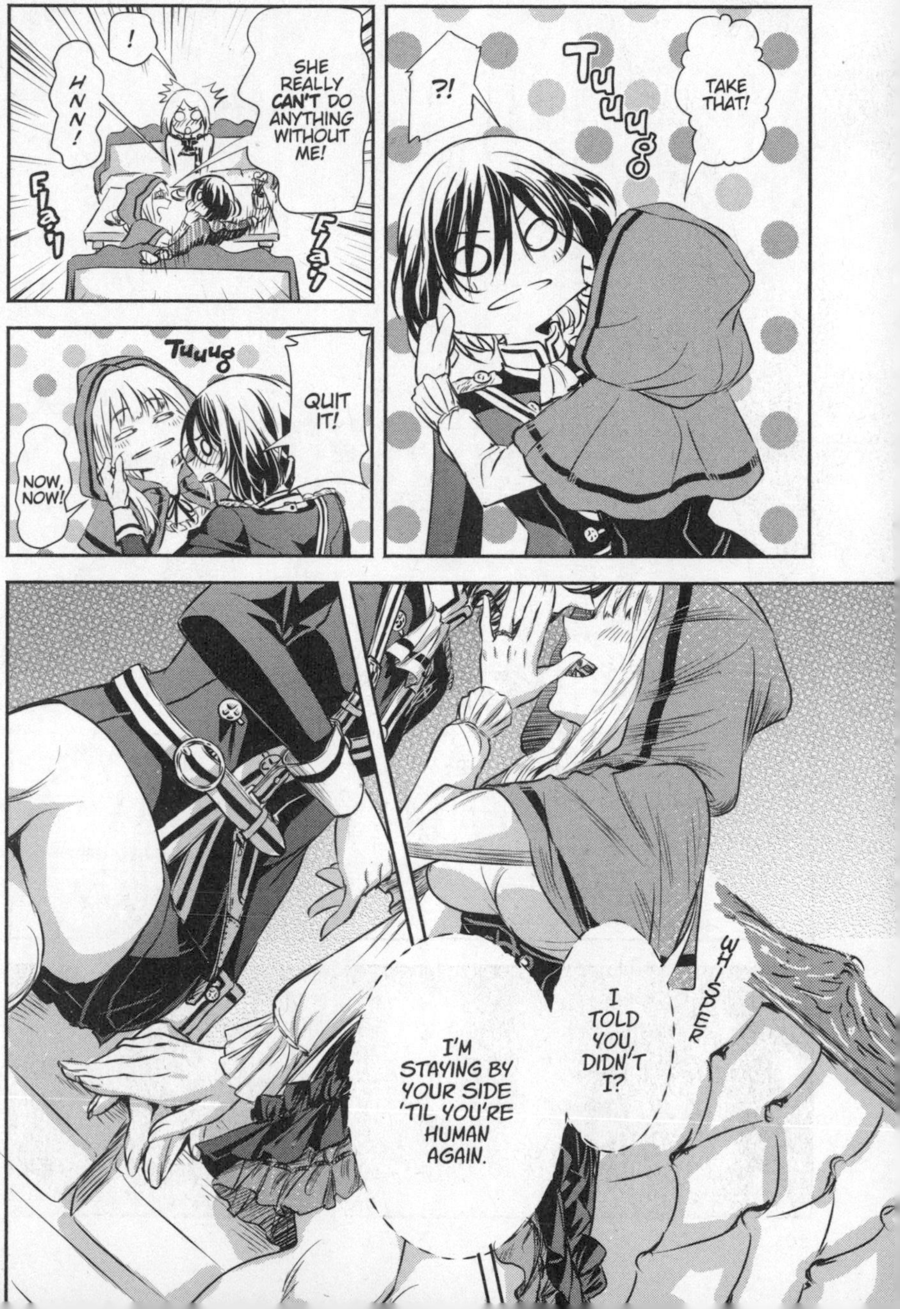
TAKE THAT!
Tuuug
?!
SHE REALLY CAN'T DO ANYTHING WITHOUT ME!
!
HNN!
Flail
Flail
QUIT IT!
Tuuug
NOW, NOW!
WHISPER
I TOLD YOU, DIDN'T I?
I'M STAYING BY YOUR SIDE 'TIL YOU'RE HUMAN AGAIN.

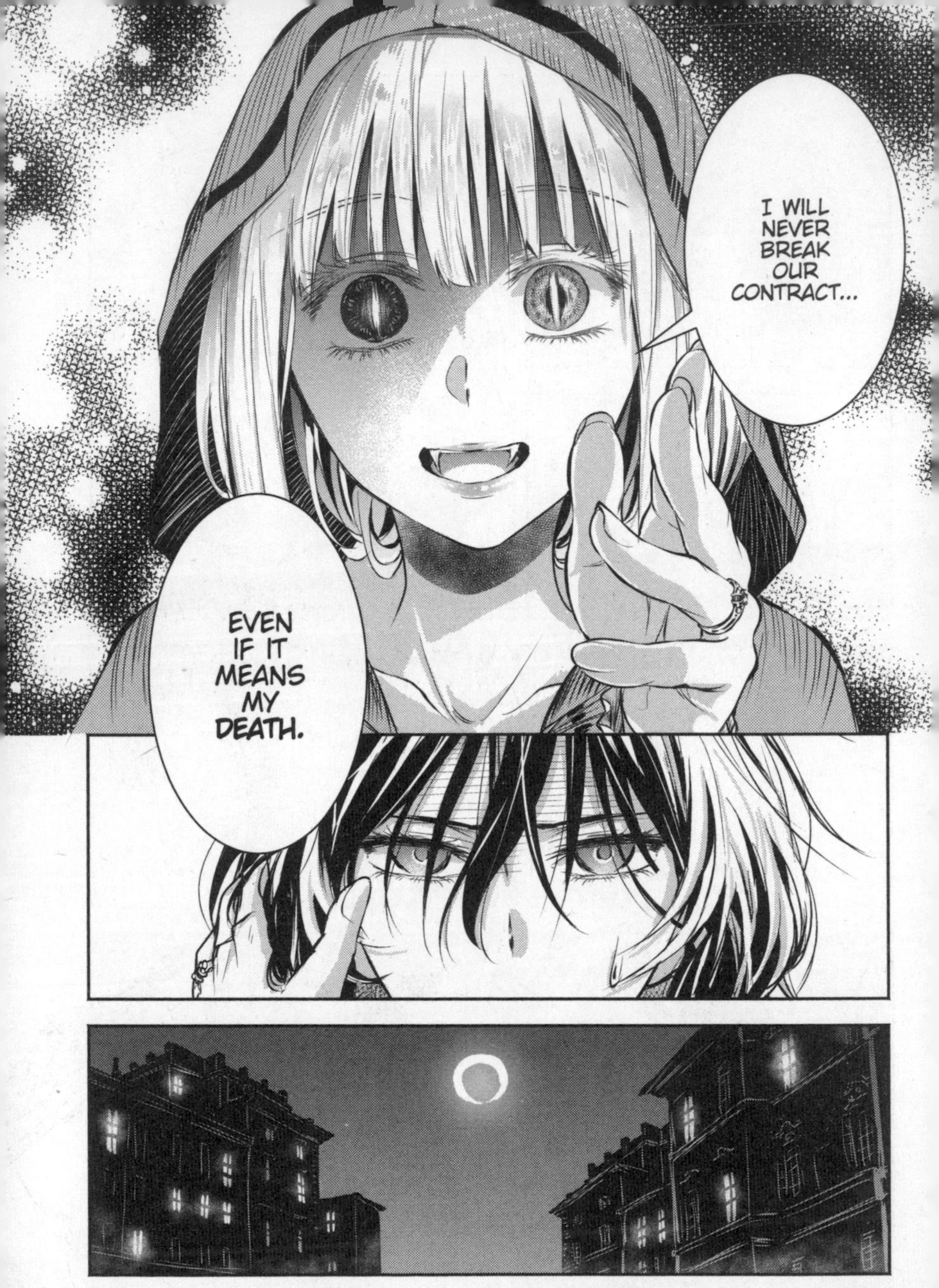
I WILL NEVER BREAK OUR CONTRACT...
EVEN IF IT MEANS MY DEATH.

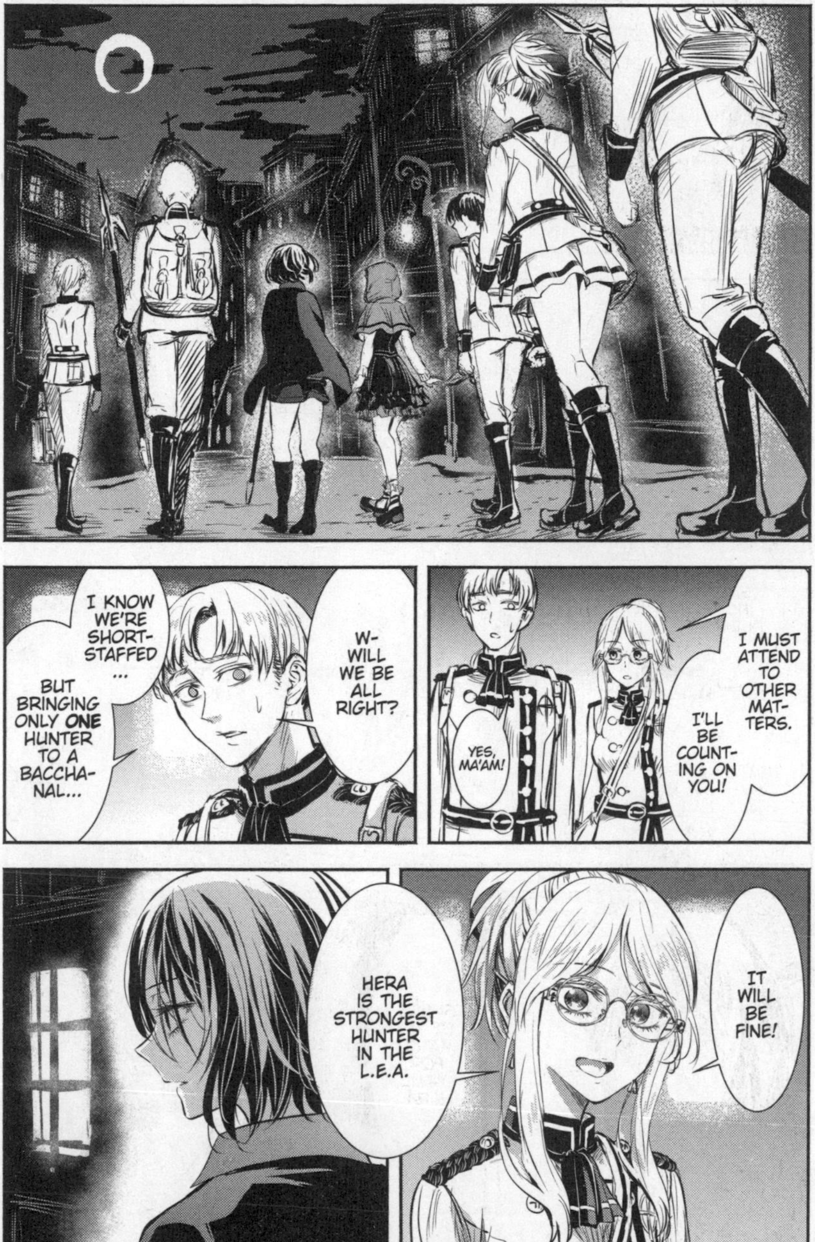
I MUST ATTEND TO OTHER MATTERS.
I'LL BE COUNTING ON YOU!
YES, MA'AM!
W-WILL WE BE ALL RIGHT?
I KNOW WE'RE SHORT-STAFFED... BUT BRINGING ONLY **ONE** HUNTER TO A BACCHANAL...
IT WILL BE FINE!
HERA IS THE STRONGEST HUNTER IN THE L.E.A.

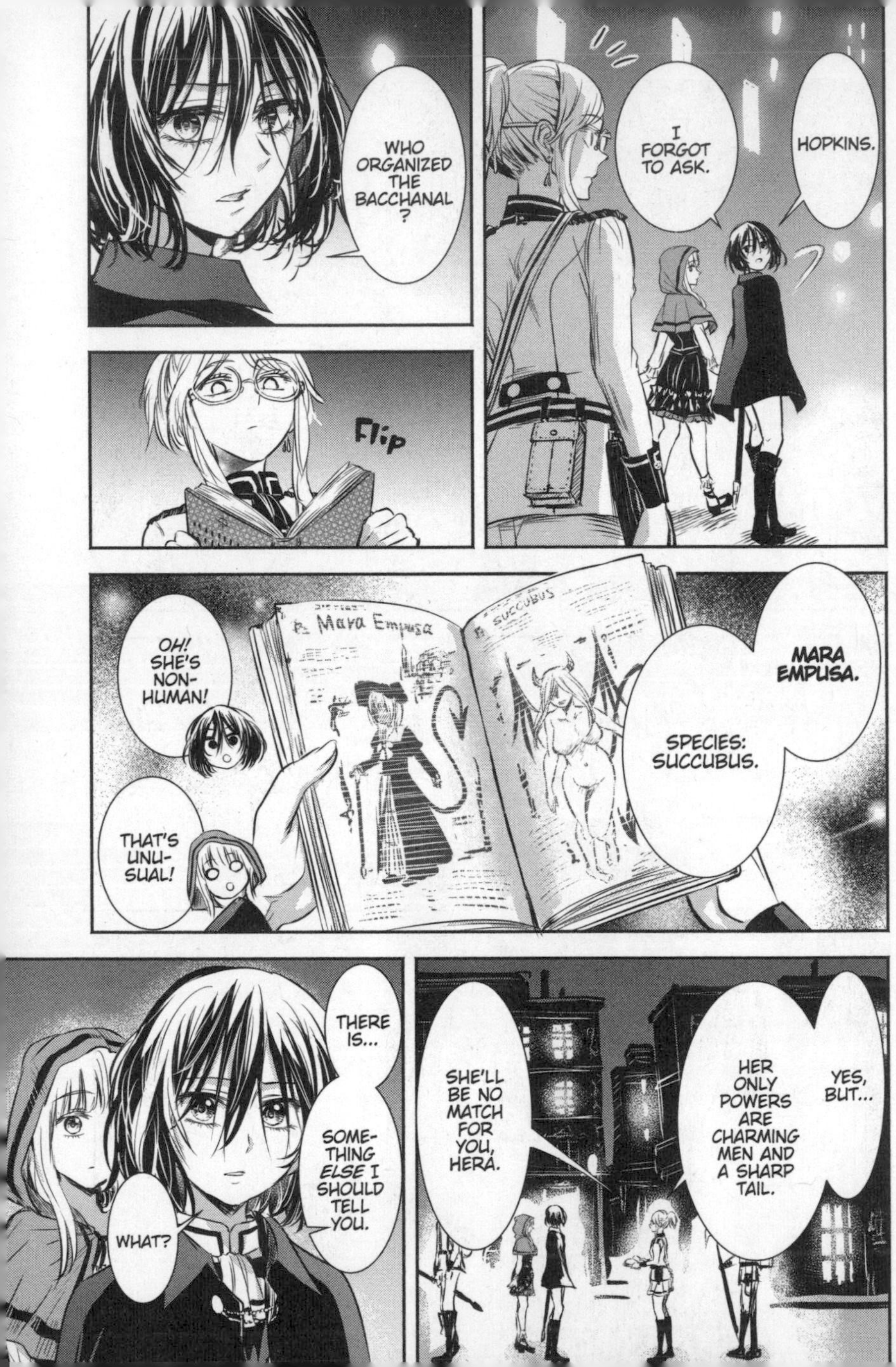
HOPKINS.
I FORGOT TO ASK.
WHO ORGANIZED THE BACCHANAL?
Flip
MARA EMPUSA.
SPECIES: SUCCUBUS.
Mara Empusa
SUCCUBUS
OH! SHE'S NON-HUMAN!
THAT'S UNU-SUAL!
YES, BUT...
HER ONLY POWERS ARE CHARMING MEN AND A SHARP TAIL.
SHE'LL BE NO MATCH FOR YOU, HERA.
THERE IS...
SOMETHING ELSE I SHOULD TELL YOU.
WHAT?

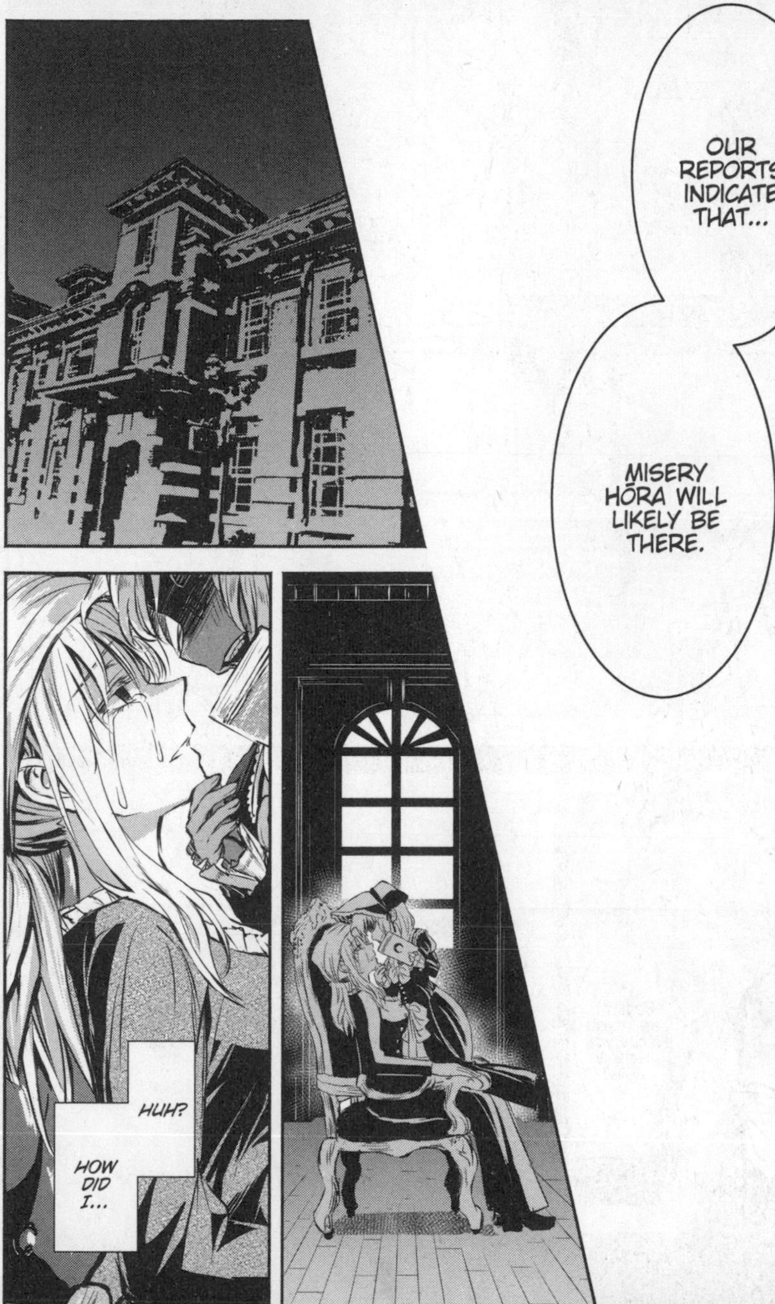
OUR REPORTS INDICATE THAT...
MISERY HŌRA WILL LIKELY BE THERE.
HUH?
HOW DID I...

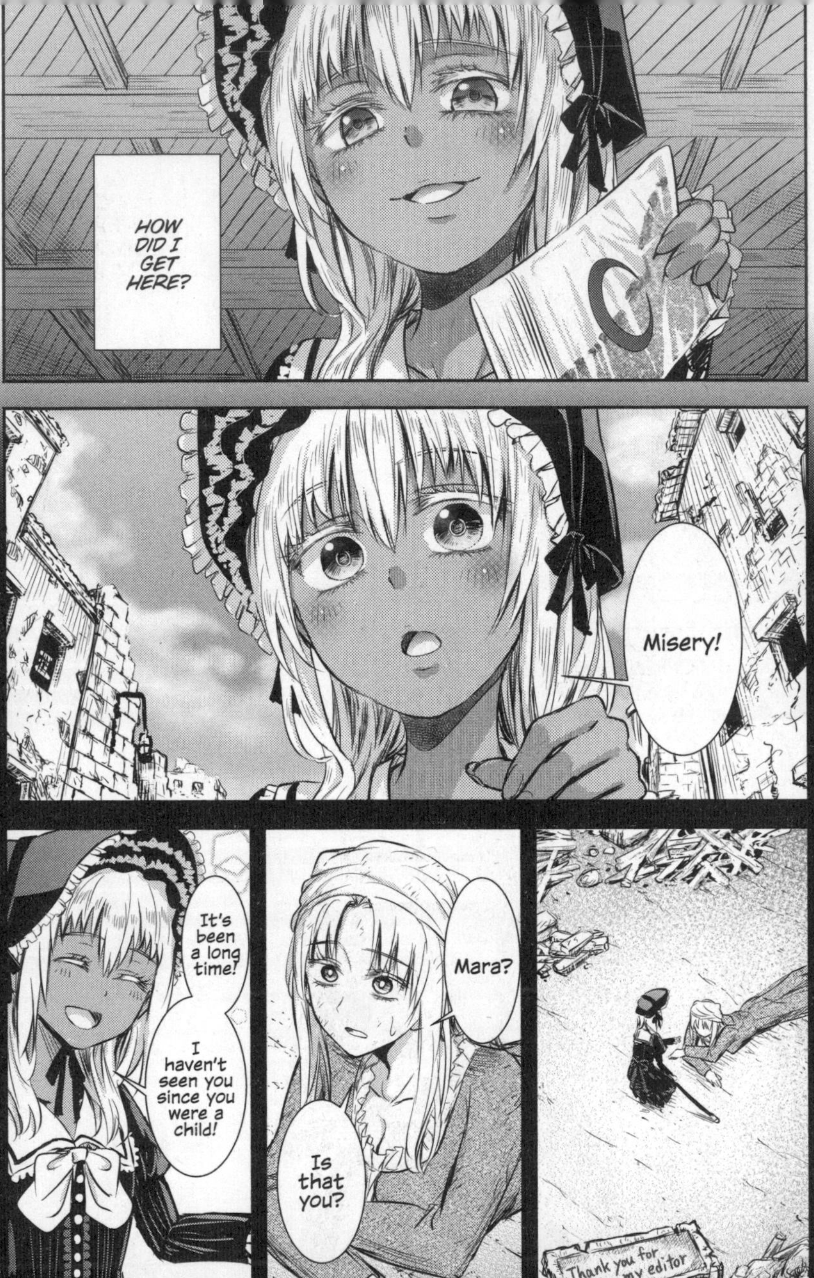
HOW DID I GET HERE?
Misery!
Thank you for my editor
Mara?
Is that you?
It's been a long time!
I haven't seen you since you were a child!

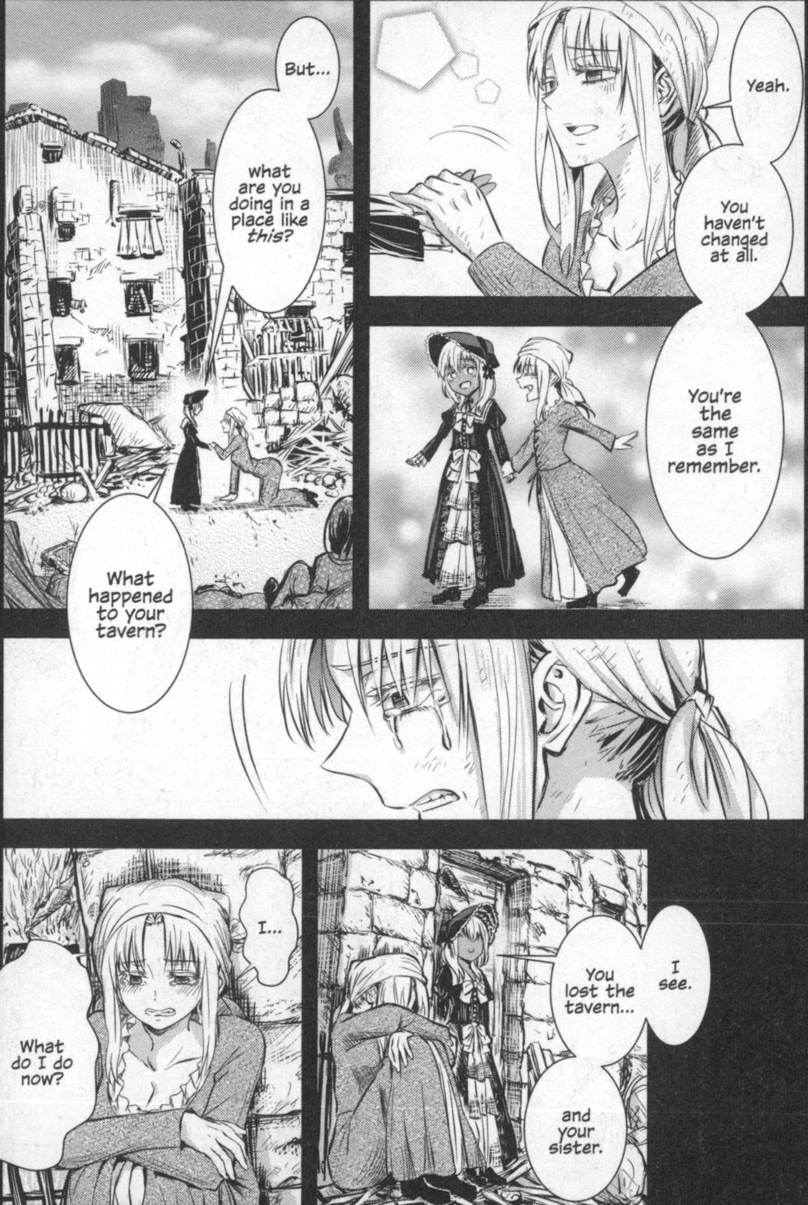
Yeah.
You haven't changed at all.
You're the same as I remember.
But...
what are you doing in a place like *this*?
What happened to your tavern?
I see.
You lost the tavern...
and your sister.
I...
What do I do now?

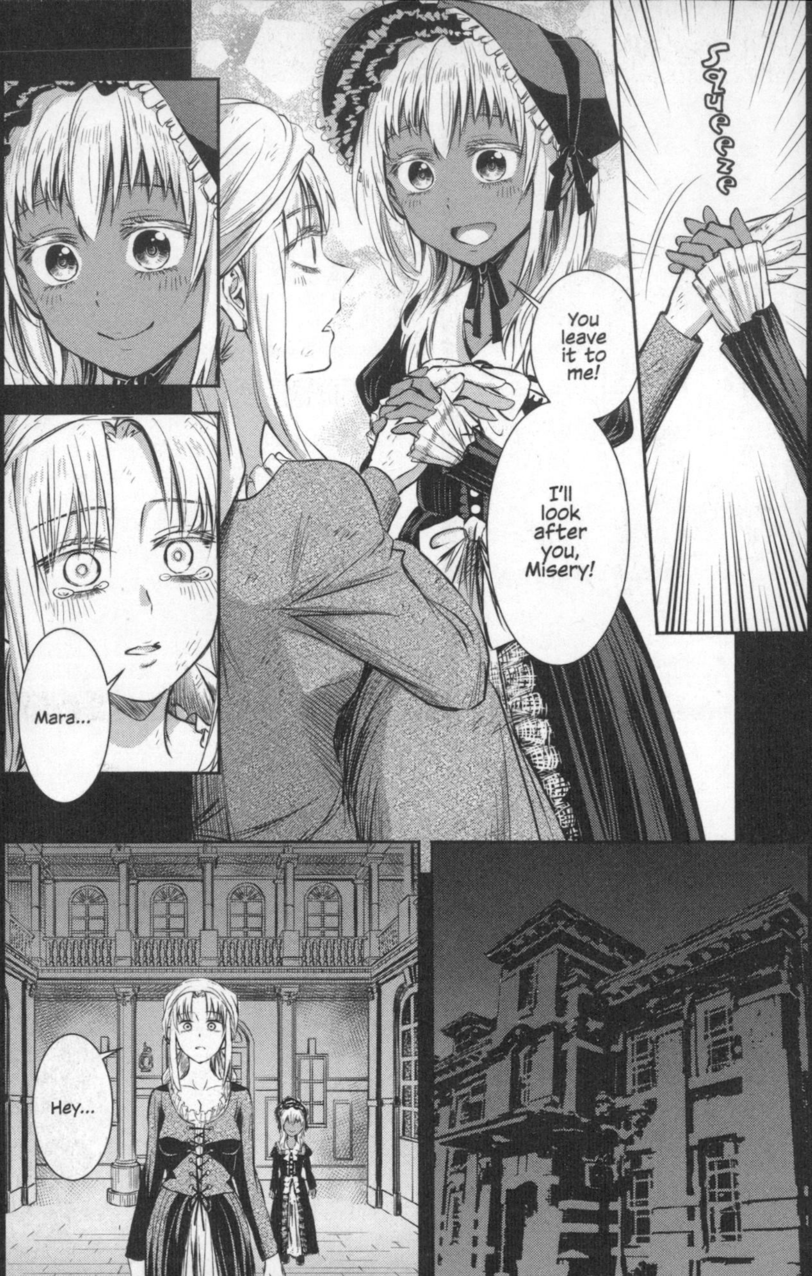
Squeeze
You leave it to me!
I'll look after you, Misery!
Mara...
Hey...

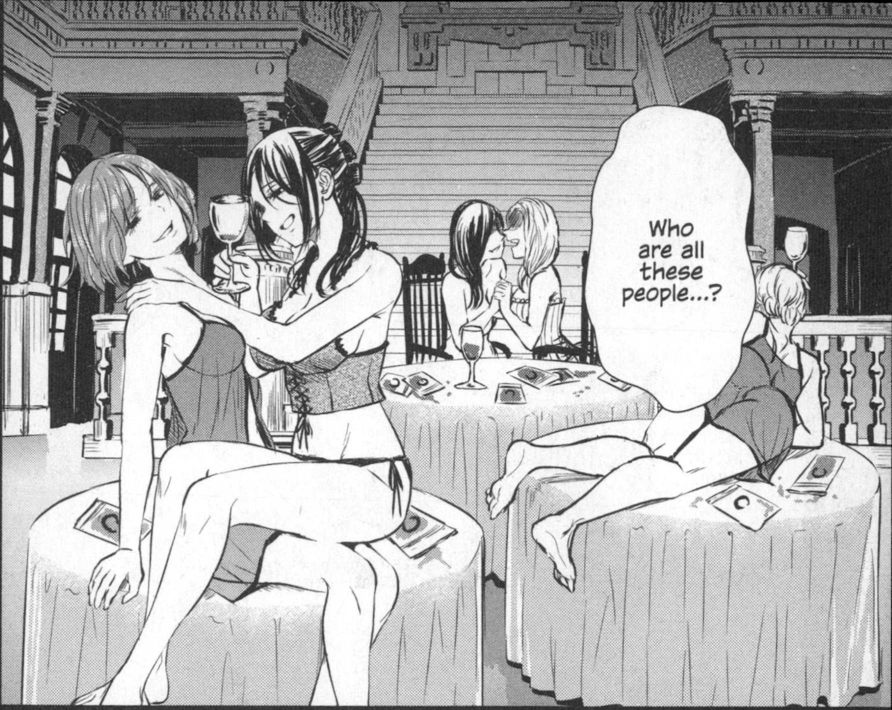
Who are all these people...?
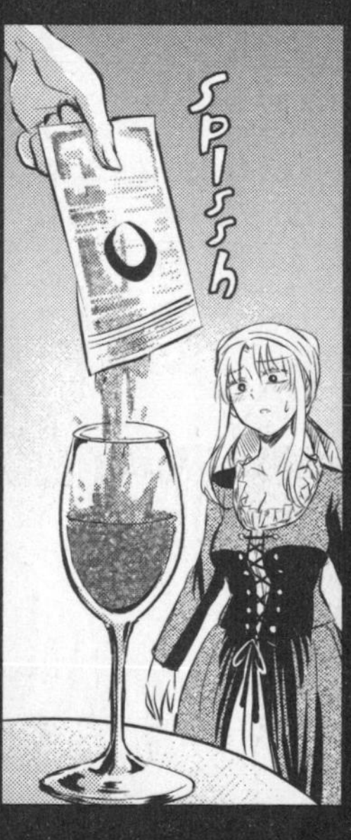
SPISSH
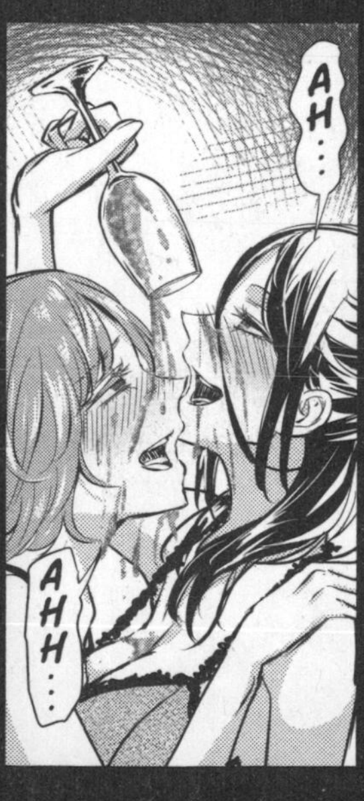
AH...
AHH...
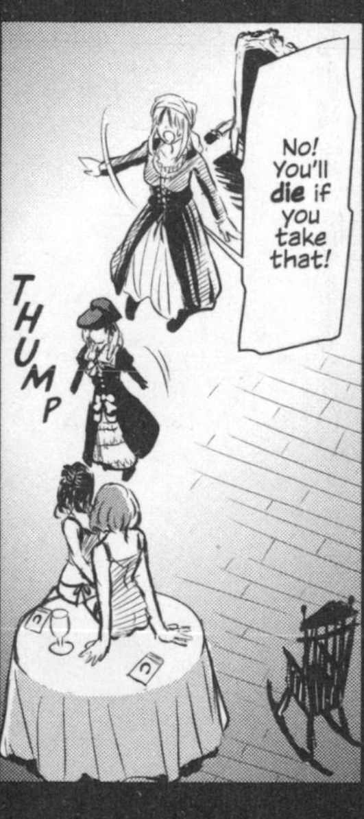
No! You'll **die** if you take that!
THUMP

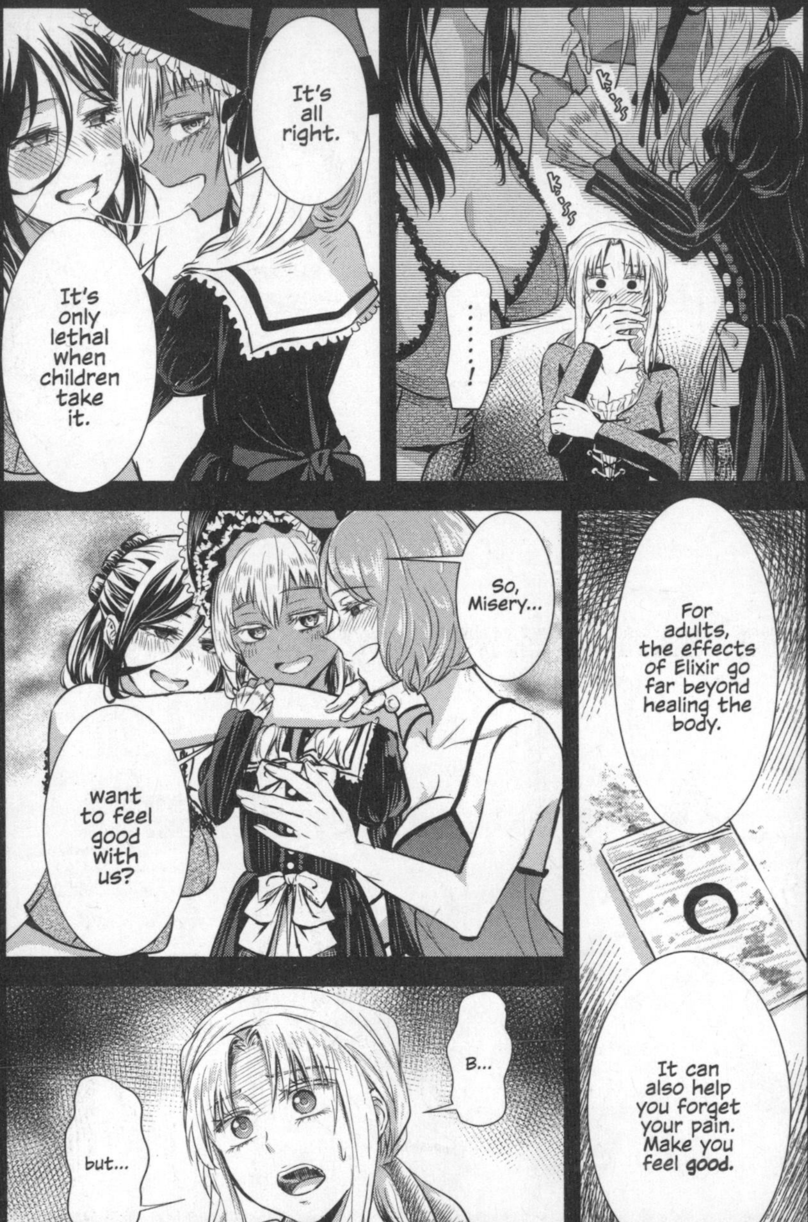
kiss
kiss
......!
It's all right.
It's only lethal when children take it.
For adults, the effects of Elixir go far beyond healing the body.
It can also help you forget your pain. Make you feel **good**.
So, Misery...
want to feel good with us?
B...
but...

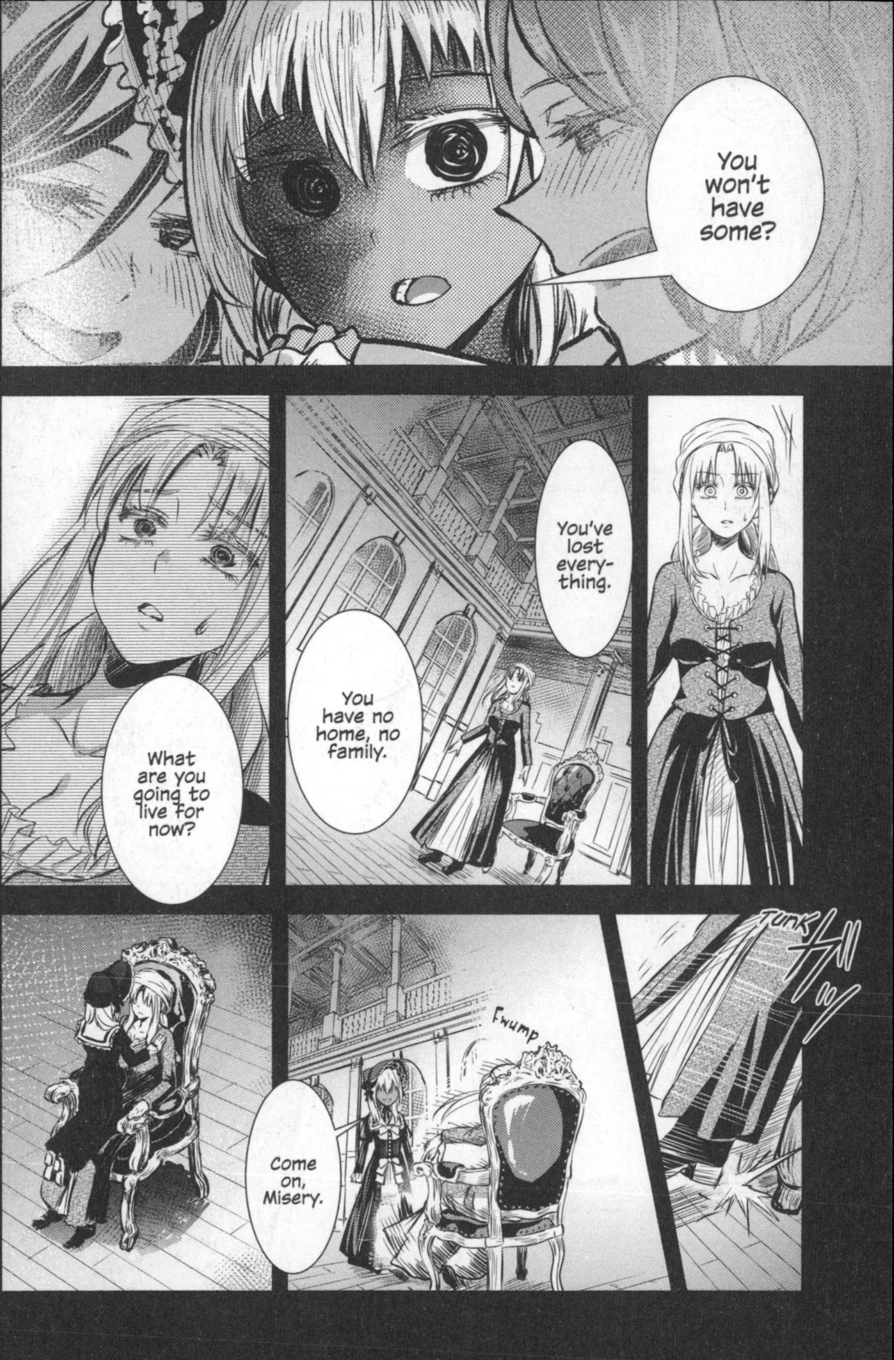
You won't have some?
You've lost everything.
You have no home, no family.
What are you going to live for now?
TUNK
Fwump
Come on, Misery.

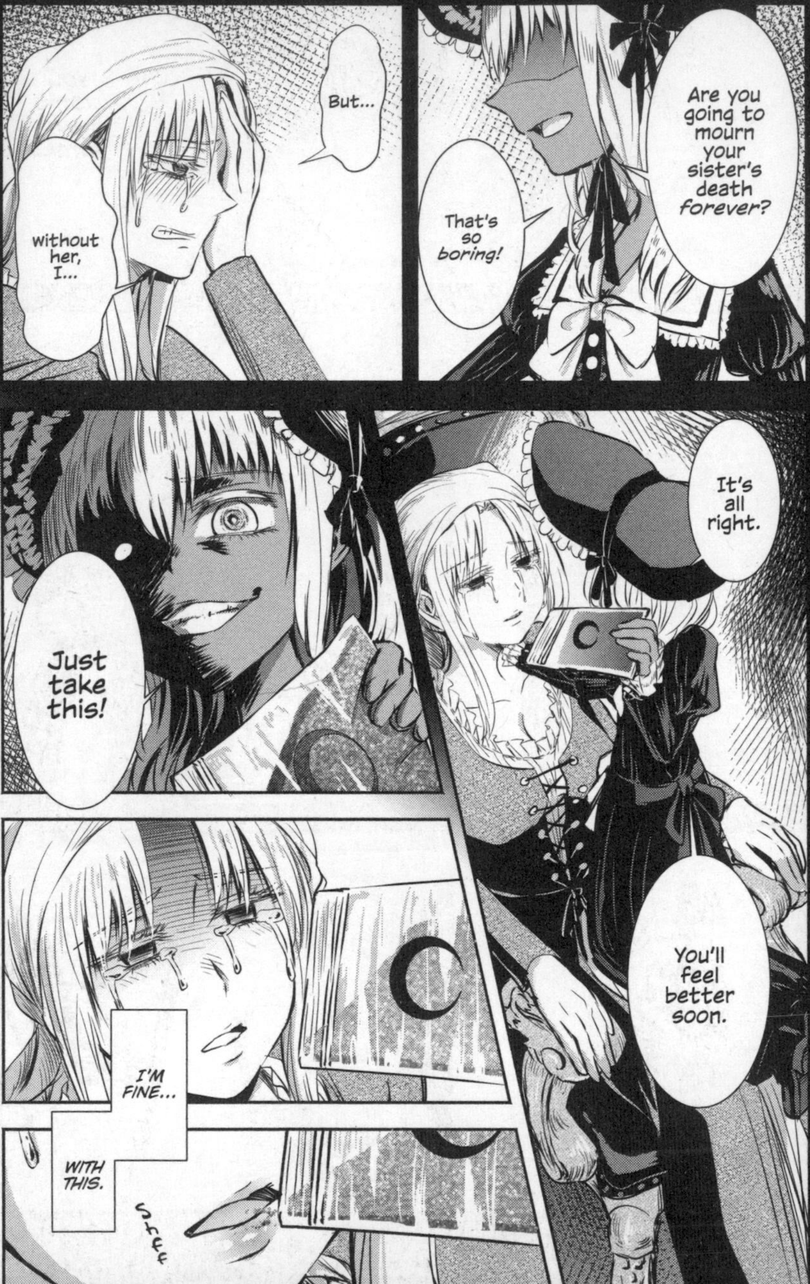
Are you going to mourn your sister's death *forever?*
That's so *boring!*
But...
without her, I...
It's all right.
You'll feel better soon.
Just take this!
I'M FINE...
WITH THIS.

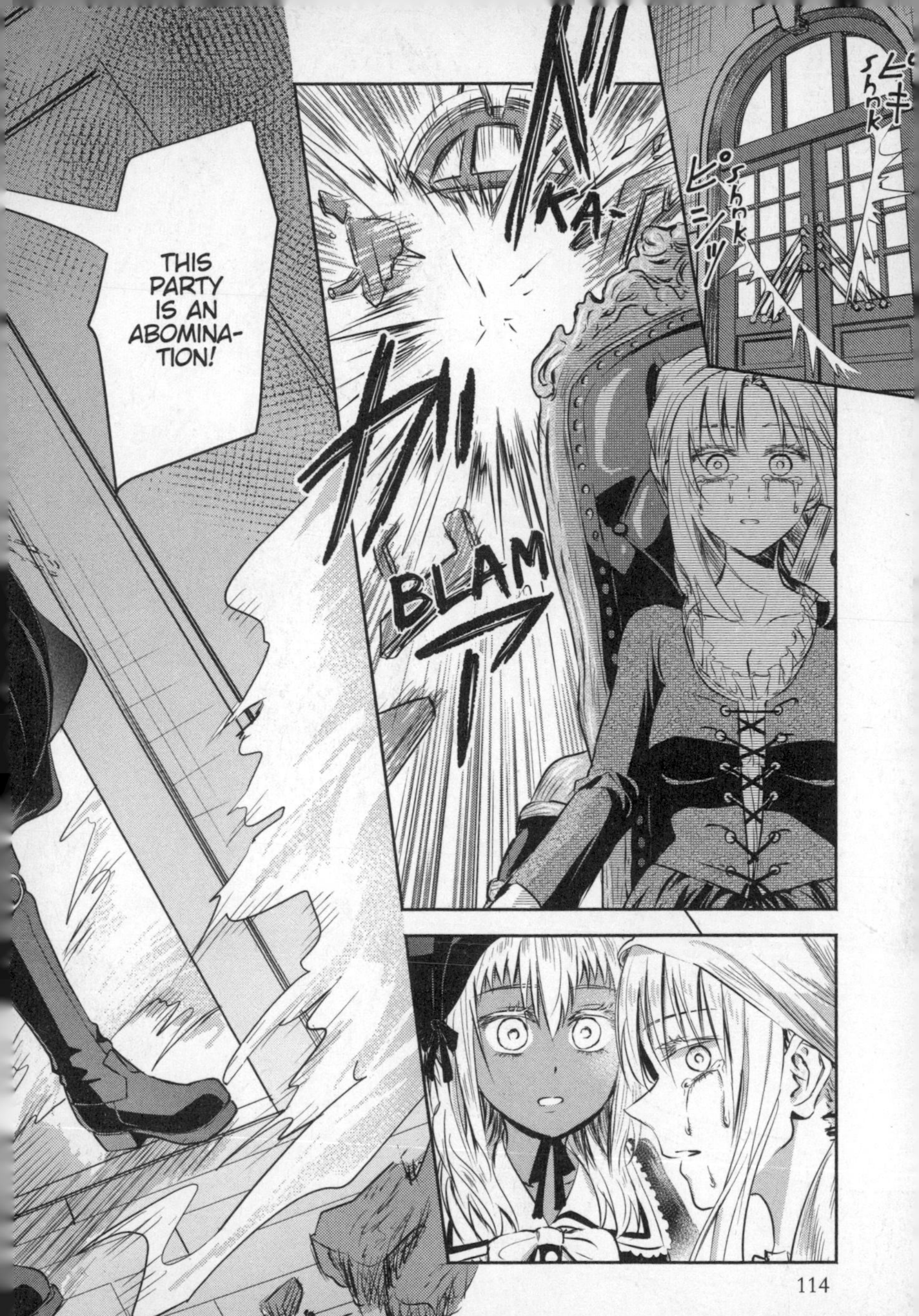

ピキ
shnk
ピシッ
shnk
KA-
BLAM
THIS PARTY IS AN ABOMINATION!

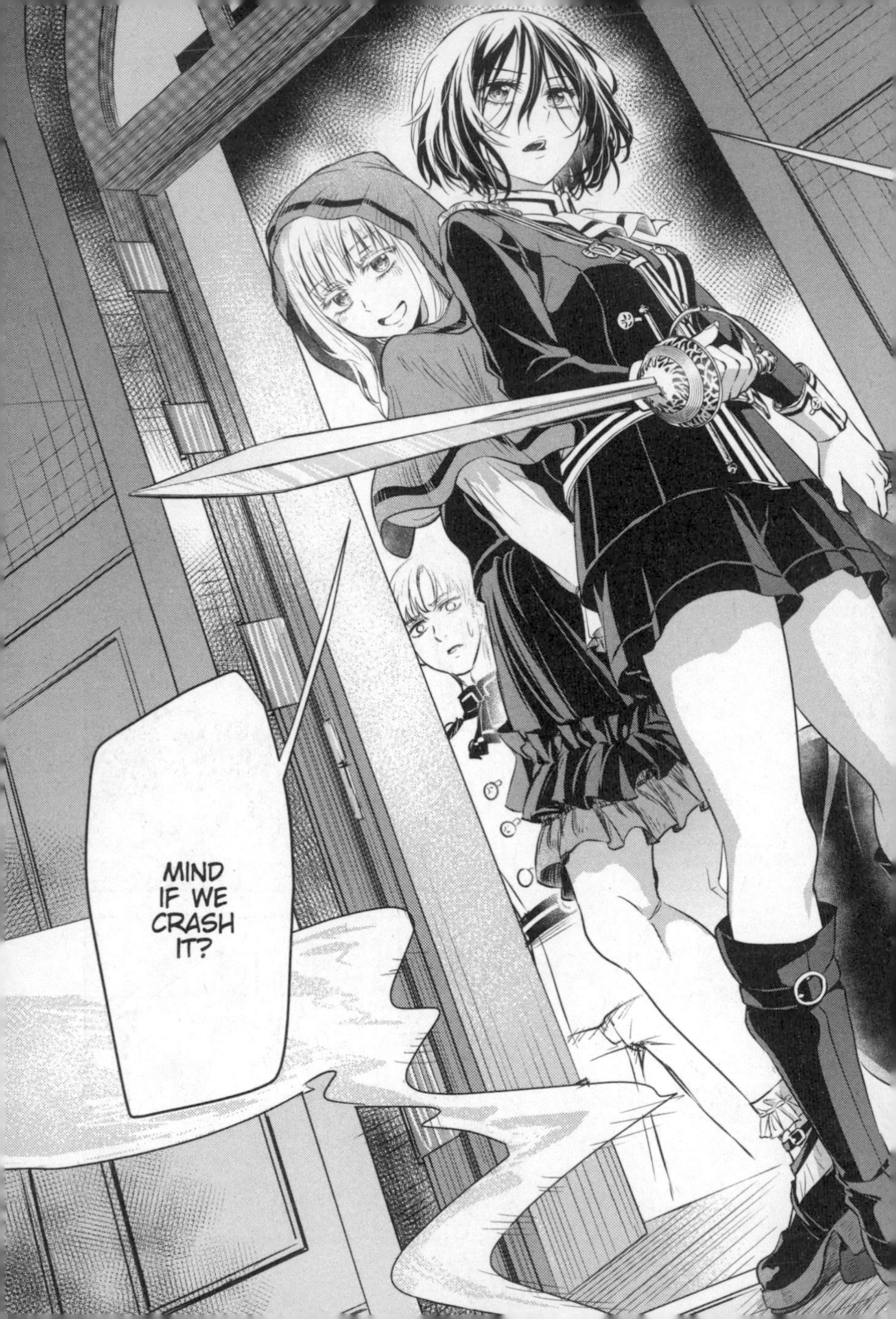
MIND IF WE CRASH IT?

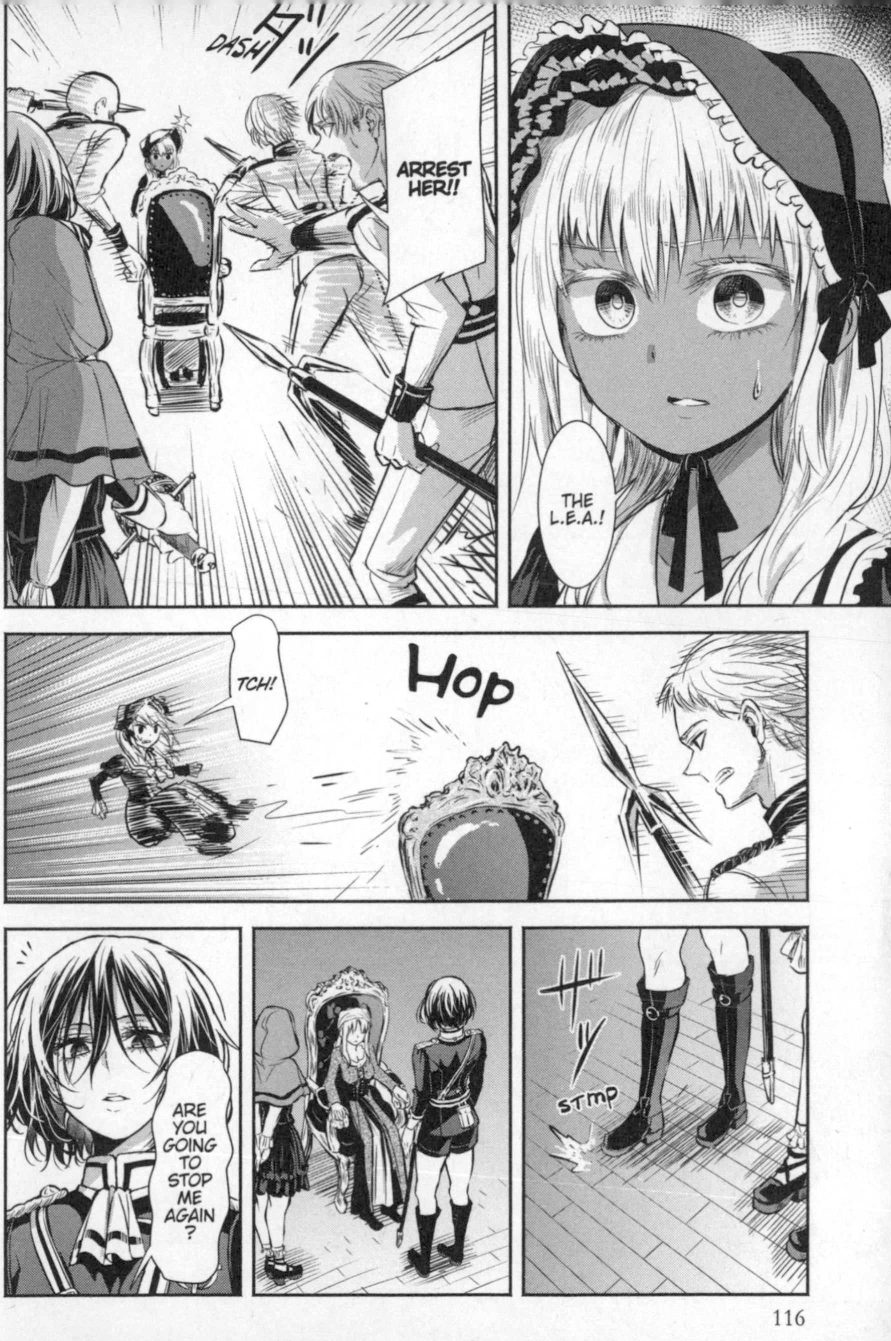
THE L.E.A.!
DASH
ARREST HER!!
Hop
TCH!
STMP
ARE YOU GOING TO STOP ME AGAIN?

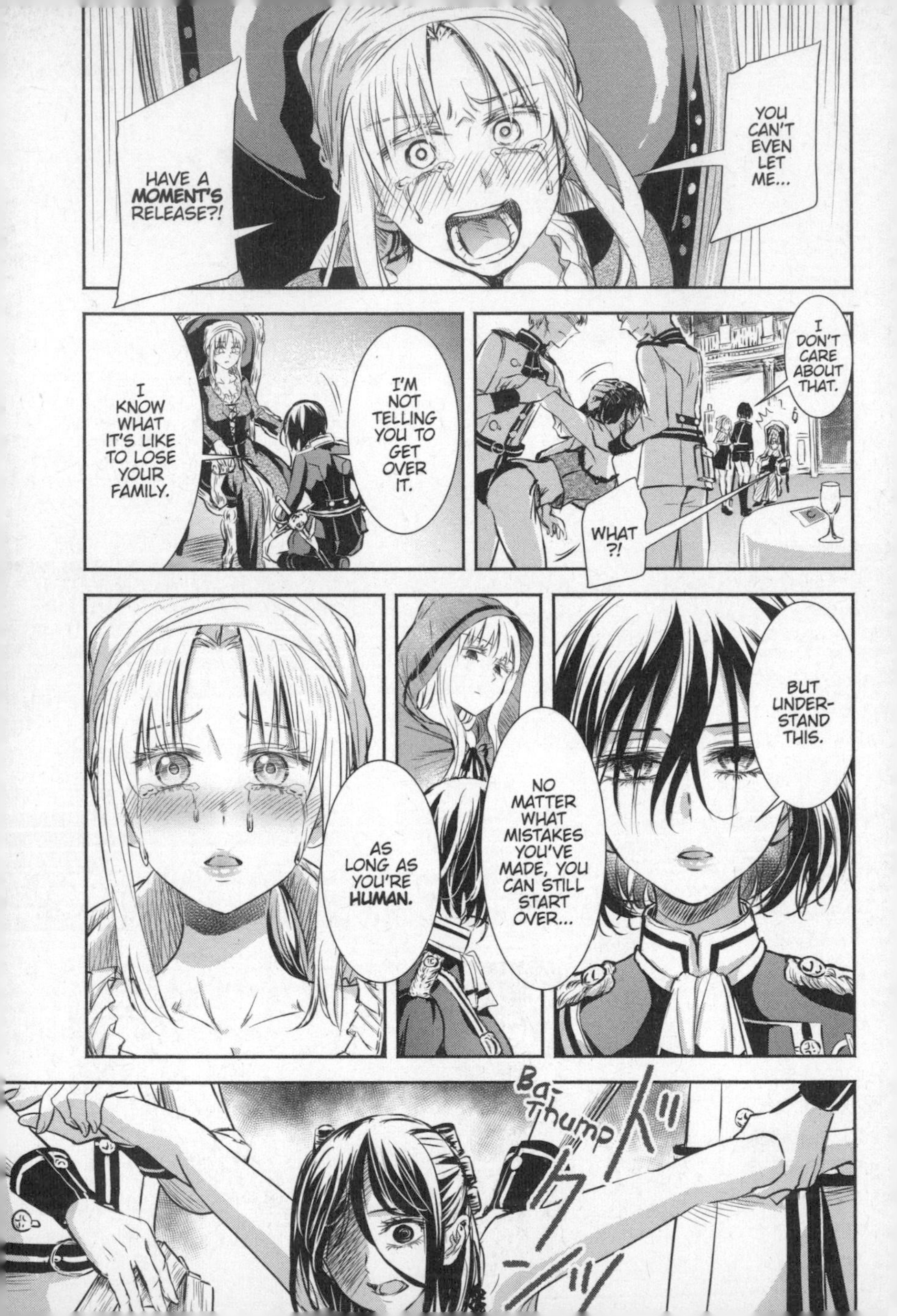
YOU CAN'T EVEN LET ME...
HAVE A **MOMENT'S** RELEASE?!
I DON'T CARE ABOUT THAT.
WHAT?!
I'M NOT TELLING YOU TO GET OVER IT.
I KNOW WHAT IT'S LIKE TO LOSE YOUR FAMILY.
BUT UNDER-STAND THIS.
NO MATTER WHAT MISTAKES YOU'VE MADE, YOU CAN STILL START OVER...
AS LONG AS YOU'RE **HUMAN.**
Ba-Thump

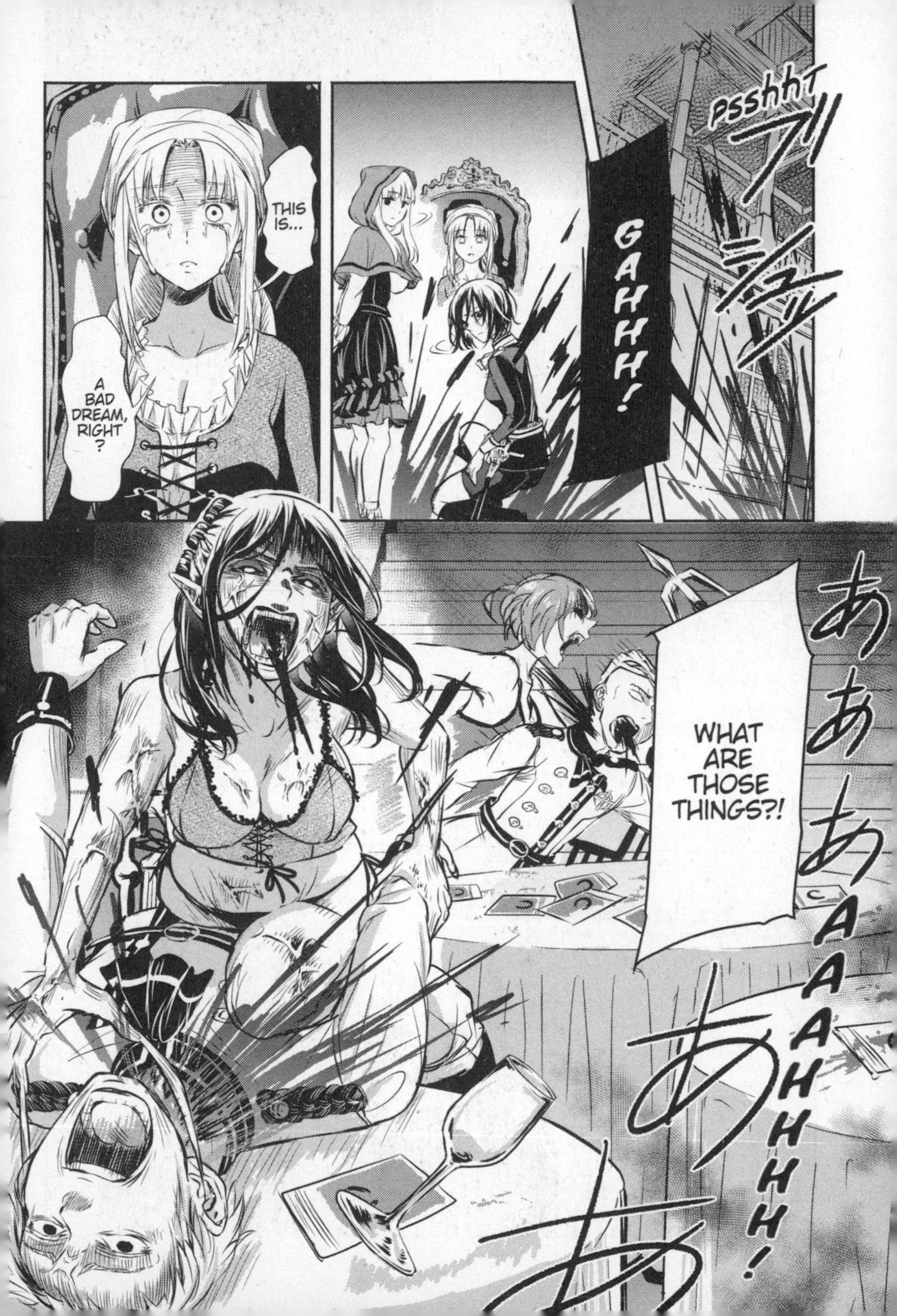
PSSHHT
GAHHHH!
THIS IS...
A BAD DREAM, RIGHT?
WHAT ARE THOSE THINGS?!
あああああ
AAAAHHHHHH!

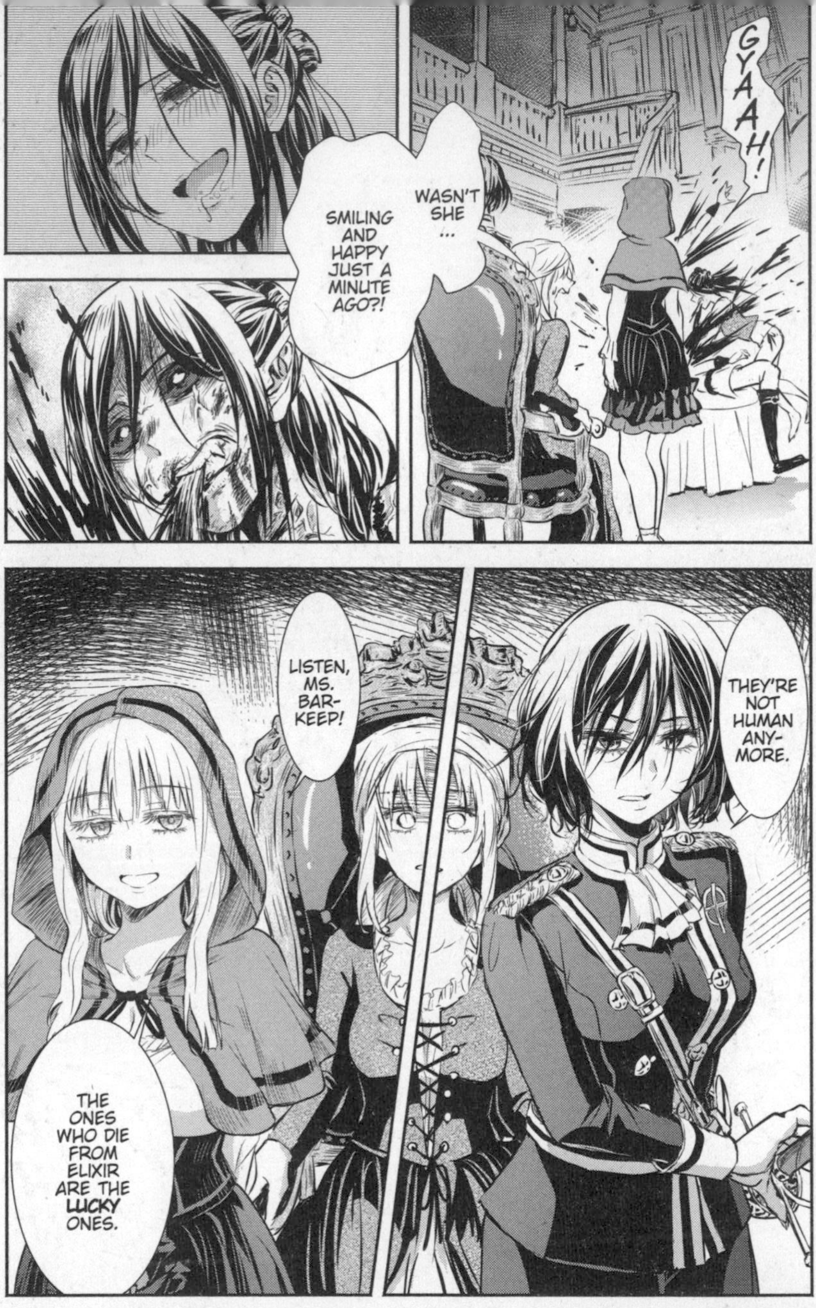
GYAAH!
WASN'T SHE ...
SMILING AND HAPPY JUST A MINUTE AGO?!
THEY'RE NOT HUMAN ANYMORE.
LISTEN, MS. BARKEEP!
THE ONES WHO DIE FROM ELIXIR ARE THE **LUCKY** ONES.

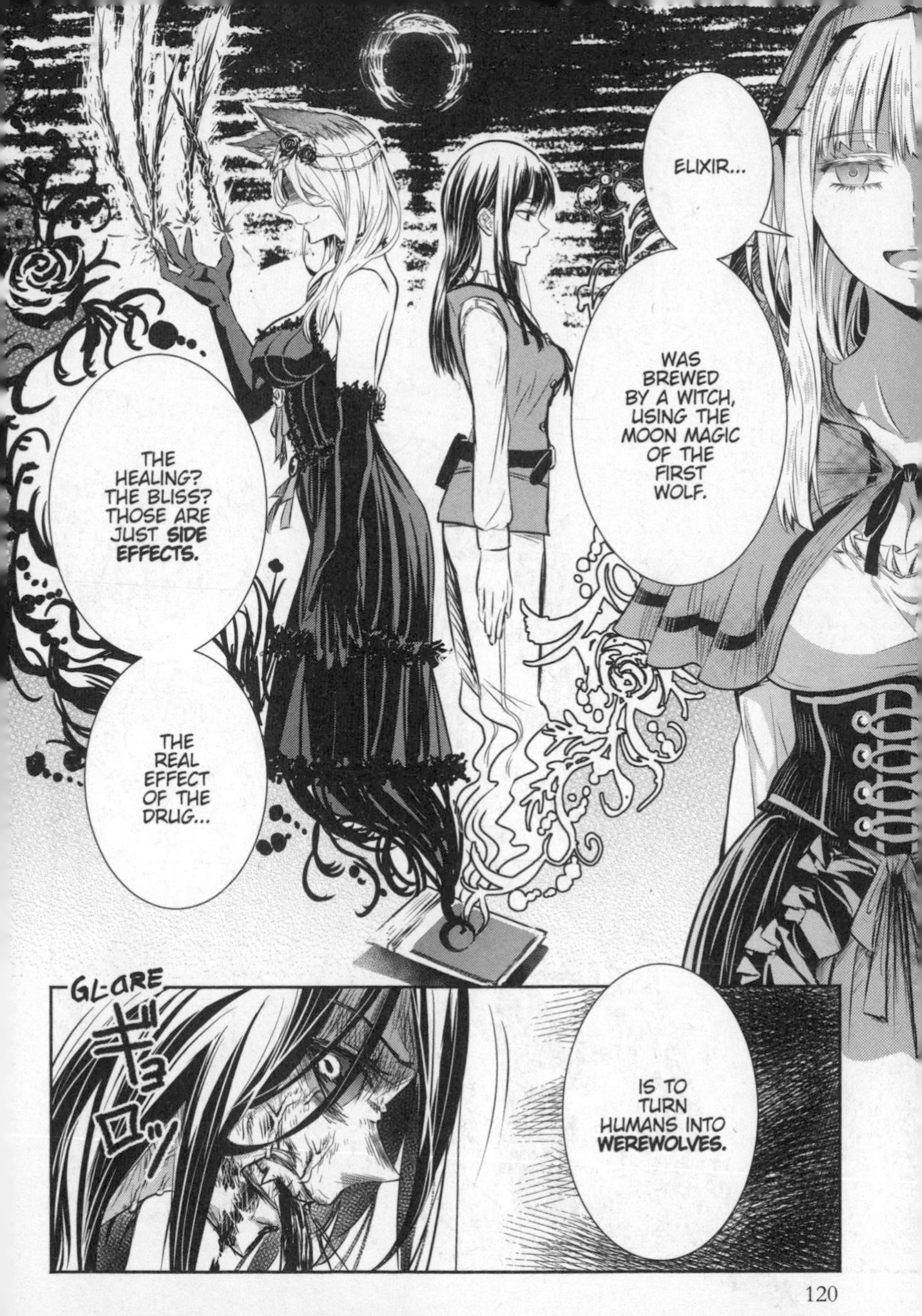
ELIXIR...
WAS BREWED BY A WITCH, USING THE MOON MAGIC OF THE FIRST WOLF.
THE HEALING? THE BLISS? THOSE ARE JUST **SIDE EFFECTS.**
THE REAL EFFECT OF THE DRUG...
IS TO TURN HUMANS INTO **WEREWOLVES.**
GL-ARE
ギョロッ

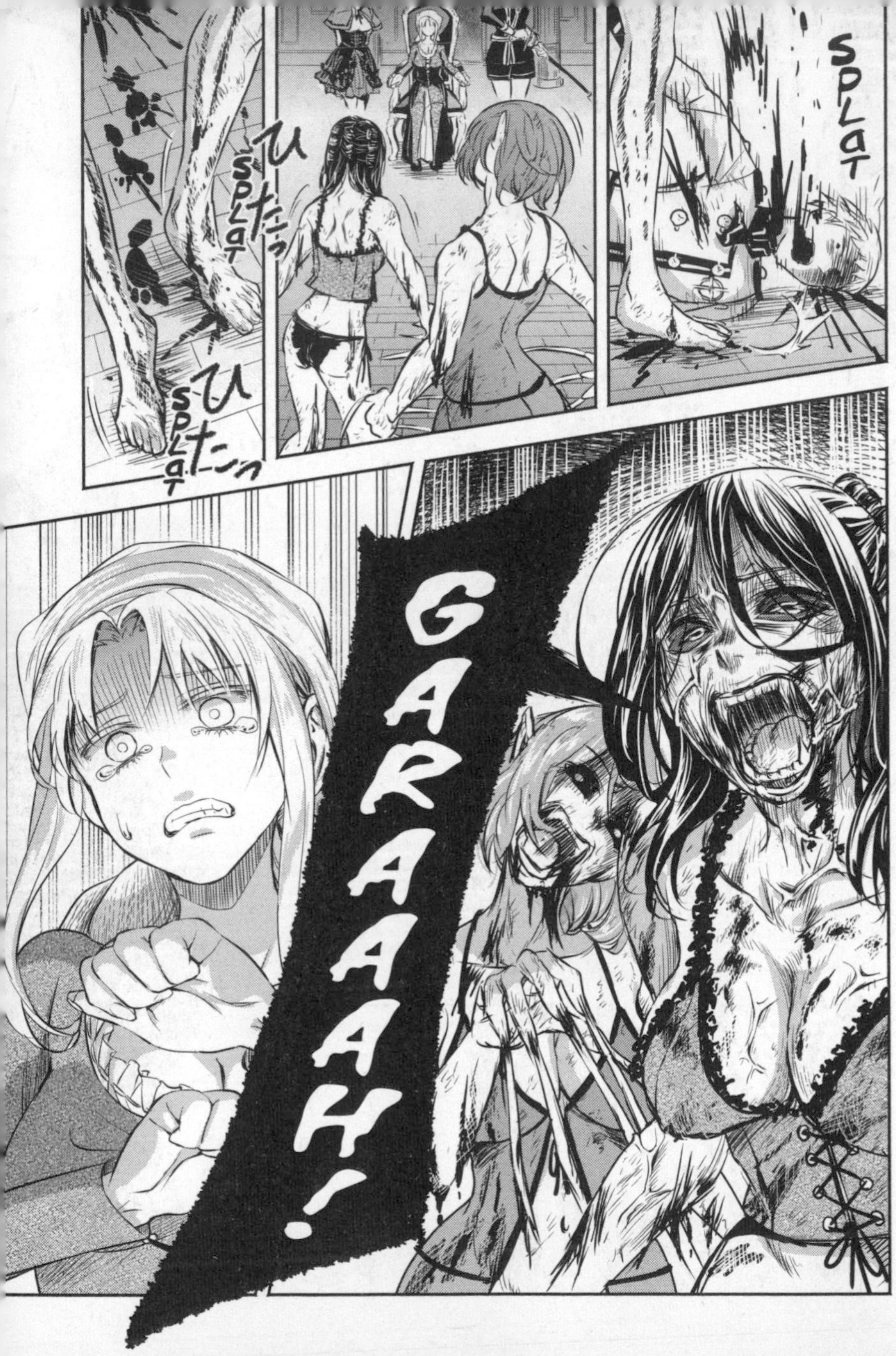
SPLAT
ひたっ
SPLAT
ひたーっ
SPLAT
GARAAAH!

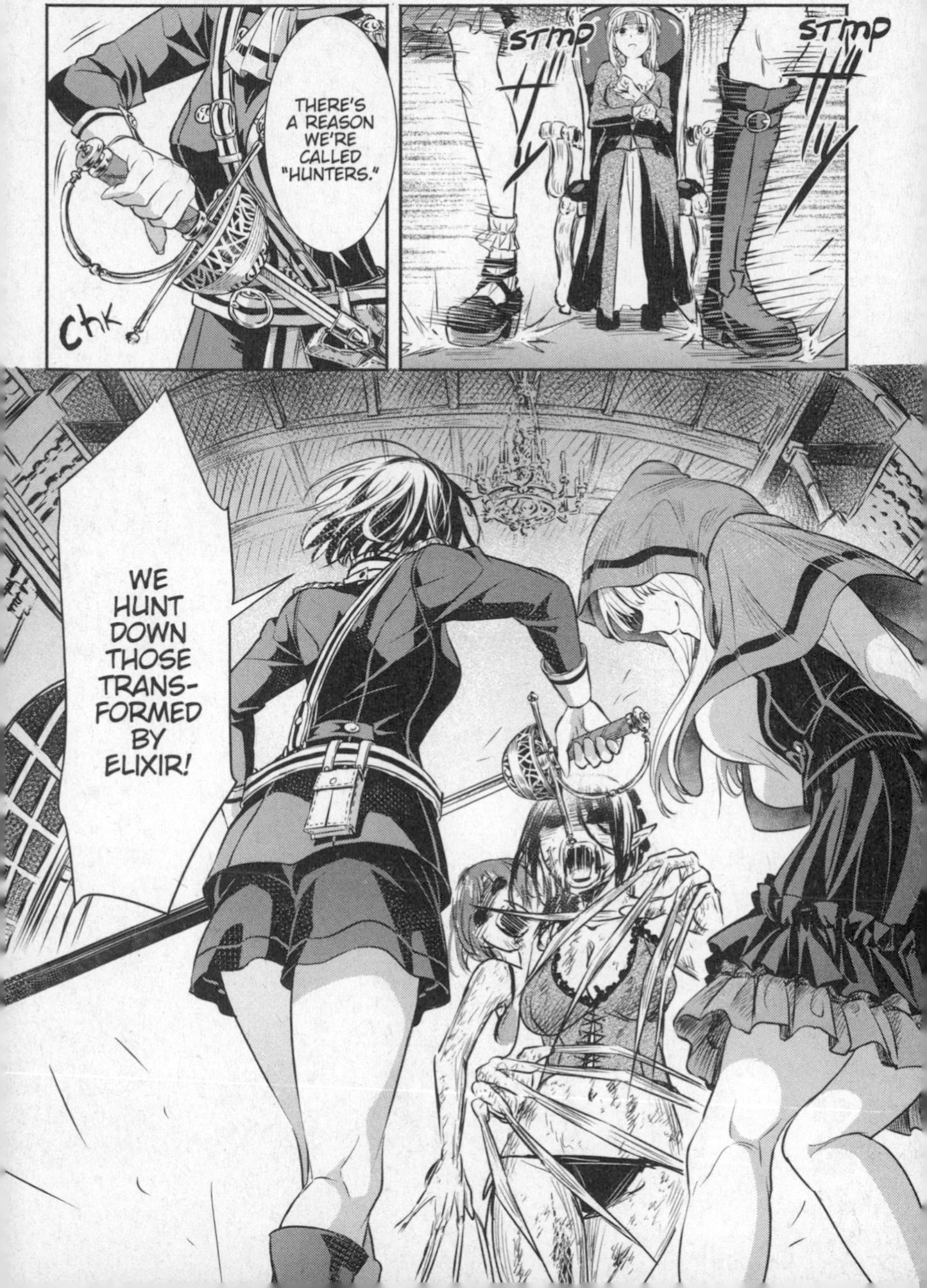
STMP
STMP
THERE'S A REASON WE'RE CALLED "HUNTERS."
Chk
WE HUNT DOWN THOSE TRANS-FORMED BY ELIXIR!

SCARLET

Moira Hopkins

【　Name　】 Moira Hopkins
【　Height　】 166cm
【　Age　　】 Unknown
【Birthday】 August 12th
【　Likes　】 Reading, rules
【Dislikes】 Licentious behavior

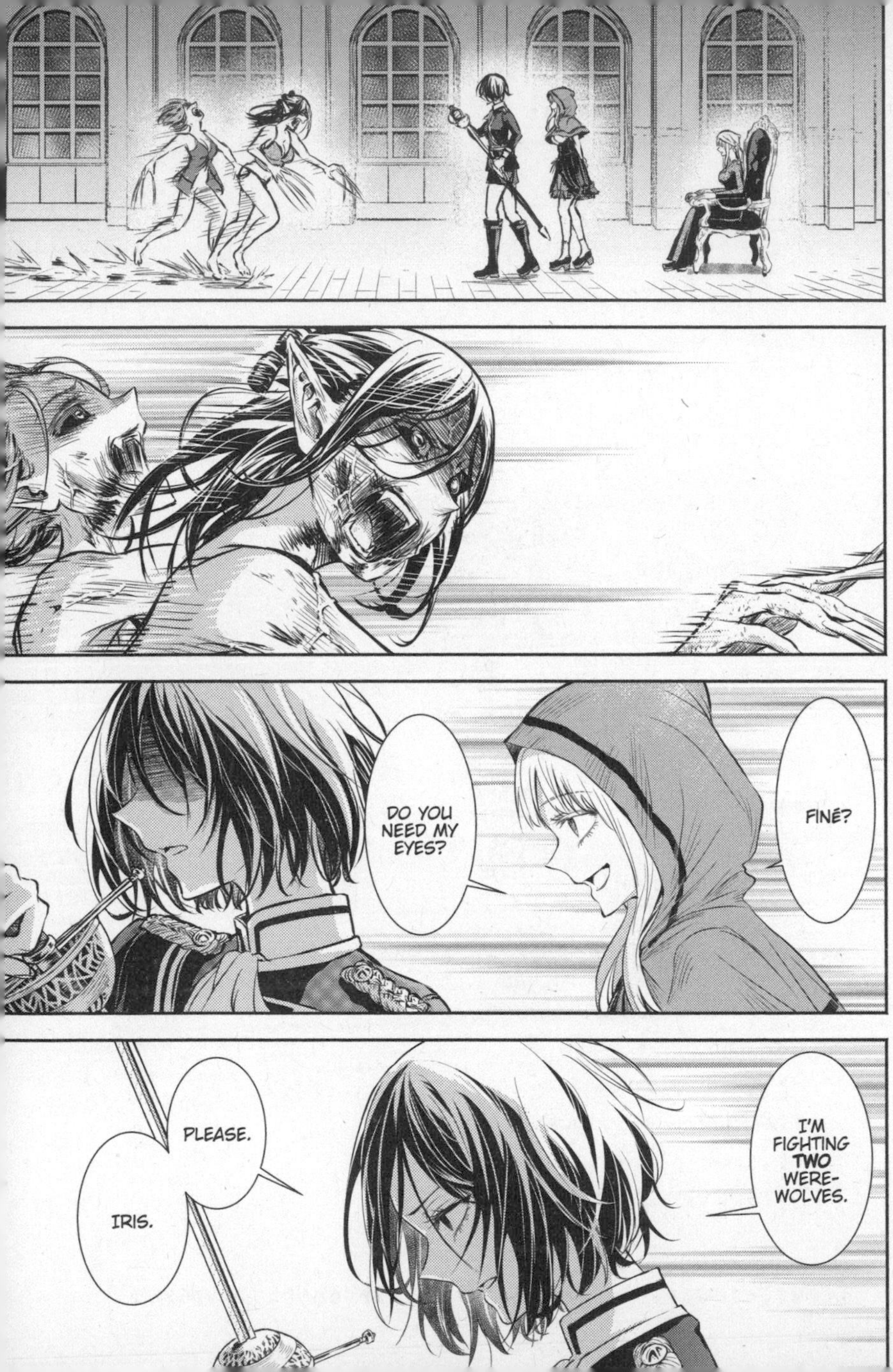
FINE?
DO YOU NEED MY EYES?
I'M FIGHTING TWO WERE-WOLVES.
PLEASE.
IRIS.

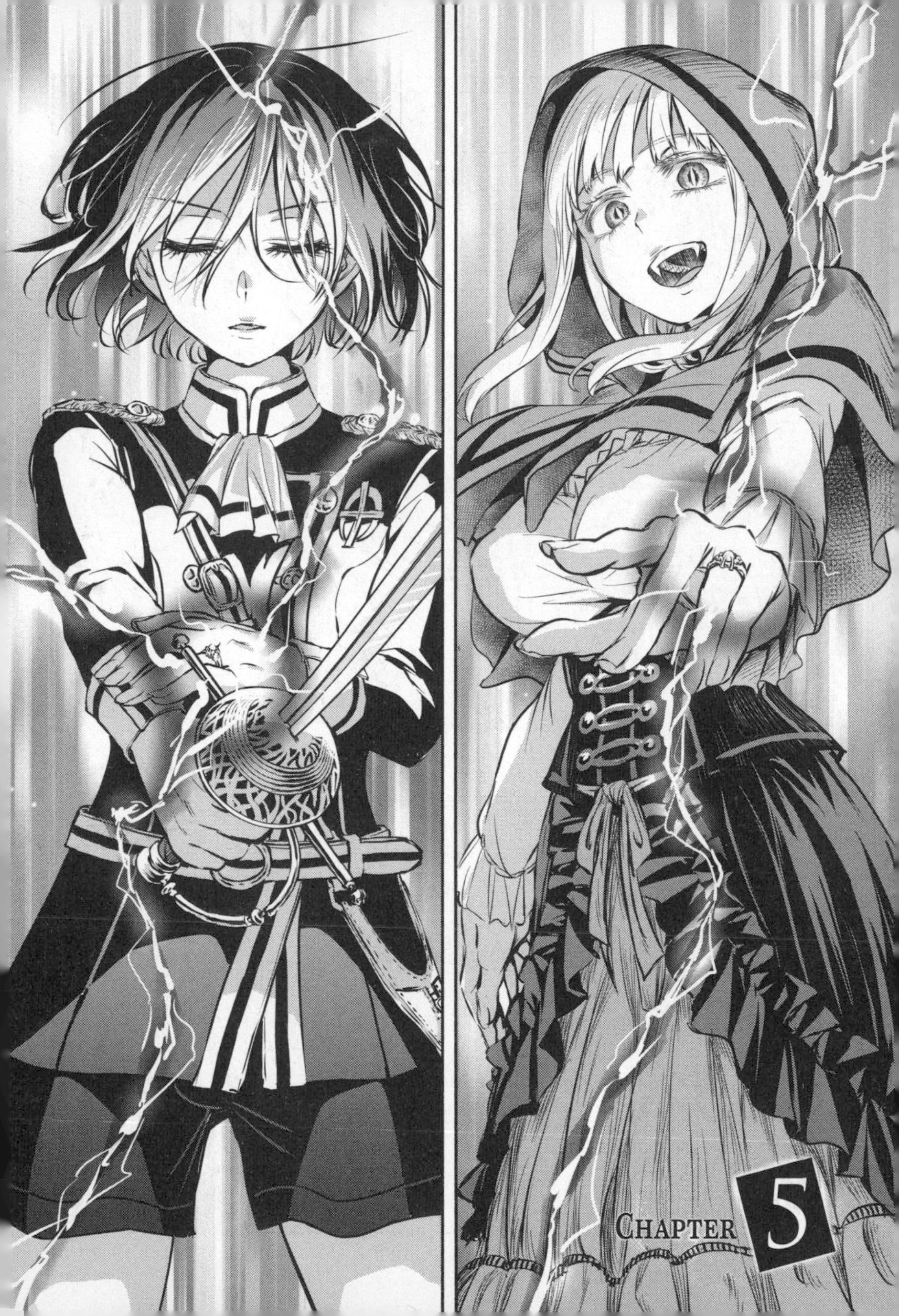
CHAPTER 5

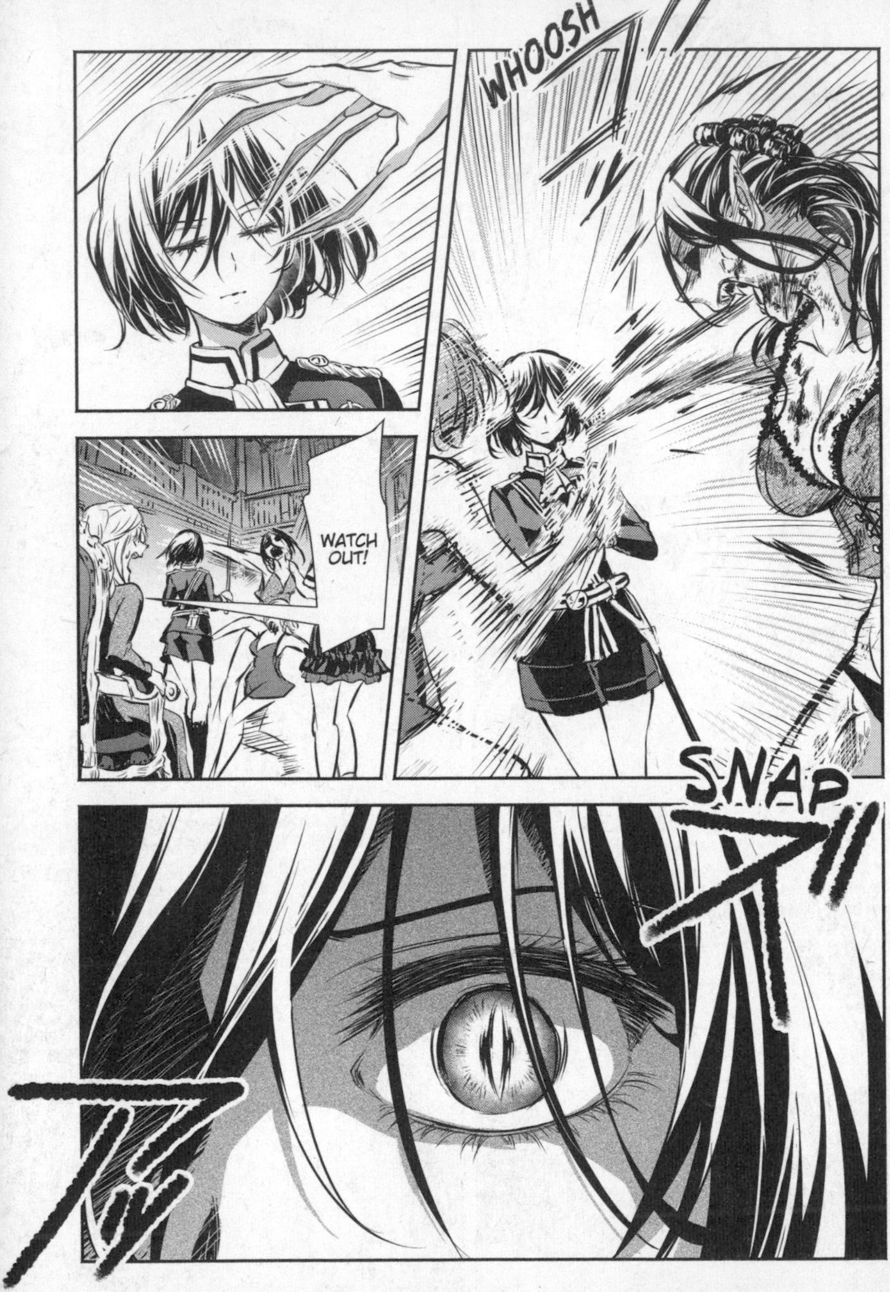
WHOOSH
WATCH OUT!
SNAP

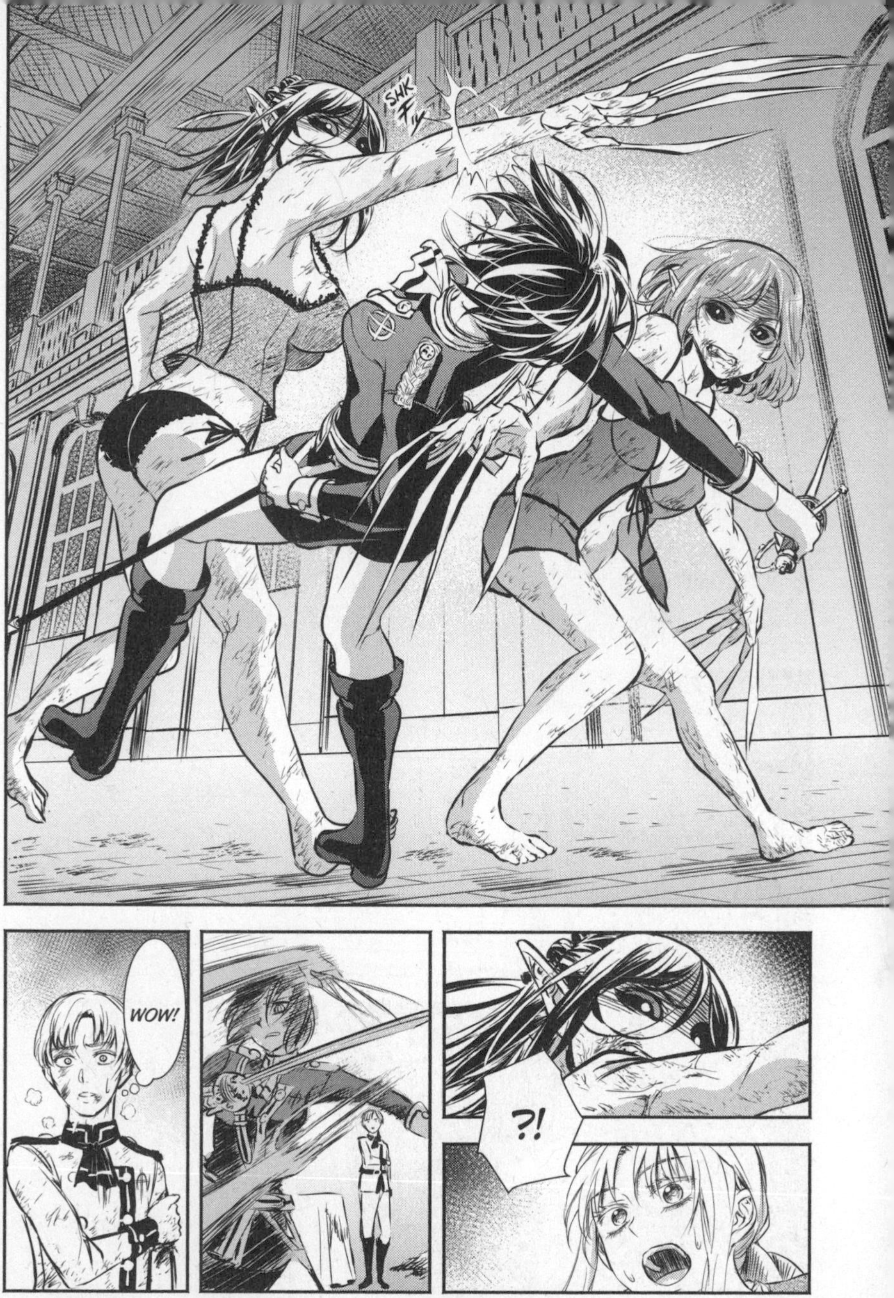
SHK
?!
WOW!

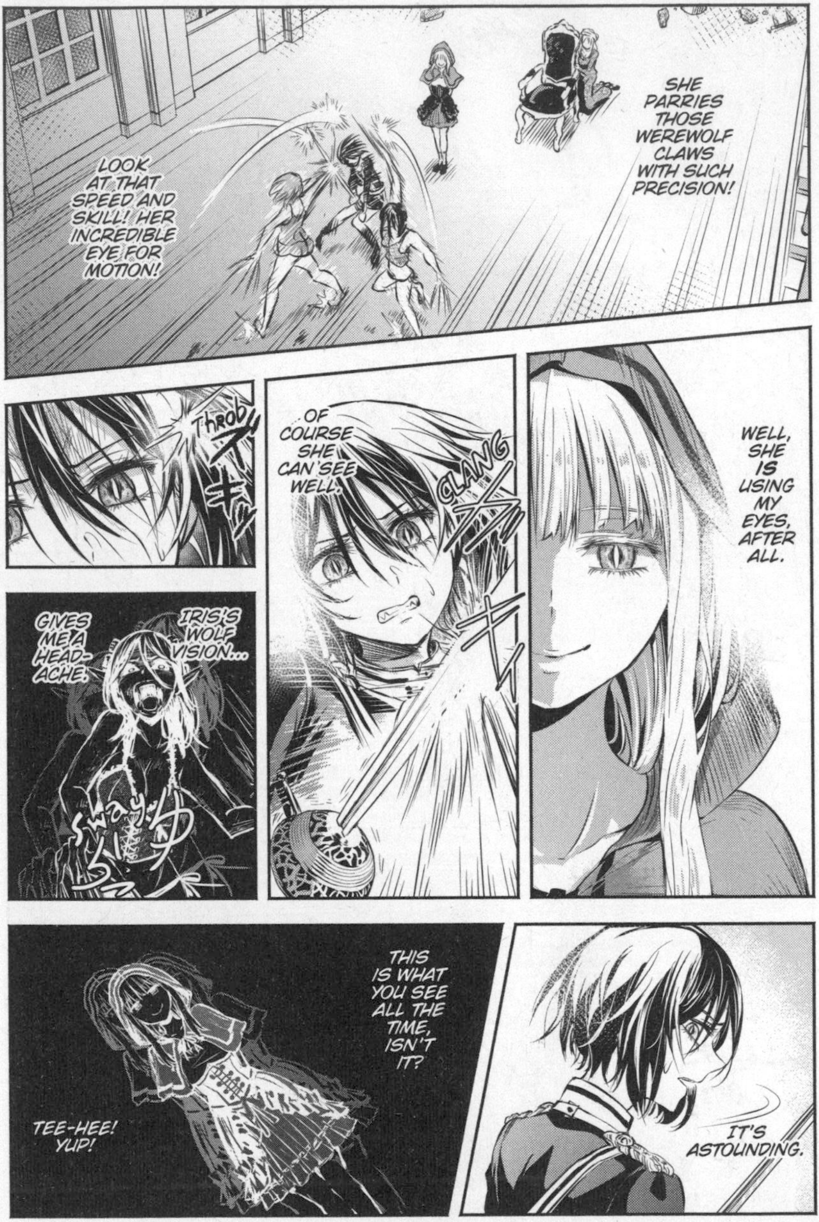
SHE PARRIES THOSE WEREWOLF CLAWS WITH SUCH PRECISION!
LOOK AT THAT SPEED AND SKILL! HER INCREDIBLE EYE FOR MOTION!
WELL, SHE IS USING MY EYES, AFTER ALL.
...OF COURSE SHE CAN SEE WELL.
CLANG
Throb
IRIS'S WOLF VISION...
GIVES ME A HEAD-ACHE.
sway
IT'S ASTOUNDING.
THIS IS WHAT YOU SEE ALL THE TIME, ISN'T IT?
TEE-HEE! YUP!

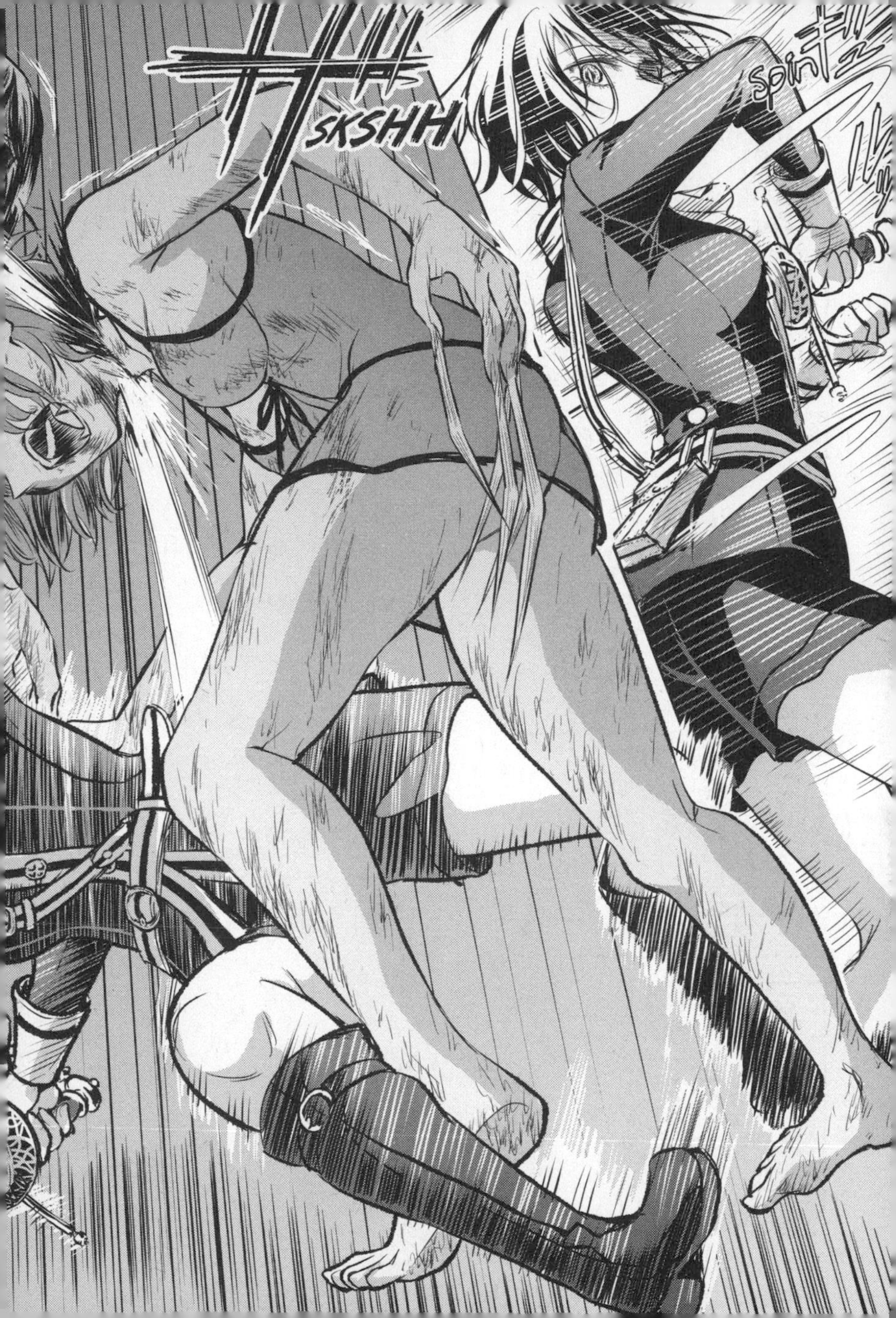
spin
SKSHH

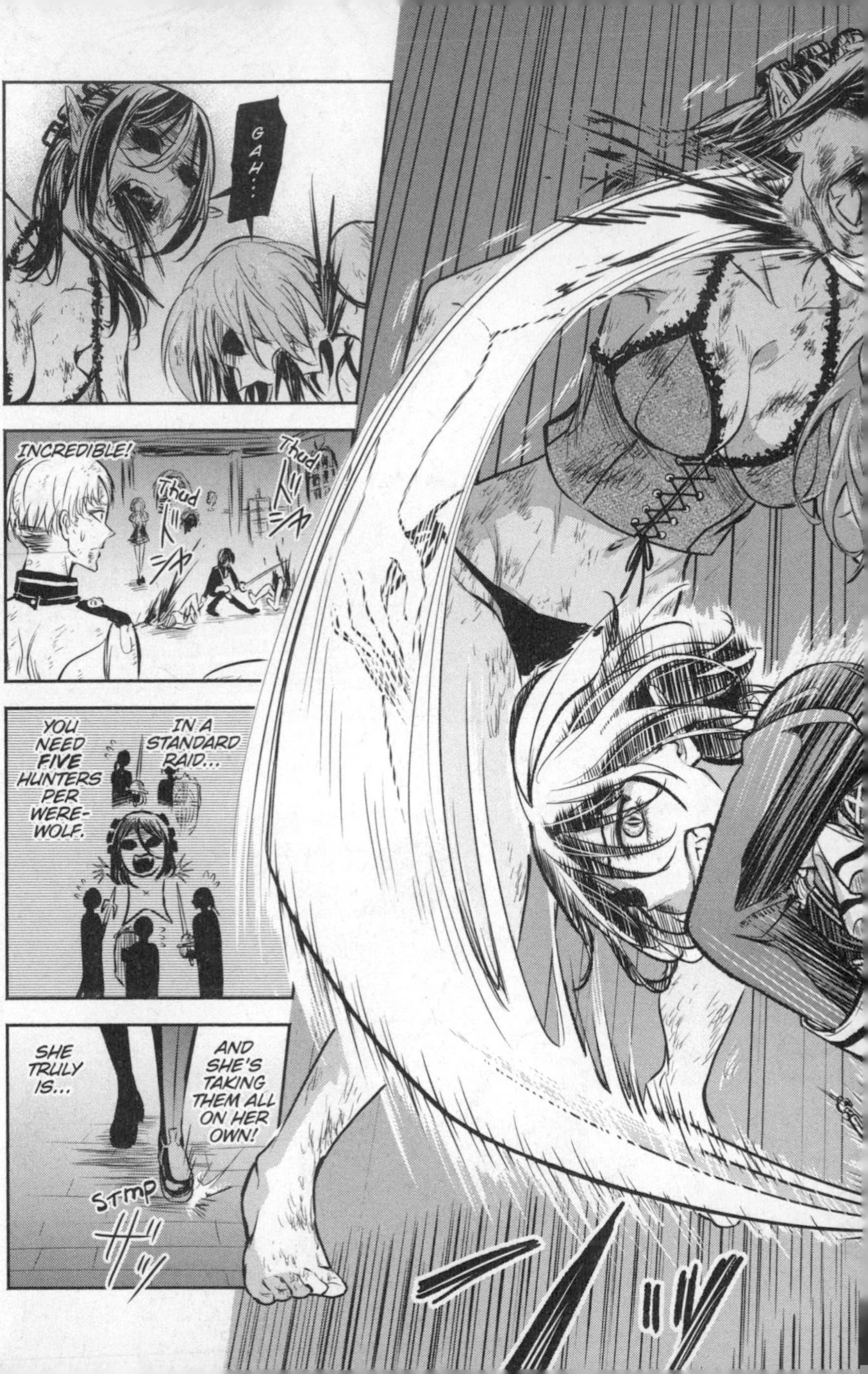
GAH...
INCREDIBLE!
Thud
Thud
IN A STANDARD RAID...
YOU NEED FIVE HUNTERS PER WERE-WOLF.
AND SHE'S TAKING THEM ALL ON HER OWN!
SHE TRULY IS...
Stmp

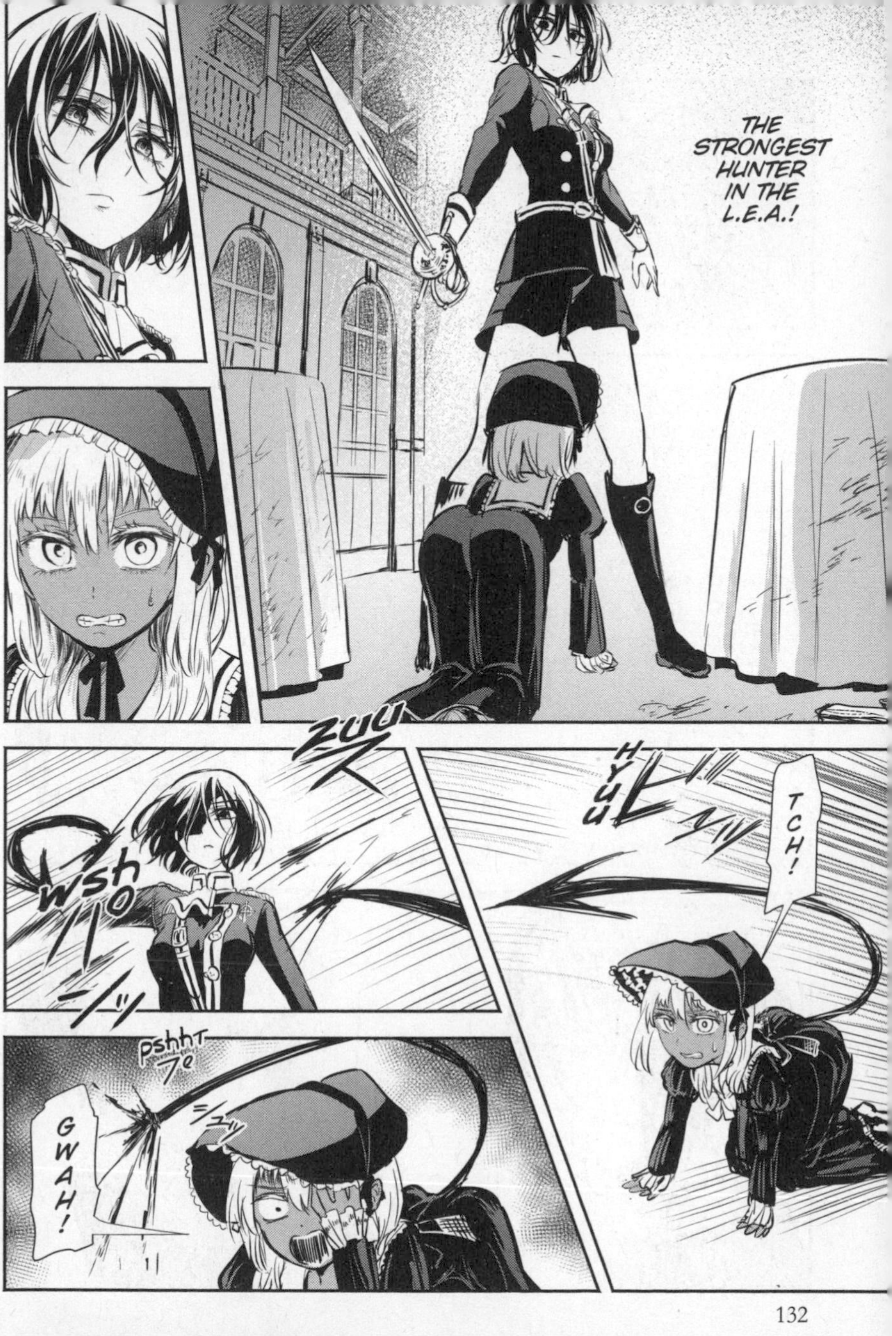
THE STRONGEST HUNTER IN THE L.E.A.!
HYUUU
TCH!
ZUUU
wsh
pshhT
GWAH!

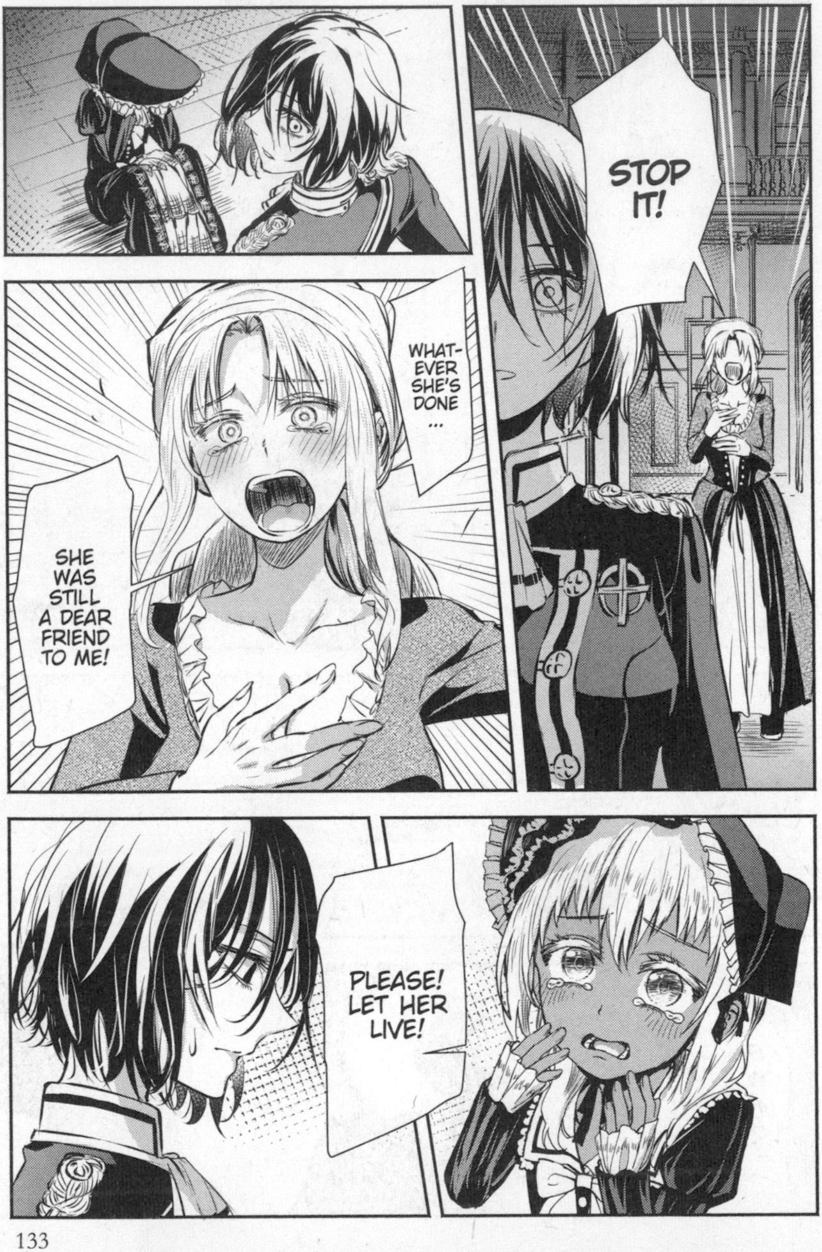
STOP IT!
WHAT-EVER SHE'S DONE ...
SHE WAS STILL A DEAR FRIEND TO ME!
PLEASE! LET HER LIVE!

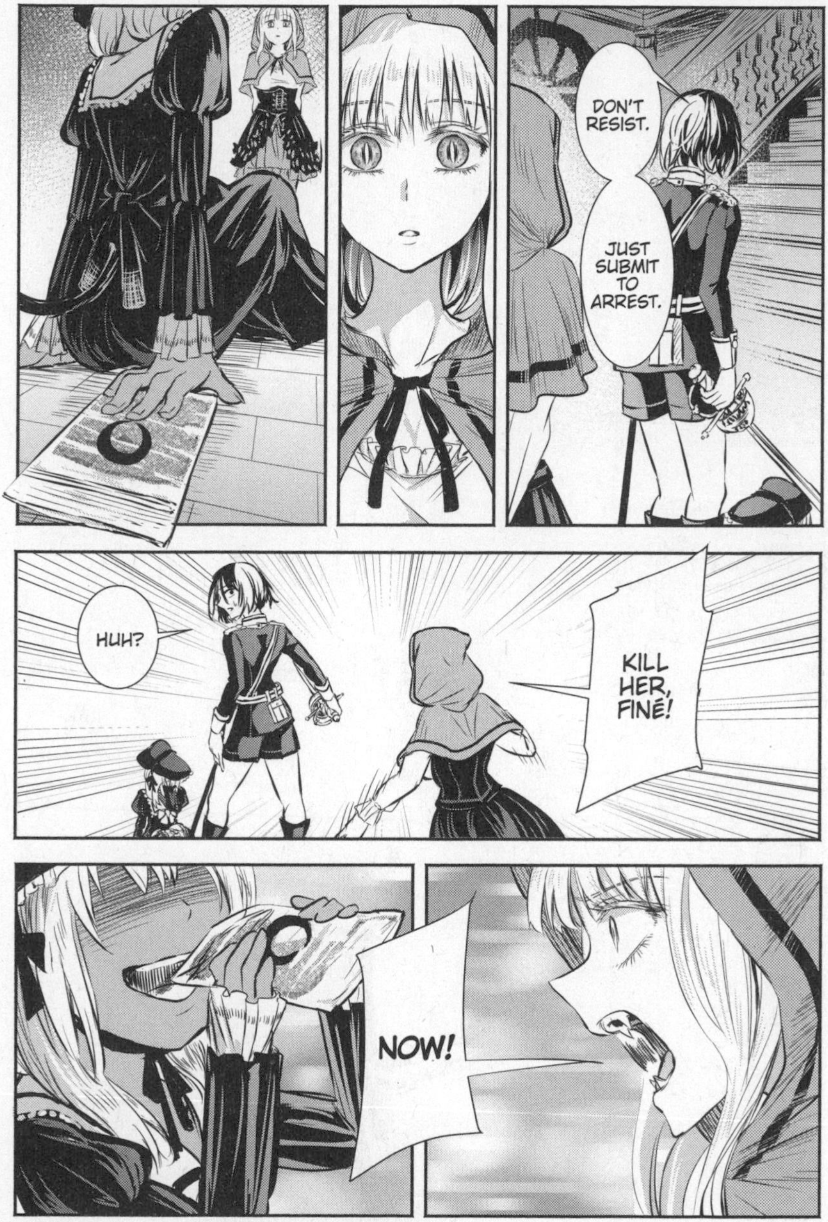
DON'T RESIST.
JUST SUBMIT TO ARREST.
KILL HER, FINÉ!
HUH?
NOW!

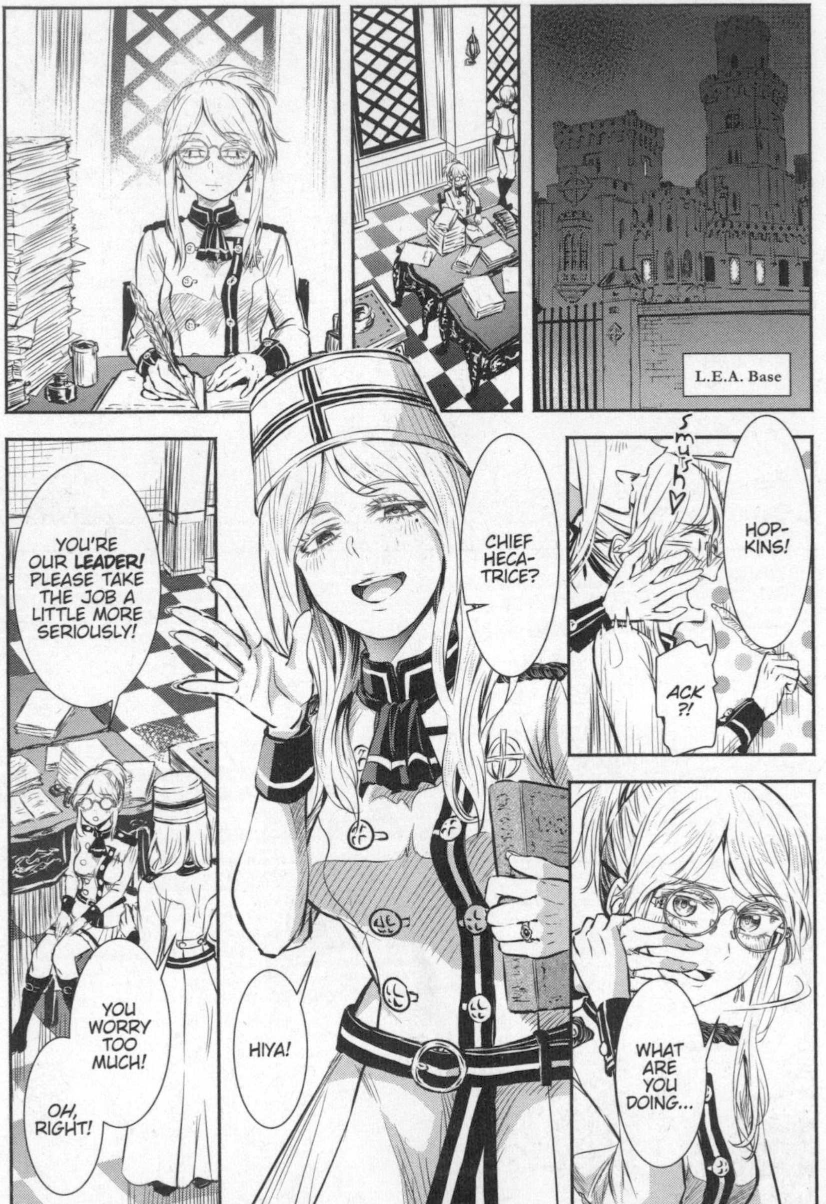
L.E.A. Base
HOP-KINS!
smush ♥
ACK?!
WHAT ARE YOU DOING...
CHIEF HECA-TRICE?
HIYA!
YOU'RE OUR **LEADER!** PLEASE TAKE THE JOB A LITTLE MORE SERIOUSLY!
YOU WORRY TOO MUCH!
OH, RIGHT!

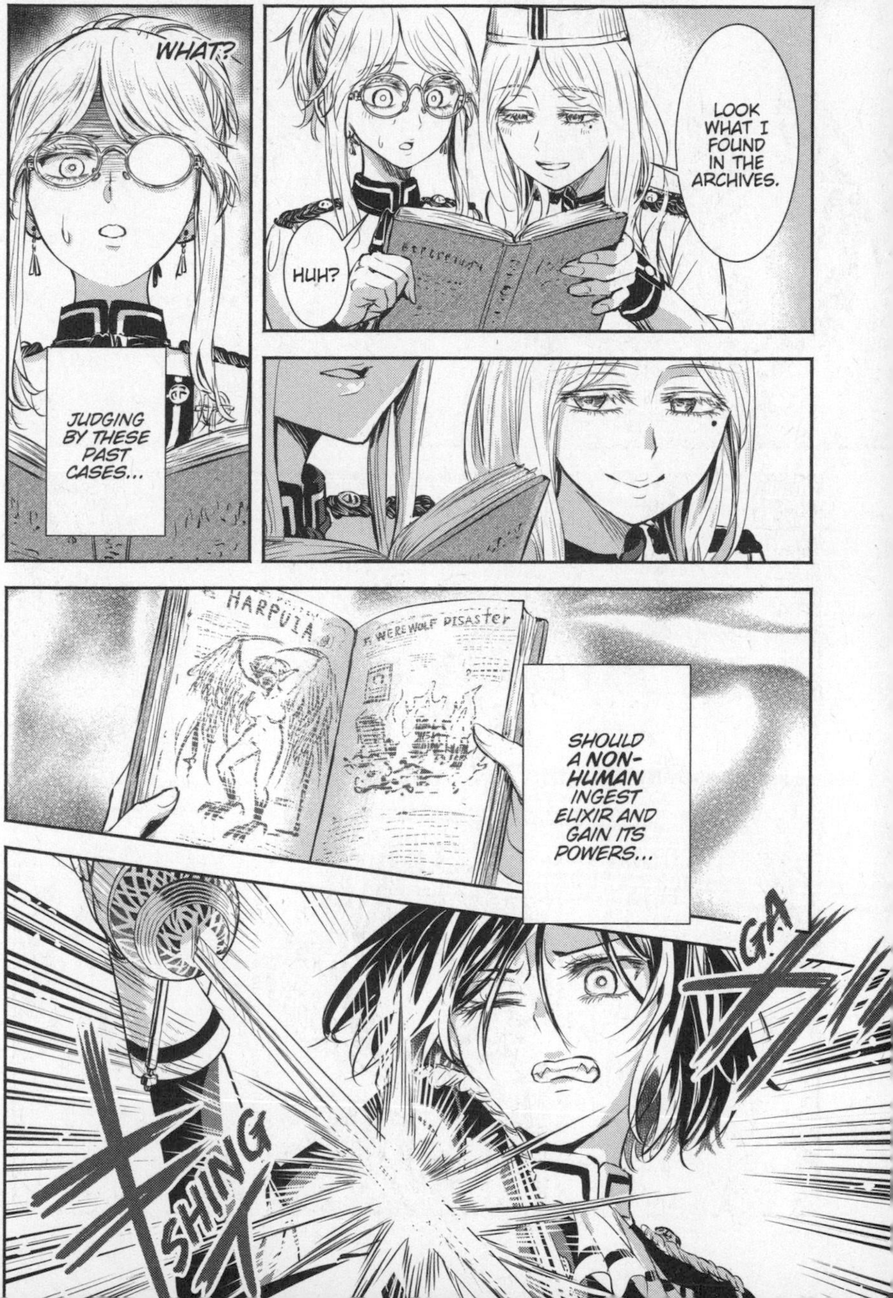
LOOK WHAT I FOUND IN THE ARCHIVES.
HUH?
WHAT?
JUDGING BY THESE PAST CASES...
HARPUIA
WEREWOLF DISASTER
SHOULD A NON-HUMAN INGEST ELIXIR AND GAIN ITS POWERS...
GA
SHING

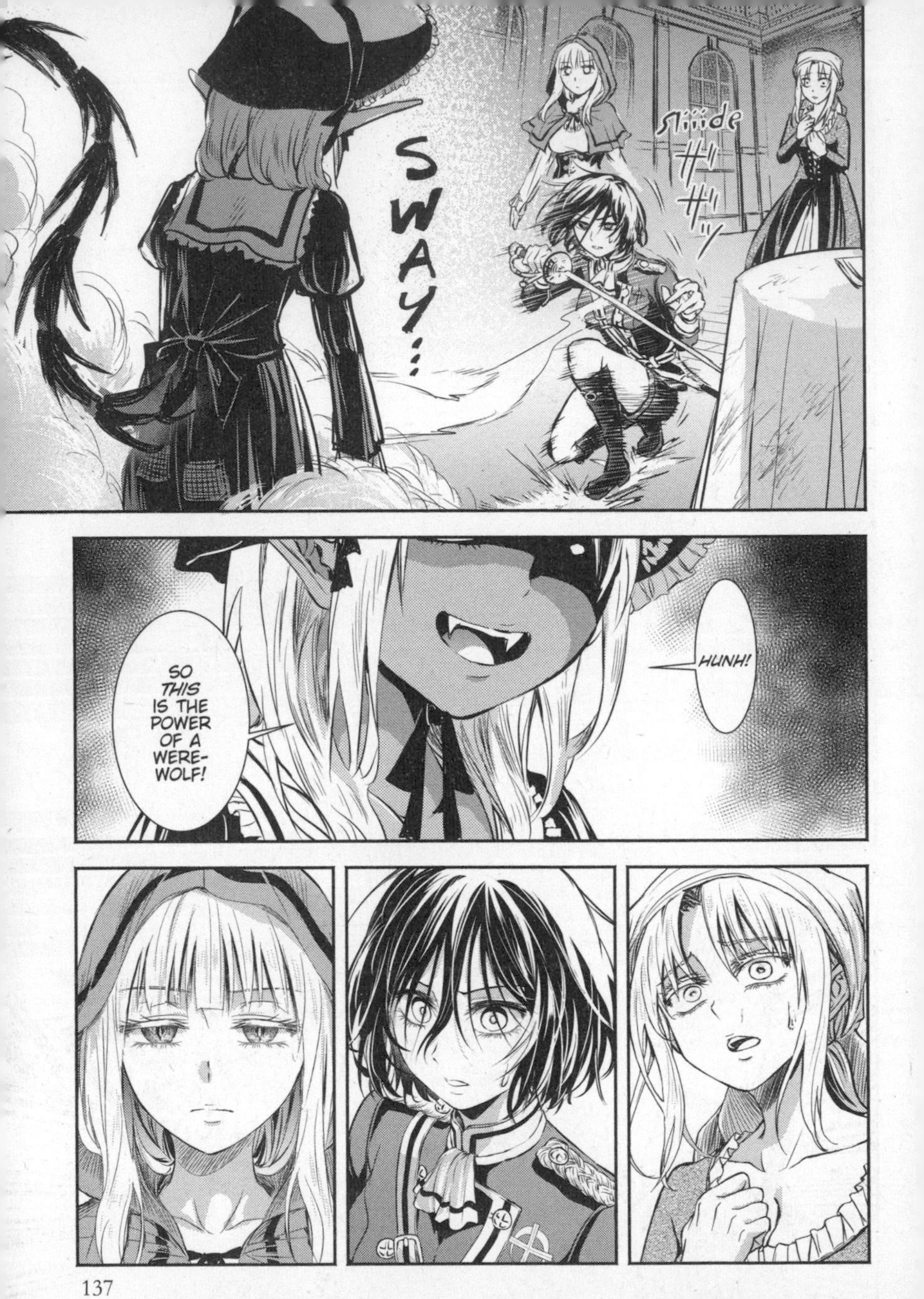
Sliiide
SWAY...
HUNH!
SO THIS IS THE POWER OF A WERE-WOLF!

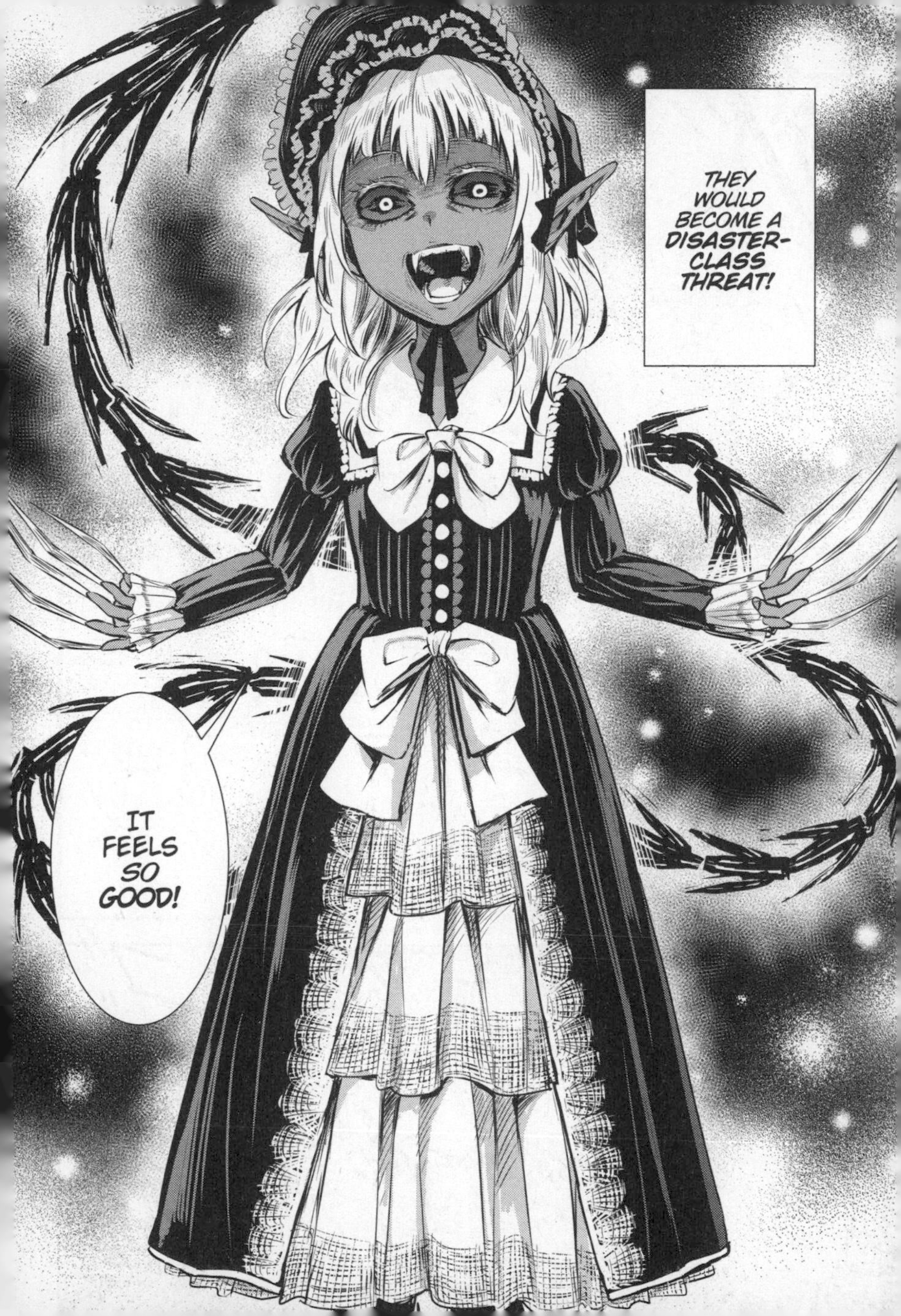
THEY WOULD BECOME A DISASTER-CLASS THREAT!
IT FEELS SO GOOD!

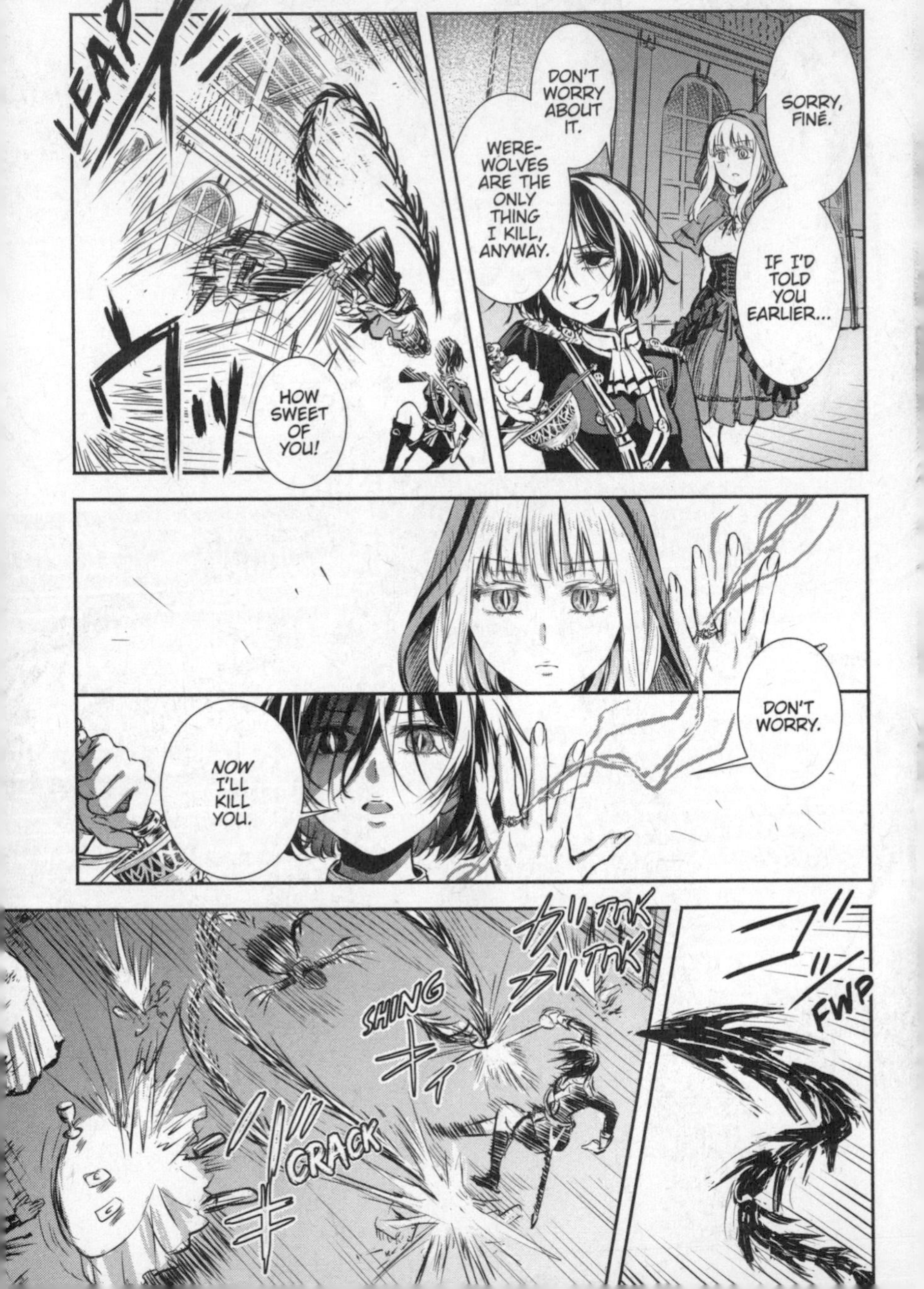
SORRY, FINÉ.
DON'T WORRY ABOUT IT.
WERE-WOLVES ARE THE ONLY THING I KILL, ANYWAY.
IF I'D TOLD YOU EARLIER...
LEAP
HOW SWEET OF YOU!
DON'T WORRY.
NOW I'LL KILL YOU.
FWP
TNK
TNK
SHING
CRACK

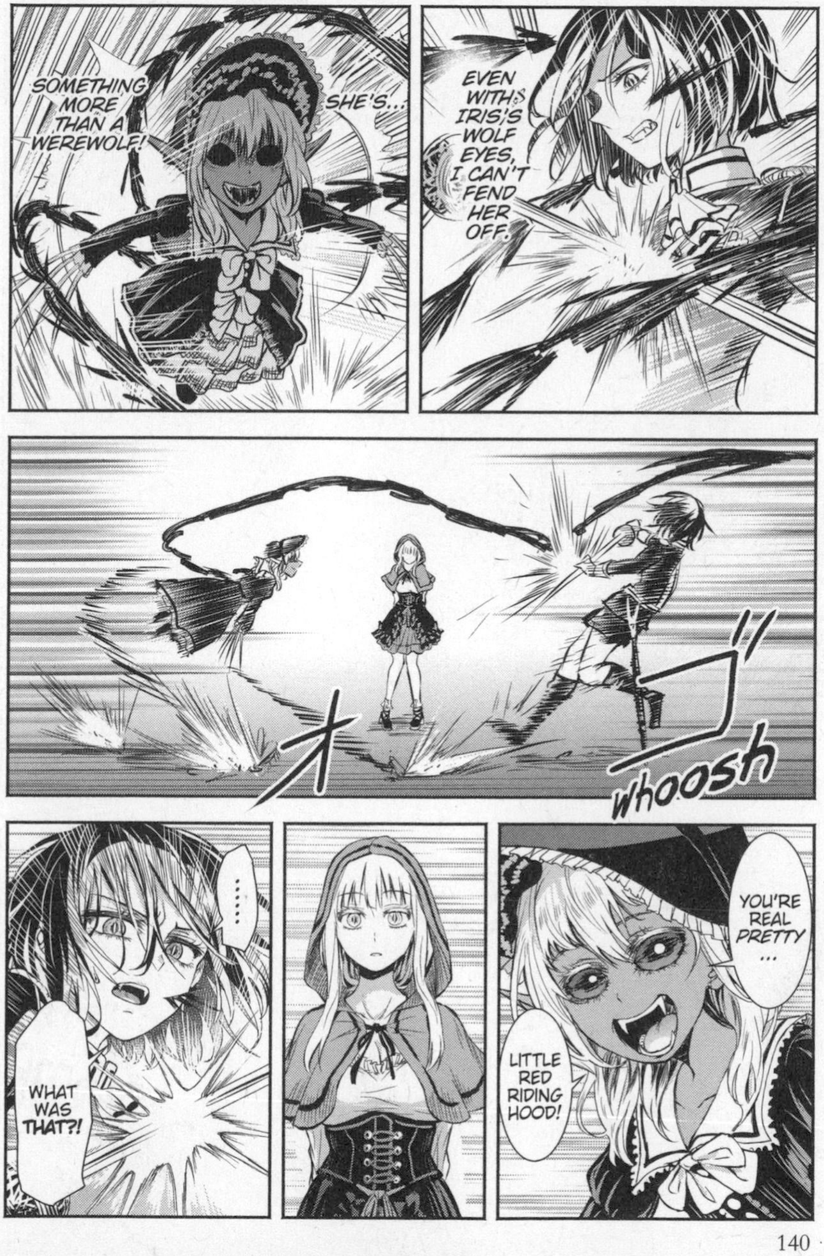
EVEN WITH IRIS'S WOLF EYES, I CAN'T FEND HER OFF.
SHE'S...
SOMETHING MORE THAN A WEREWOLF!
whoosh
YOU'RE REAL PRETTY...
LITTLE RED RIDING HOOD!
......
WHAT WAS THAT?!

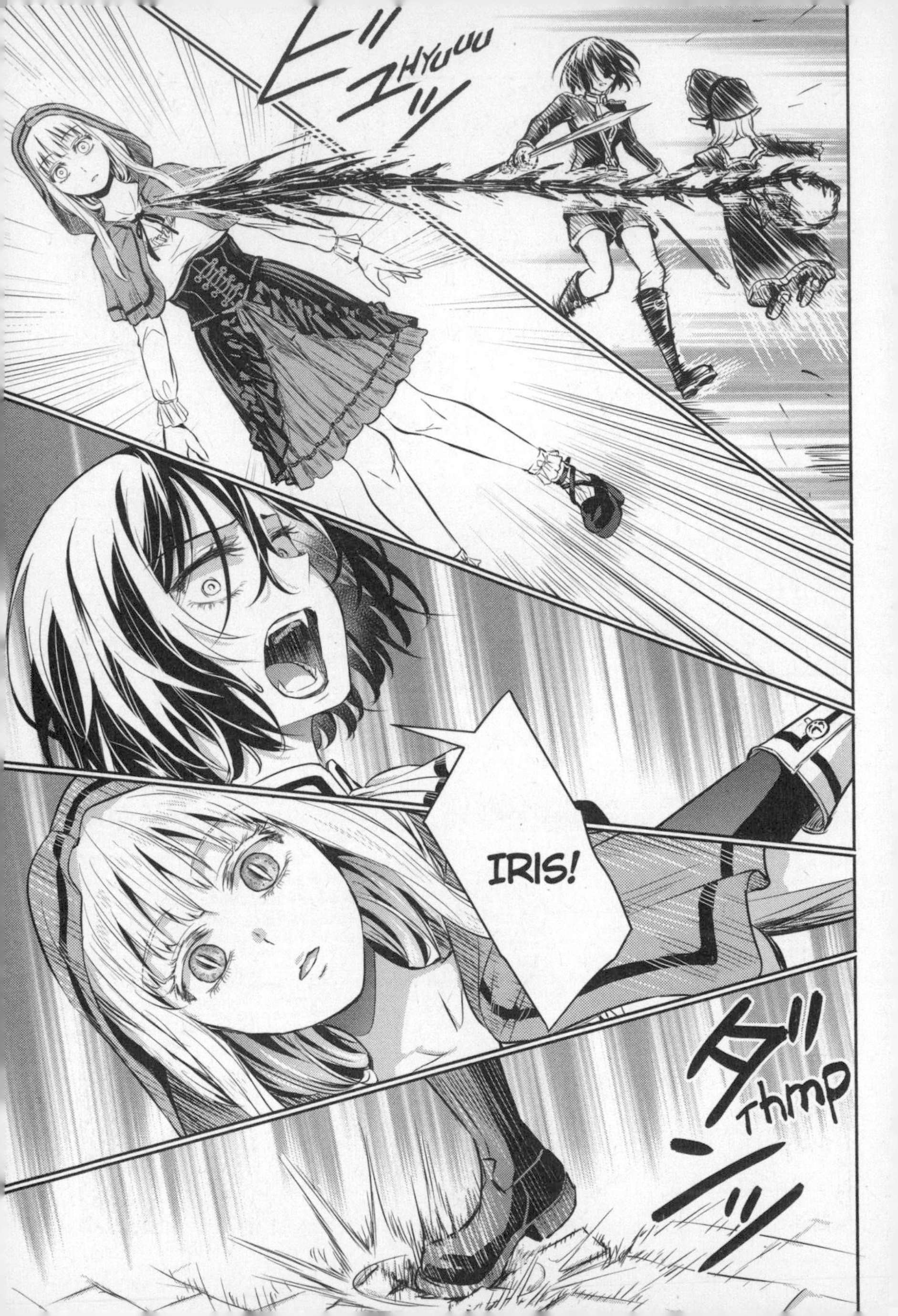
ZHYUUU
IRIS!
thmp

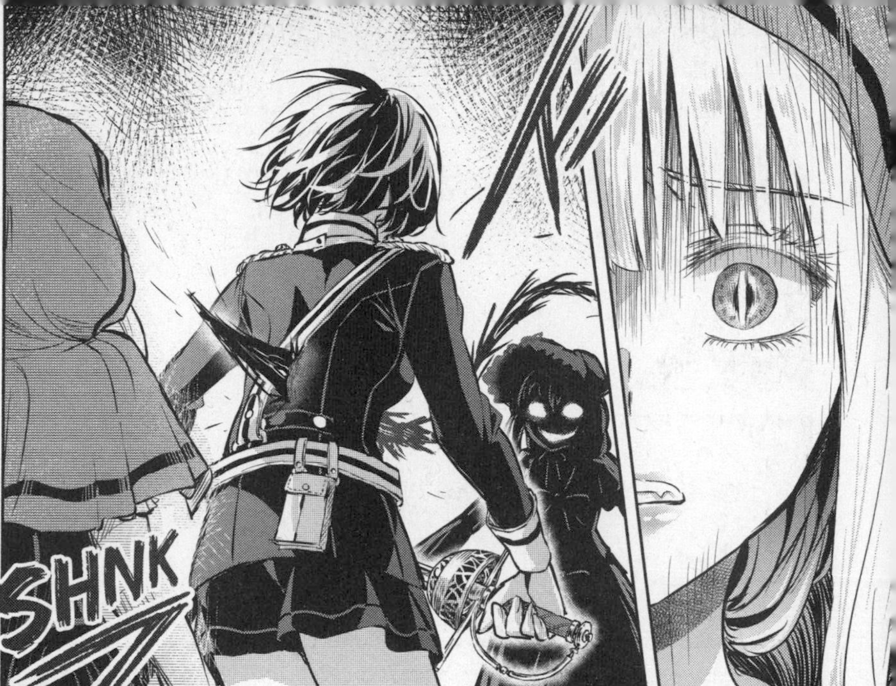
SHNK

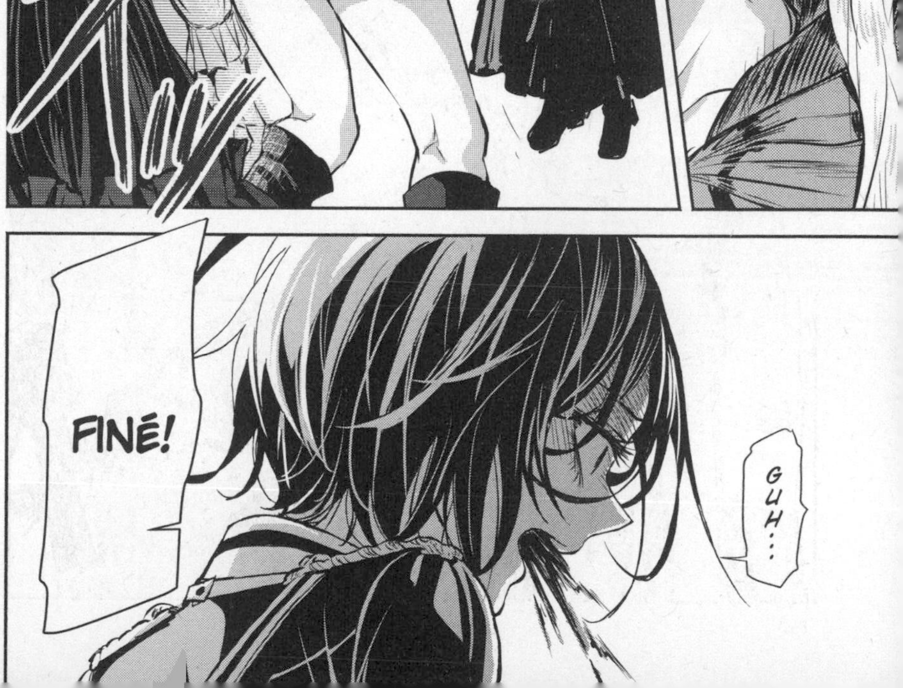
GUH...
FINÉ!

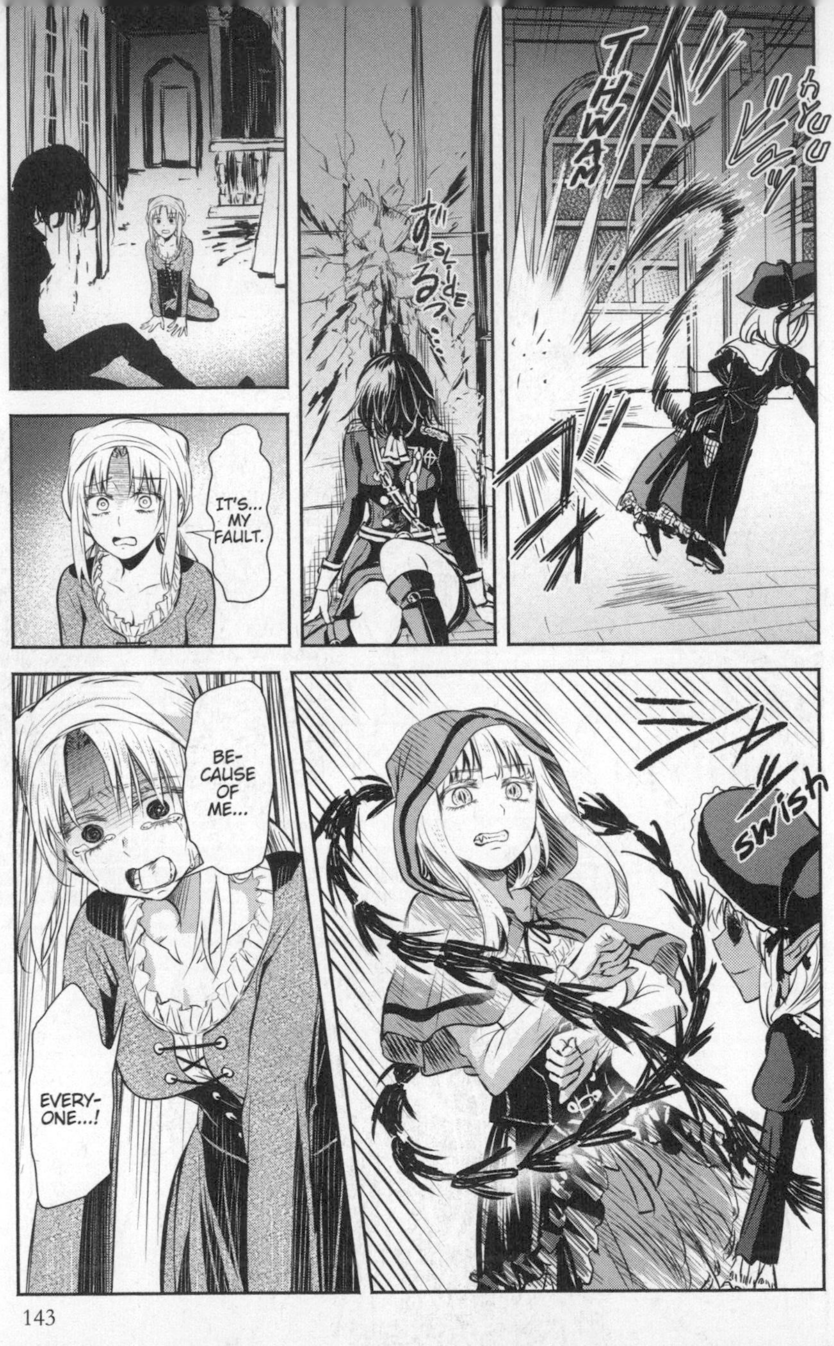
HYUU
THWAM
SLIDE
IT'S... MY FAULT.
swish
BE-CAUSE OF ME...
EVERY-ONE...!

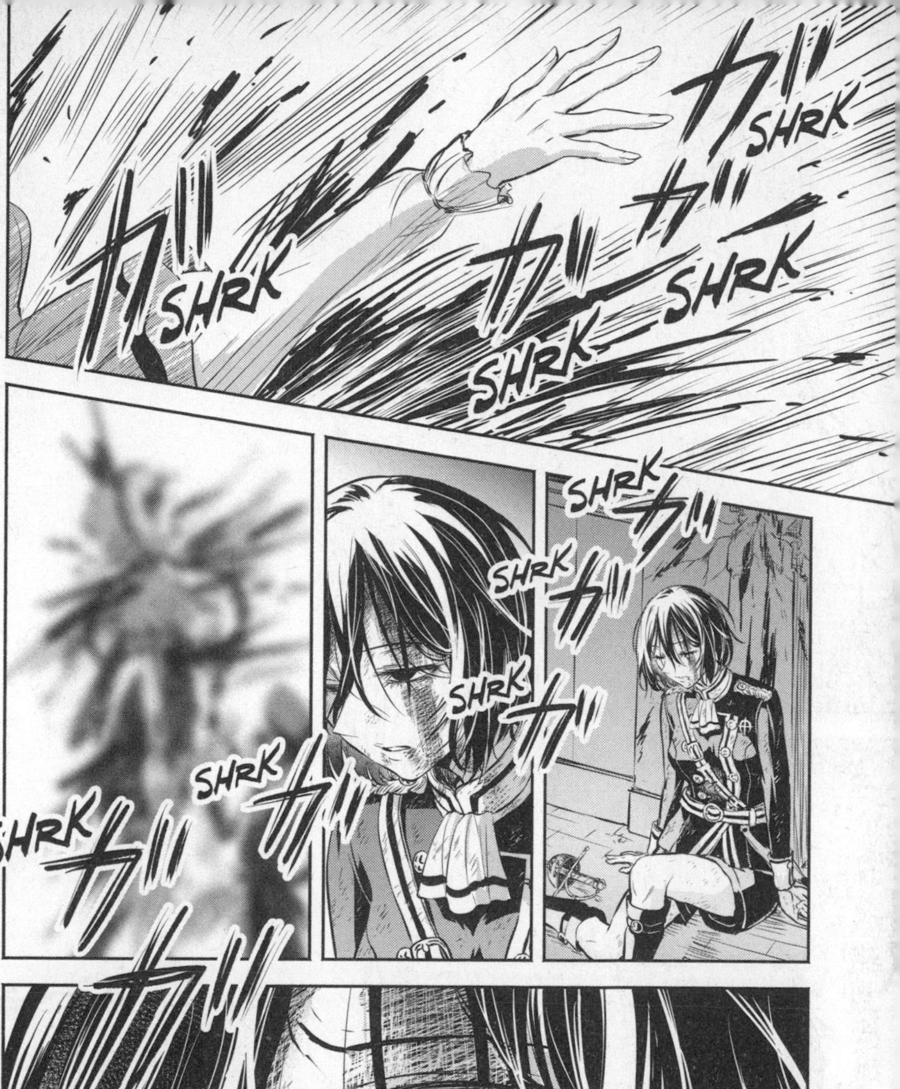
SHRK
SHRK
SHRK
SHRK
SHRK
SHRK
SHRK
SHRK
SHRK
SHRK

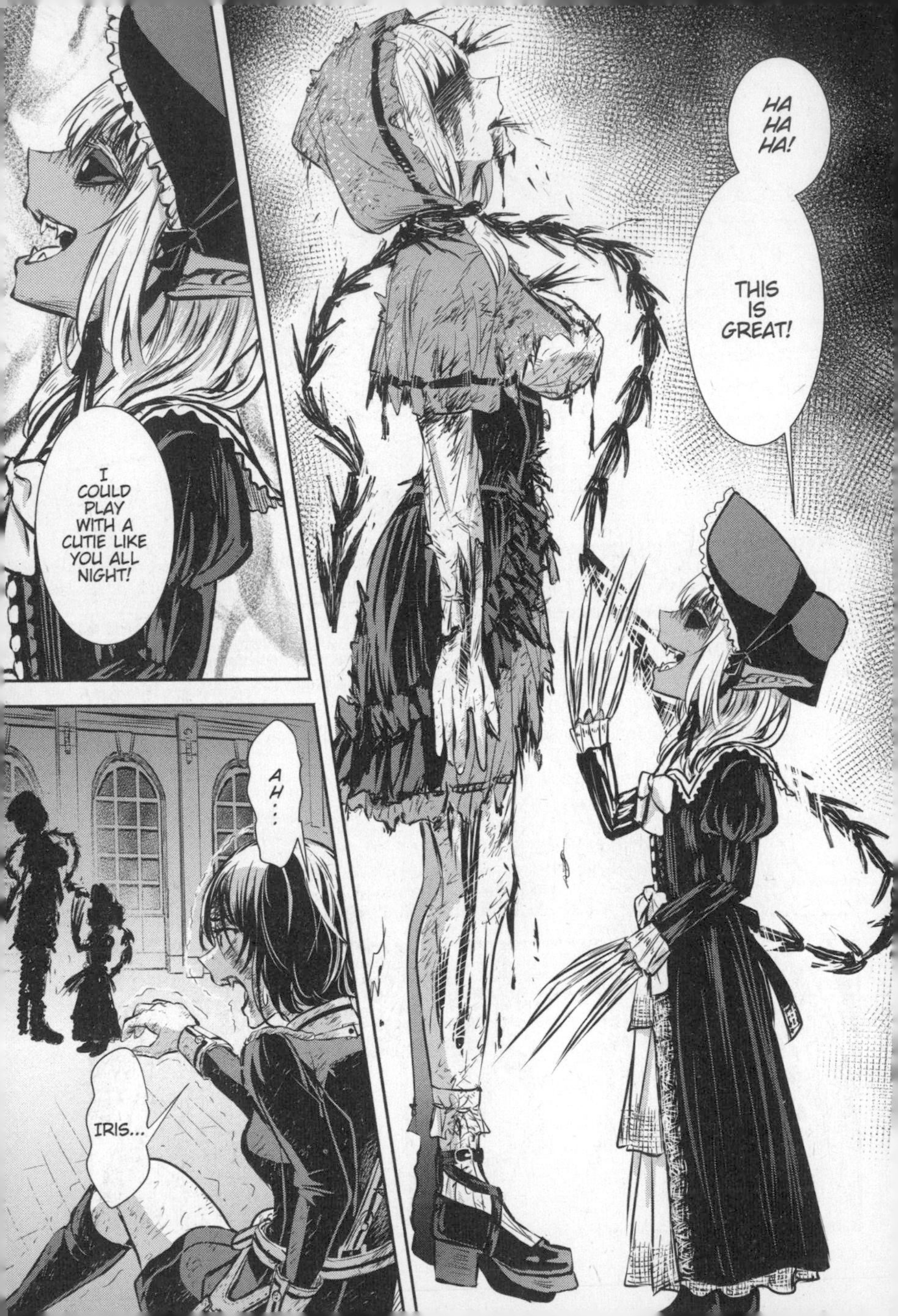
HA HA HA! THIS IS GREAT!
I COULD PLAY WITH A CUTIE LIKE YOU ALL NIGHT!
AH...
IRIS...

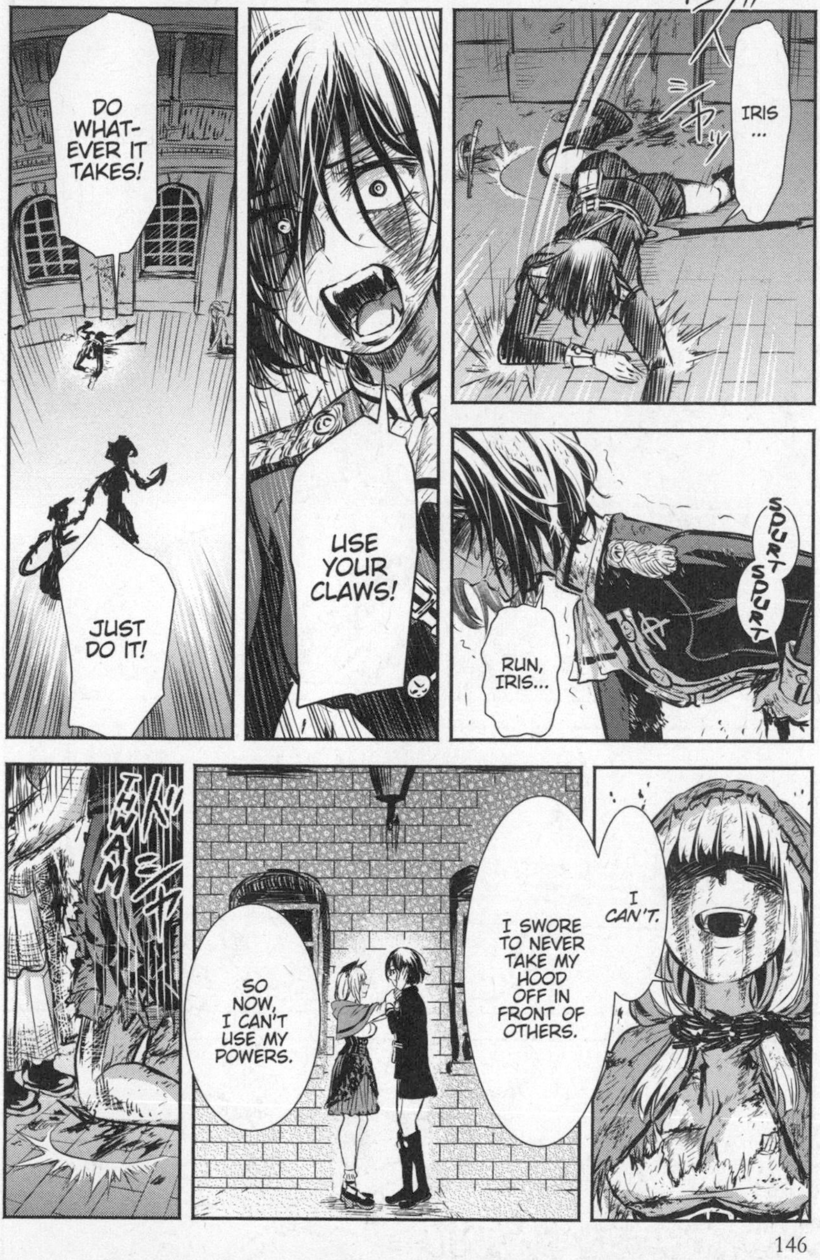
Thud
IRIS ...
SPURT SPURT
RUN, IRIS...
USE YOUR CLAWS!
DO WHATEVER IT TAKES!
JUST DO IT!
I CAN'T.
I SWORE TO NEVER TAKE MY HOOD OFF IN FRONT OF OTHERS.
SO NOW, I CAN'T USE MY POWERS.
THWAM

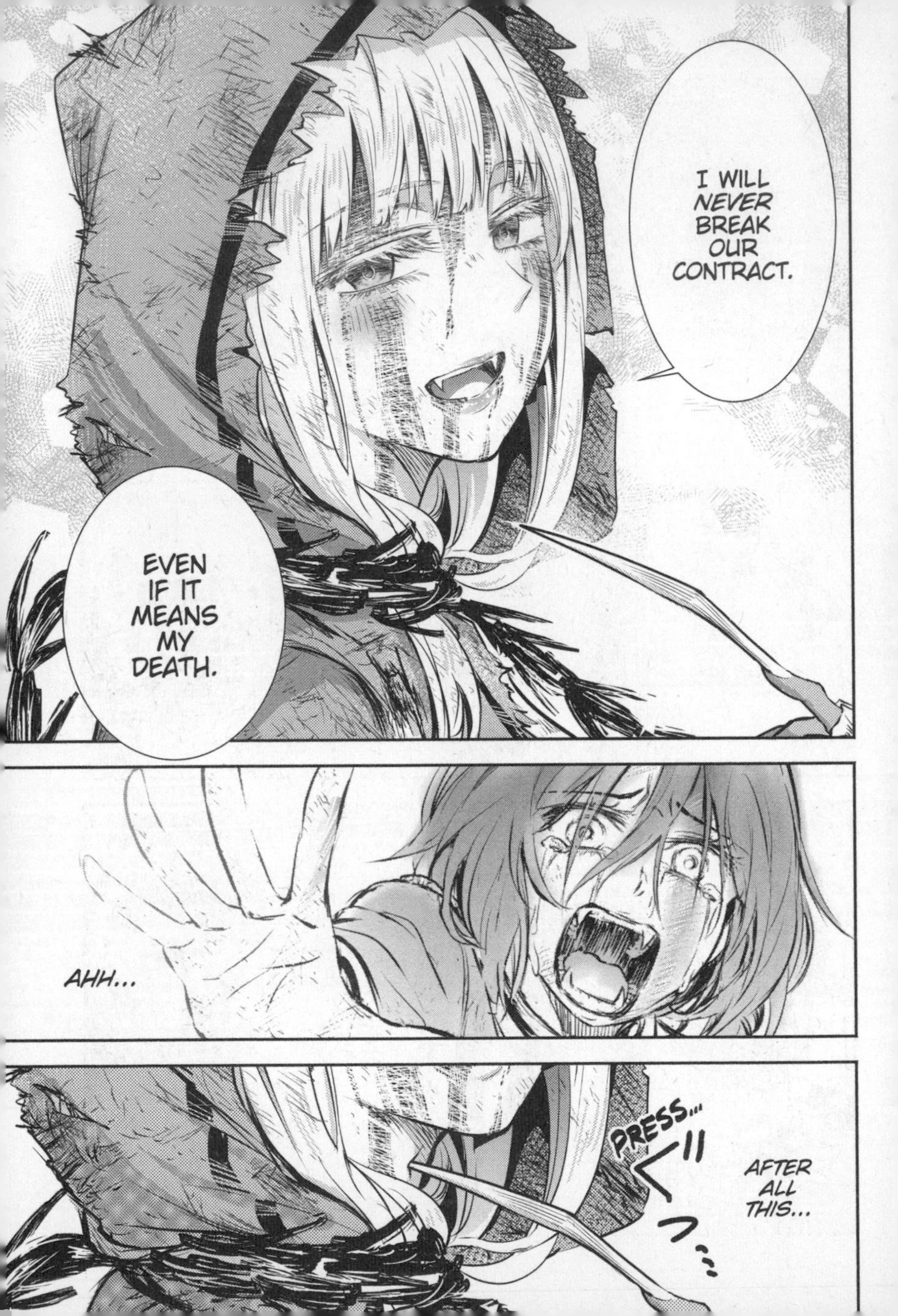
I WILL NEVER BREAK OUR CONTRACT.
EVEN IF IT MEANS MY DEATH.
AHH...
AFTER ALL THIS...
PRESS...

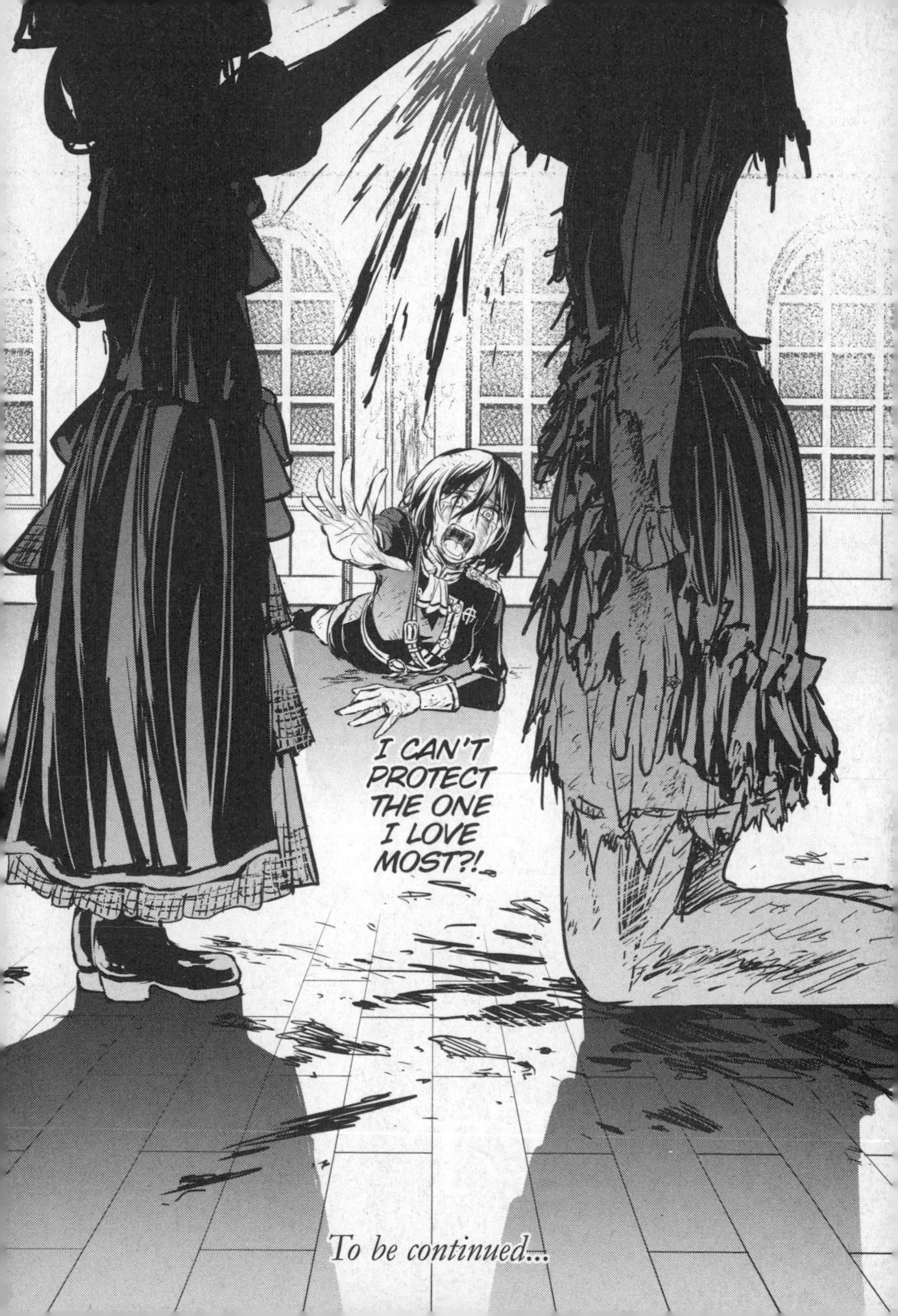
I CAN'T PROTECT THE ONE I LOVE MOST?!

To be continued...

SCARLET

SCARLET

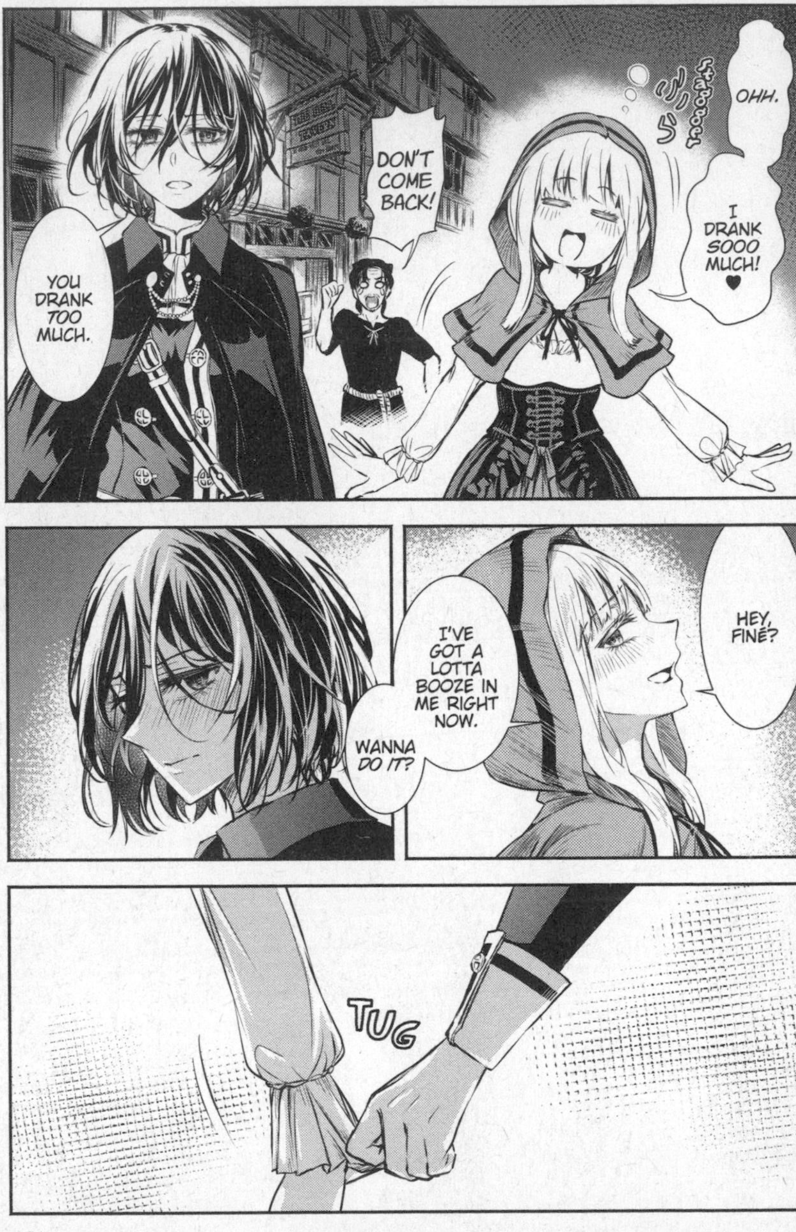
OHH.
I DRANK SOOO MUCH! ♥
DON'T COME BACK!
YOU DRANK *TOO* MUCH.
HEY, FINÉ?
I'VE GOT A LOTTA BOOZE IN ME RIGHT NOW.
WANNA DO IT?
TUG

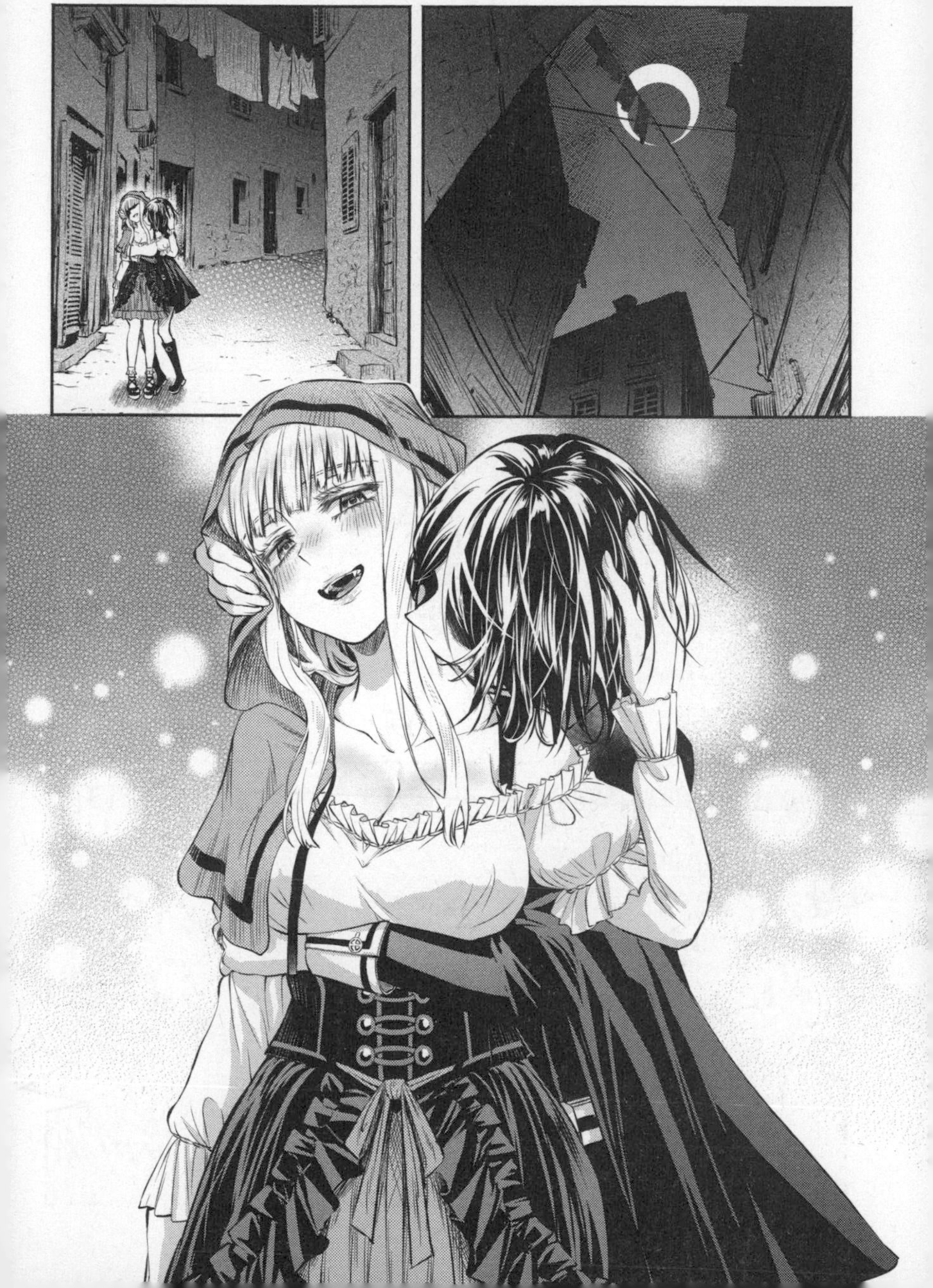

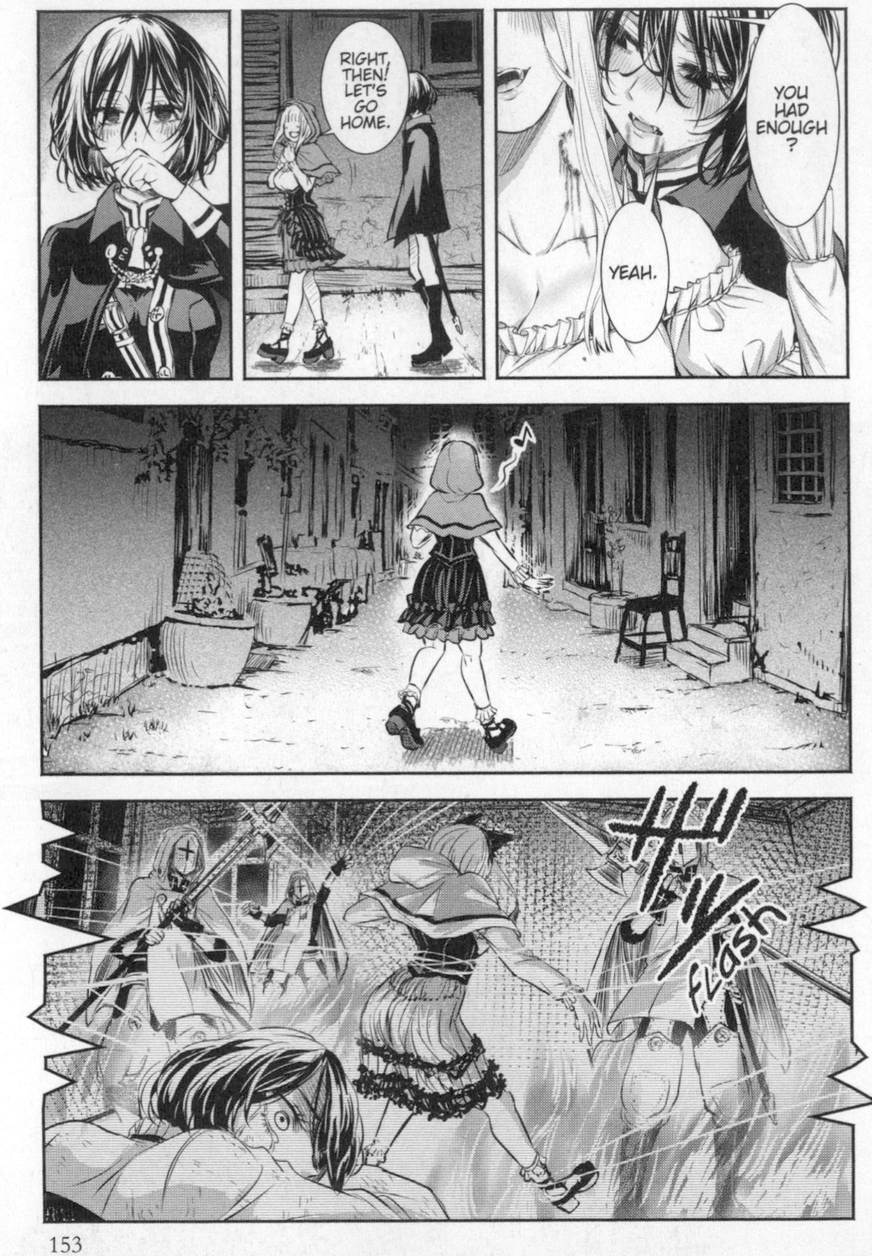
YOU HAD ENOUGH?
YEAH.
RIGHT, THEN! LET'S GO HOME.
flash

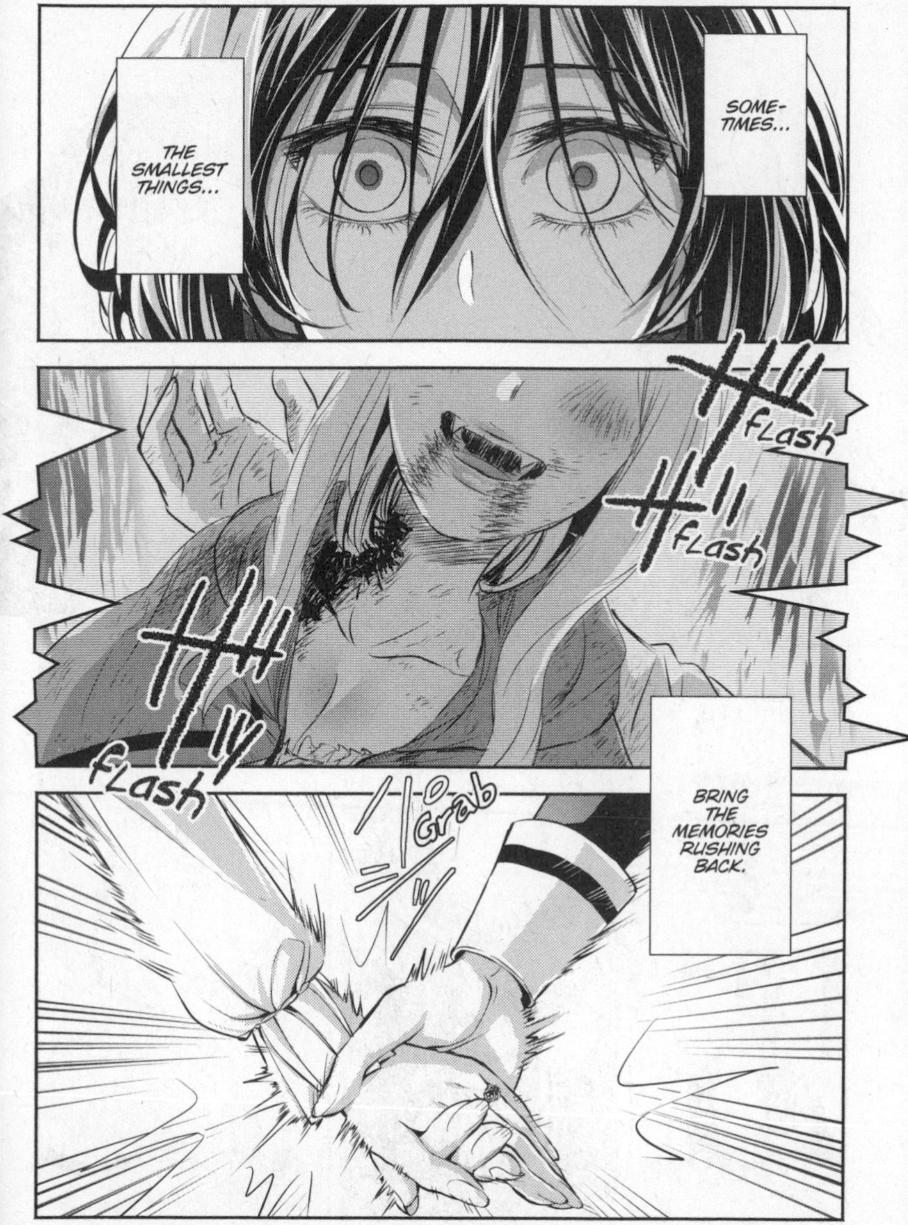
SOME-TIMES...
THE SMALLEST THINGS...
FLASH
FLASH
FLASH
BRING THE MEMORIES RUSHING BACK.
GRAB

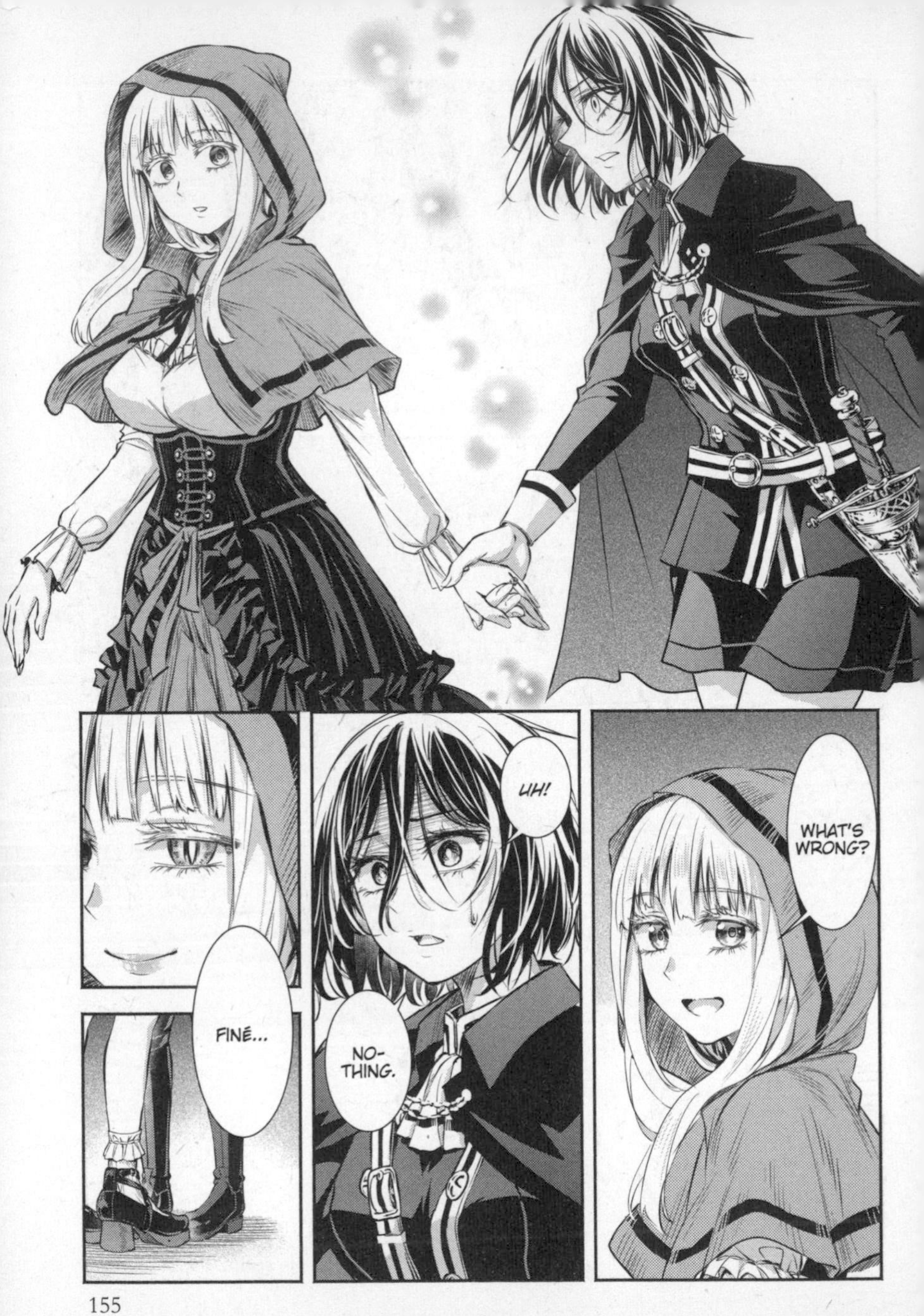
WHAT'S WRONG?
UH!
NO-THING.
FINÉ...

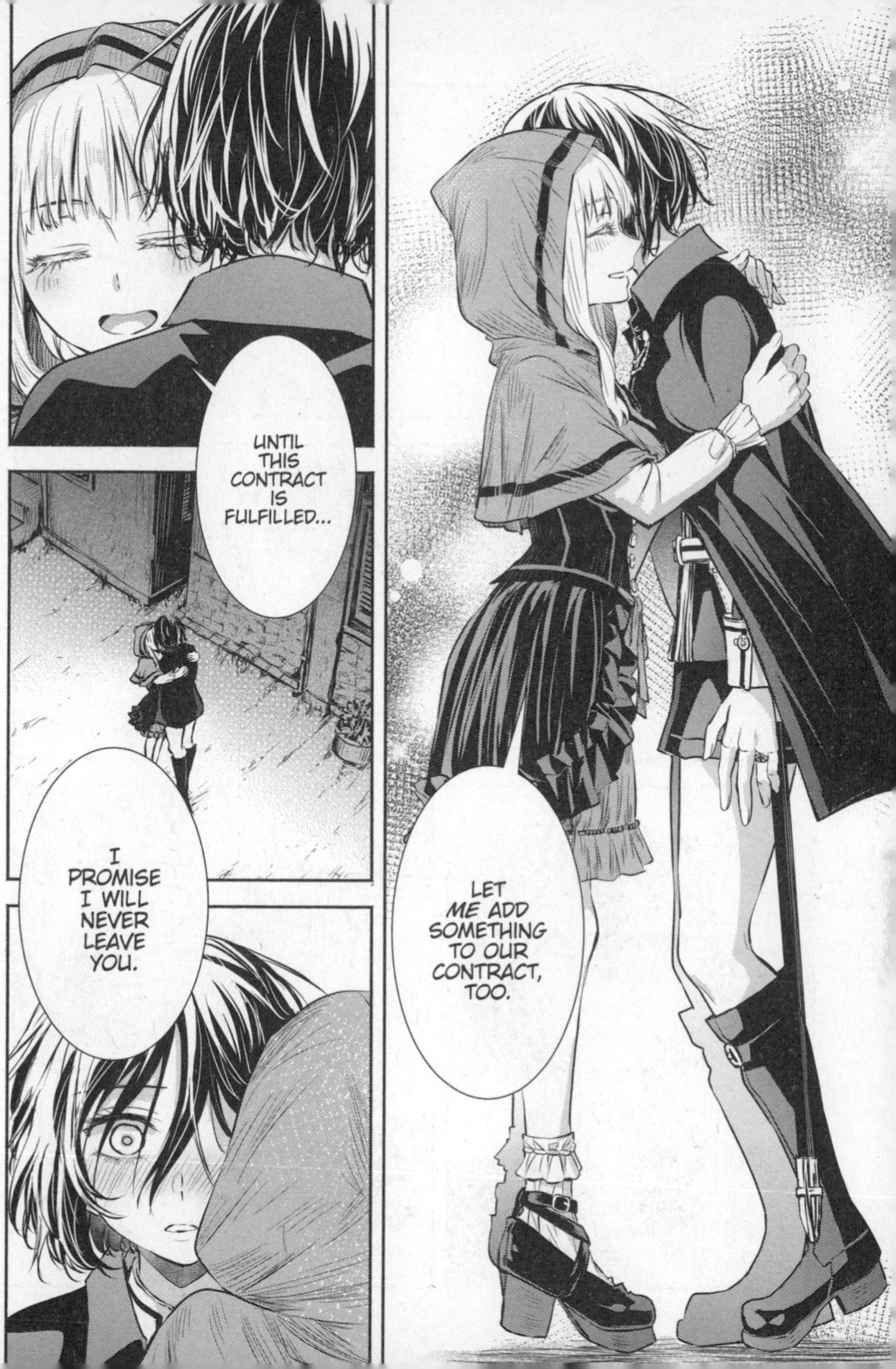
LET ME ADD SOMETHING TO OUR CONTRACT, TOO.
UNTIL THIS CONTRACT IS FULFILLED...
I PROMISE I WILL NEVER LEAVE YOU.

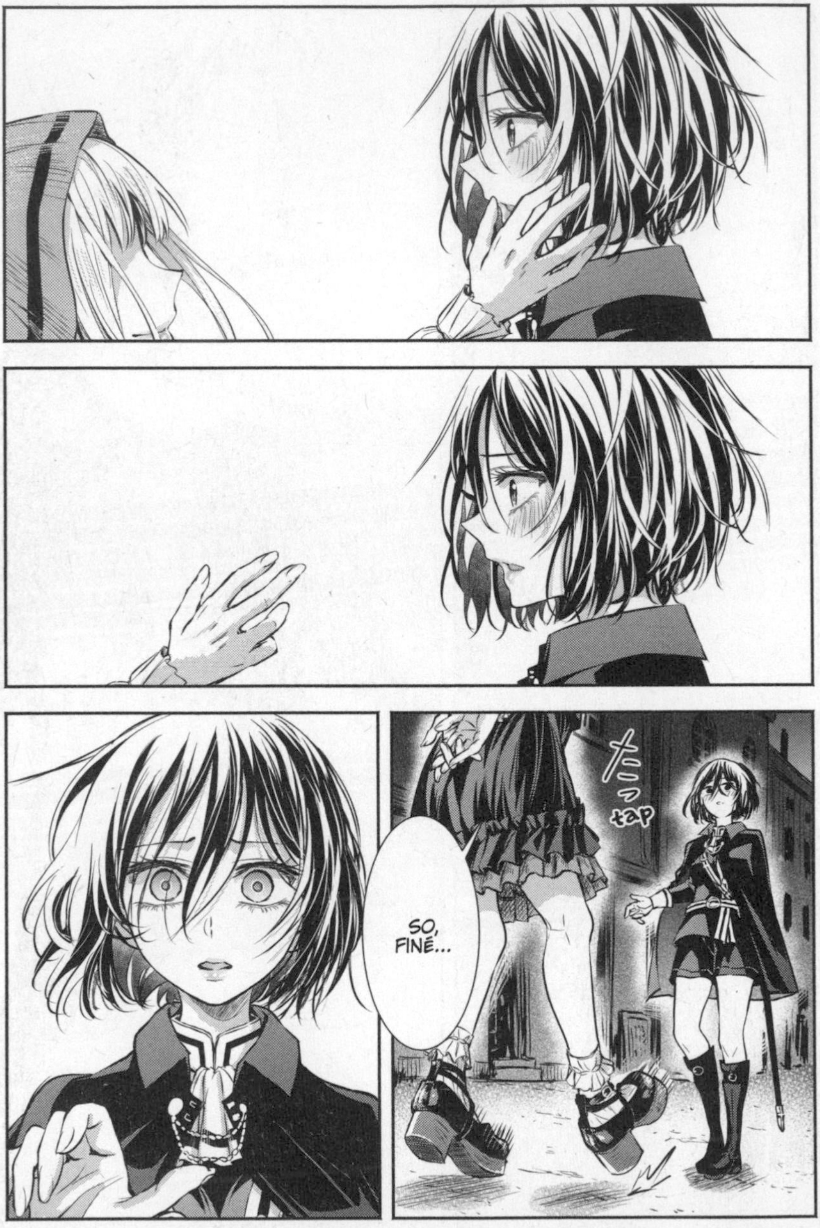
たっ
tap
SO, FINÉ...

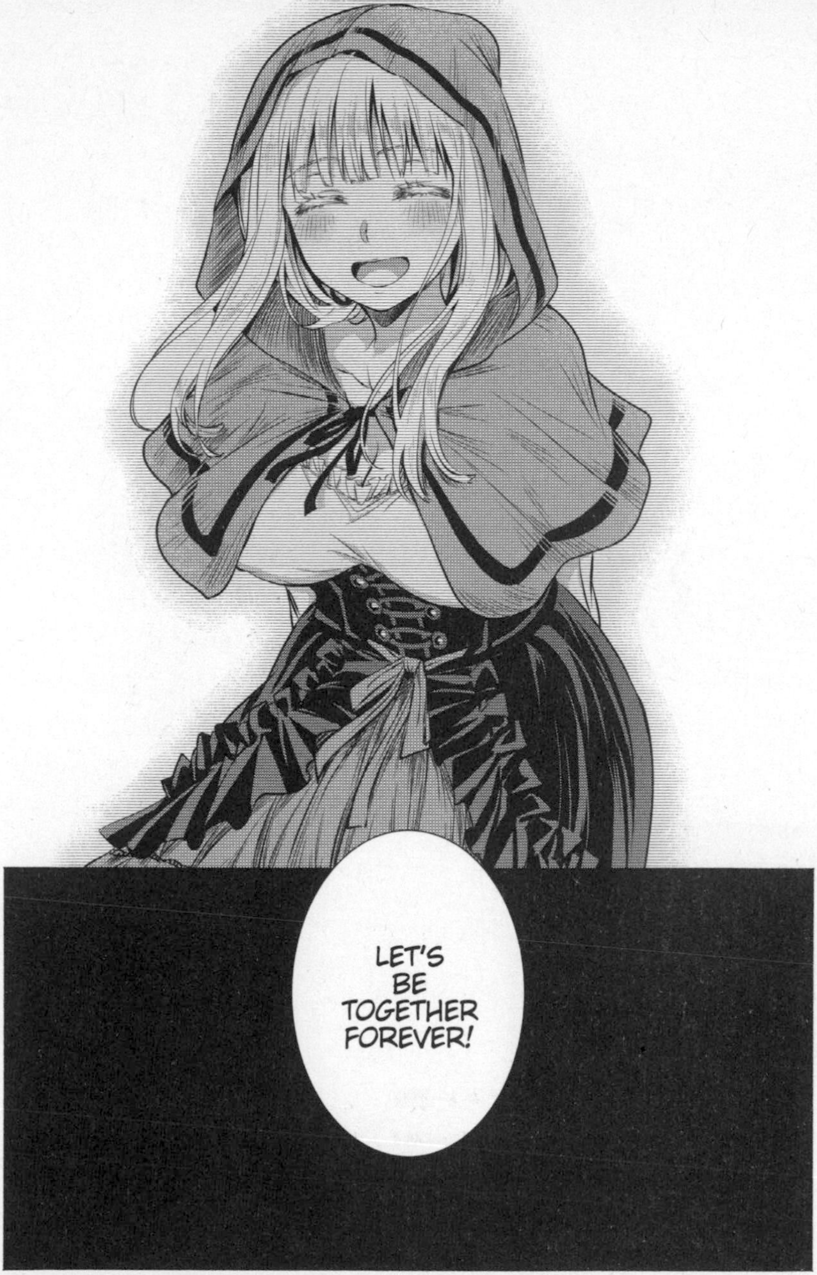
LET'S BE TOGETHER FOREVER!

♦ INITIAL PUBLICATION ♦

CHAPTER 1.... *Comic Yuri Hime,* Nov. 2018 issue

CHAPTER 2.... *Comic Yuri Hime,* Dec. 2018 issue

CHAPTER 3.... *Comic Yuri Hime,* Jan. 2019 issue

CHAPTER 4.... *Comic Yuri Hime,* Feb. 2019 issue

CHAPTER 5.... *Comic Yuri Hime,* Mar. 2019 issue

Afterword

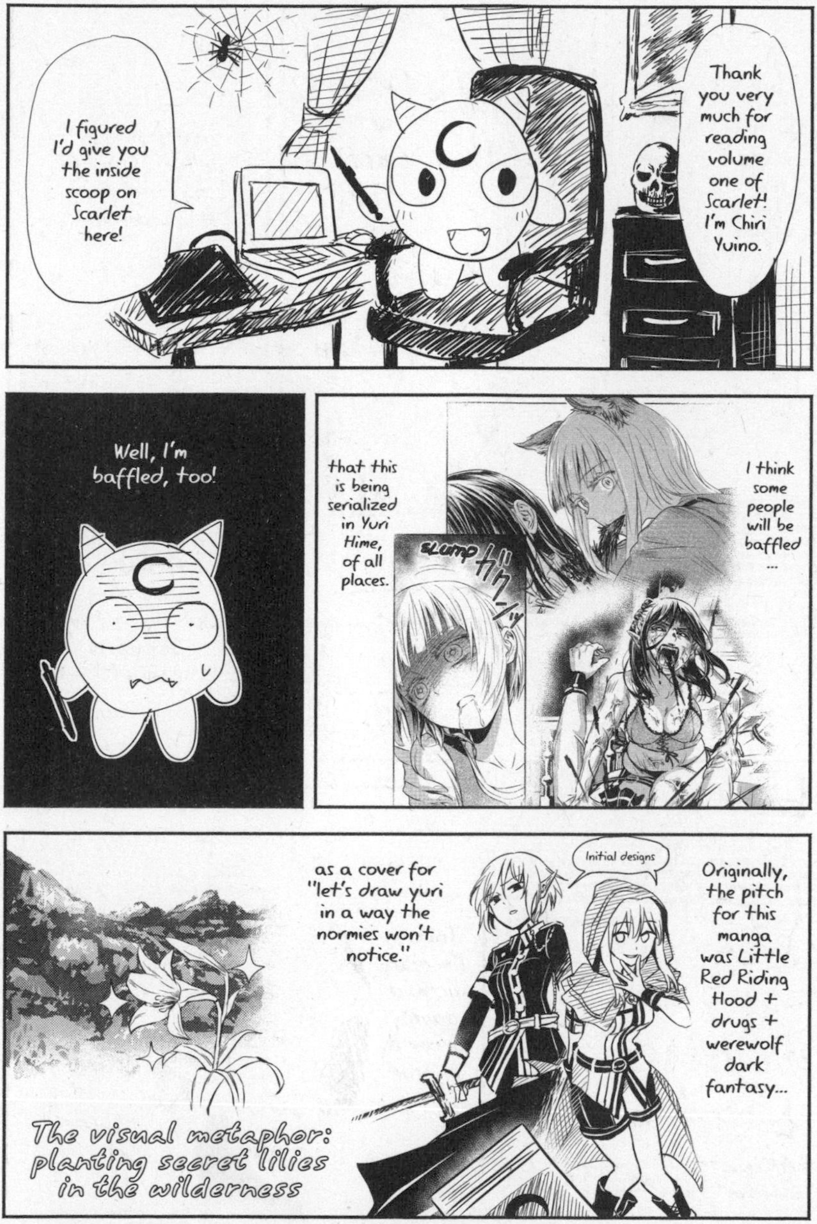

Thank you very much for reading volume one of Scarlet! I'm Chiri Yuino.
I figured I'd give you the inside scoop on Scarlet here!
I think some people will be baffled ...
that this is being serialized in Yuri Hime, of all places.
slump
Well, I'm baffled, too!
Originally, the pitch for this manga was Little Red Riding Hood + drugs + werewolf dark fantasy...
Initial designs
as a cover for "let's draw yuri in a way the normies won't notice."
The visual metaphor: planting secret lilies in the wilderness

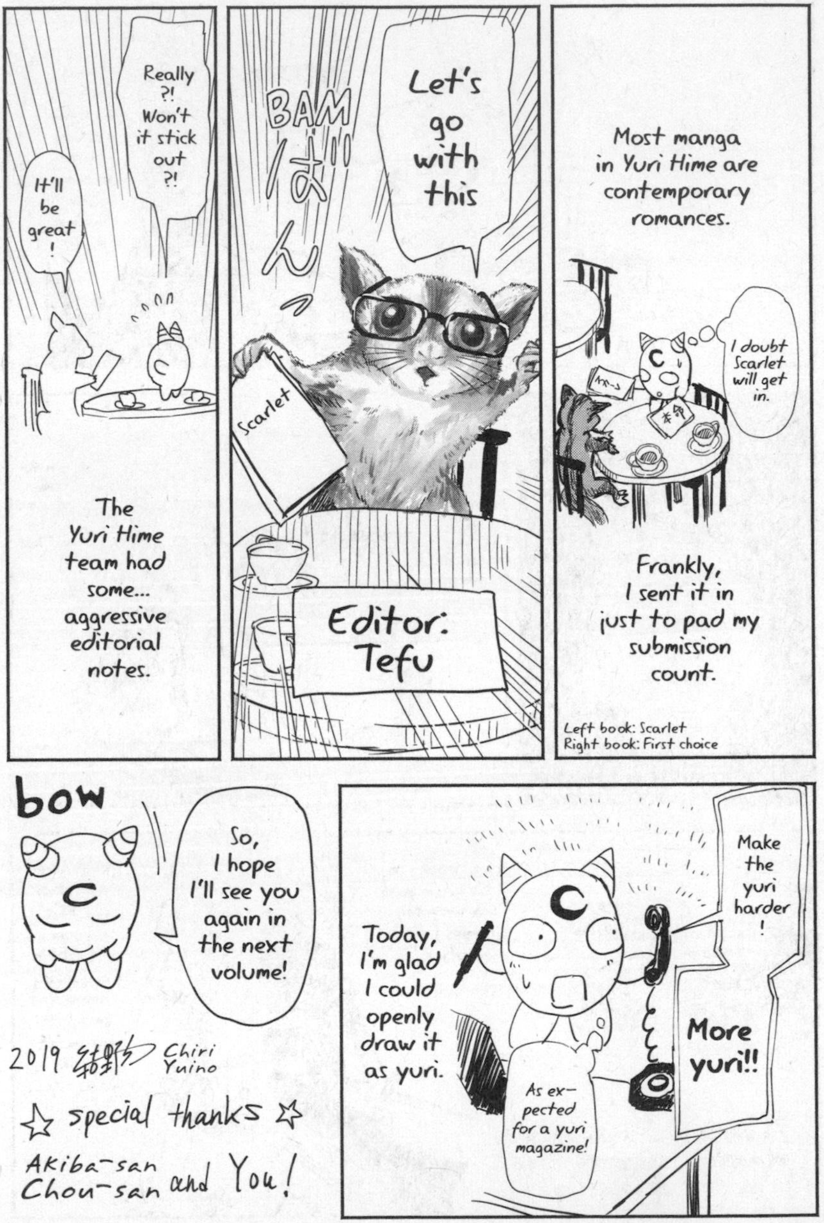
Most manga in Yuri Hime are contemporary romances.
I doubt Scarlet will get in.
Frankly, I sent it in just to pad my submission count.
Left book: Scarlet
Right book: First choice
Let's go with this
BAM
Scarlet
Editor: Tefu
Really?! Won't it stick out?!
It'll be great!
The Yuri Hime team had some... aggressive editorial notes.
Make the yuri harder!
More yuri!!
Today, I'm glad I could openly draw it as yuri.
As ex-pected for a yuri magazine!
So, I hope I'll see you again in the next volume!
bow
2019 Chiri Yuino
special thanks
Akiba-san
Chou-san and You!

Next volume!!

AT OVER 100 YEARS OLD, SHE'S EASILY THE WORLD'S OLDEST IDOL!
IRIS

To save the world from a dangerous drug...

and to keep smiles on all your faces...

SHE'LL DRAW YOU IN WITH THOSE DEAD-FISH EYES!
FINÉ

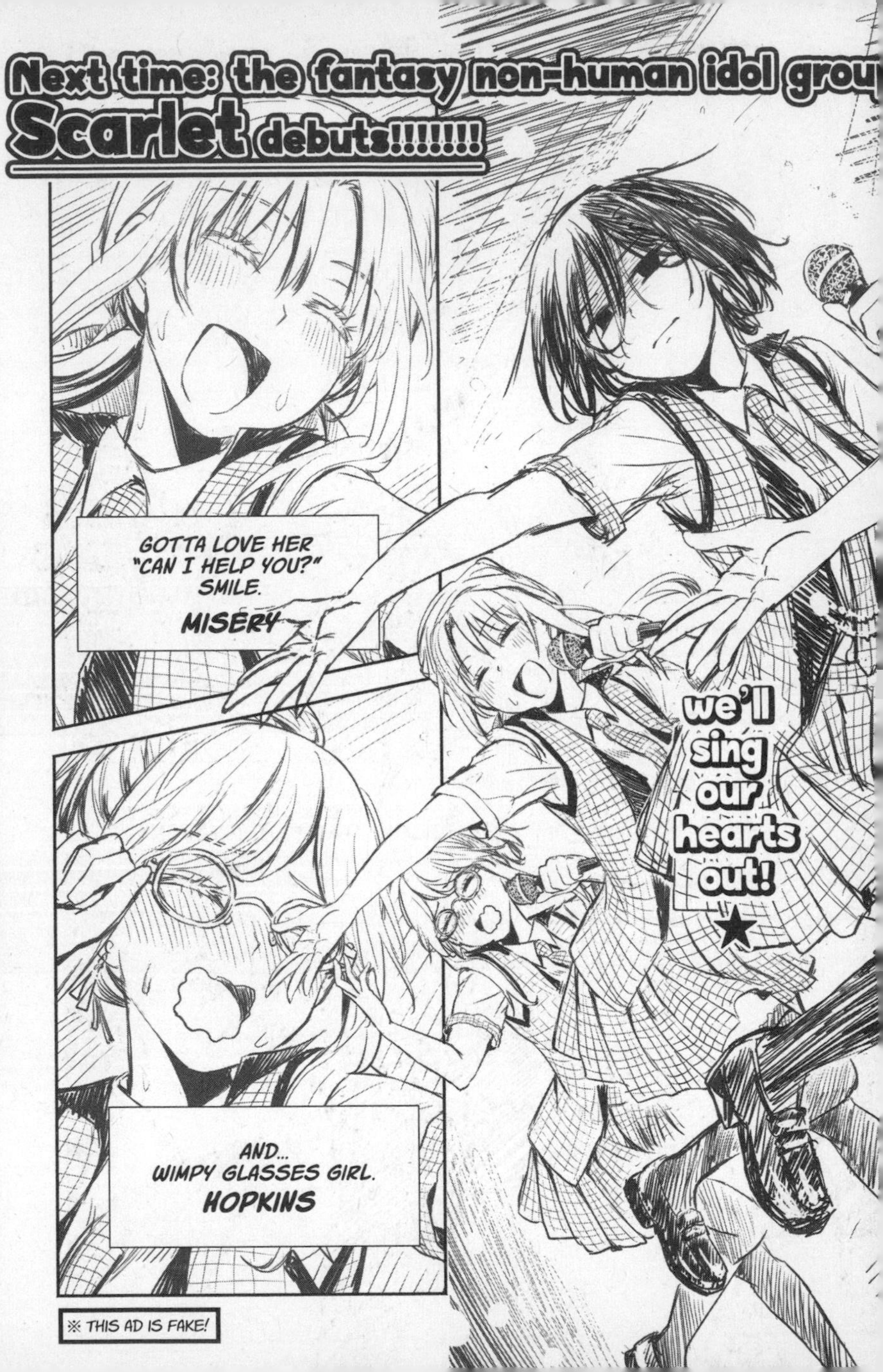
Next time: the fantasy non-human idol group
Scarlet debuts!!!!!!!!
we'll sing our hearts out! ★
GOTTA LOVE HER "CAN I HELP YOU?" SMILE.
MISERY
AND... WIMPY GLASSES GIRL.
HOPKINS
※ THIS AD IS FAKE!

SEVEN SEAS ENTERTAIN

SCARLET

story and art by **CHIRI YUINO** **VOLUME 1**

TRANSLATION
Jennifer Ward

ADAPTATION
Marykate Jasper

LETTERING AND RETOUCH
Simone Harrison

COVER DESIGN
Nicky Lim

PROOFREADER
Casey Lucas

EDITOR
Shannon Fay

PREPRESS TECHNICIAN
Rhiannon Rasmussen-Silverstein

PRODUCTION MANAGER
Lissa Pattillo

MANAGING EDITOR
Julie Davis

ASSOCIATE PUBLISHER
Adam Arnold

PUBLISHER
Jason DeAngelis

SCARLET VOL. 1

First published in Japan in 2019 by Ichijinsha Inc., Tokyo.
Publication rights for this English edition arranged through Kodansha Ltd., Tokyo.

Seven Seas press and purchase enquiries can be sent to Marketing Manager Lianne Sentar at press@gomanga.com. Information regarding the distribution and purchase of digital editions is available from Digital Manager CK Russell at digital@gomanga.com.

ISBN: 978-1-64505-296-8

Printed in Canada

First Printing: February 2020

10 9 8 7 6 5 4 3 2 1

FOLLOW US ONLINE: ***www.sevenseasentertainment.com***

READING DIRECTIONS

This book reads from ***right to left***, Japanese style. If this is your first time reading manga, you start reading from the top right panel on each page and take it from there. If you get lost, just follow the numbered diagram here. It may seem backwards at first, but you'll get the hang of it! Have fun!!

1
2
3
4
5
6
7
8
9

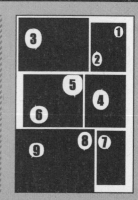